BLACKS
AND CRIME

BLACKS AND CRIME

A Function of Class

JAMES A. CHAMBERS

PRAEGER

Westport, Connecticut
London

Library of Congress Cataloging-in-Publication Data

Chambers, James A.
    Blacks and crime : a function of class / James A. Chambers.
       p.   cm.
    Includes bibliographical references and index.
    ISBN 0–275–94937–0 (alk. paper)
      1. Criminal behavior—United States. 2. Afro-American criminals.
    3. Race discrimination—United States. 4. Social exchange.
    I. Title.
    HV6791.C46   1995
    364.3′496073—dc20   94–8338

British Library Cataloguing in Publication Data is available.

Library of Congress Catalog Card Number: 94–8338
ISBN: 0–275–94937–0

First published in 1995

Praeger Publishers, 88 Post Road West, Westport, CT   06881
An imprint of Greenwood Publishing Group, Inc.

Printed in the United States of America

The paper used in this book complies with the
Permanent Paper Standard issued by the National
Information Standards Organization (Z39.48–1984).

10 9 8 7 6 5 4 3 2 1

Specifically to my loving, caring, and long time roommate, my wife, who makes all things possible.

Contents

Figures and Tables

FIGURES

TABLES

Preface

Initially this text was intended to be a general introduction to the administration of justice. This effort threatened to contain all the standard concepts, jargons, and models. Because a book of that nature would be the dullest task I could ever under take, I decided to address issues that interest me and basically ignore the rest. Therefore, this book is confined to a few key problems and their interrelatedness. The final product is not so much a consecutive narrative but rather a series of chapters on closely connected themes regarding class, Blacks, and crime. The underlying assumption throughout is that the exploitation by a dominant class through a philosophy of social exchange is the causative factor for differential behavior. It details a domination through the use and application of philosophical values. An analysis of these enables one to more coherently analyze behavior and the attempts to maintain social control. Responses to these attempts to maintain order are specified in the social exchange apparatus and are manifested to a large extent, not in conforming behavior but rather in crime, delinquency, riots, and other forms of rebellion. Hence, the title, *Blacks and Crime:*

A Function of Class.

More succinctly, this book examines some of the social forces that influence Black responses to differential societal conditions. These responses, rather than nihilism, have been attempts to alter the elements of social exchange. The issue of social exchange and its impact on Whites similarly situated is also discussed.

The reader needs to remember that an abstract theory formulated on the macro level can not explain the variations when applied on a micro level. However, we can use macro theory to explain variations of its adaptability in a social order. The macro theory contains four independent variables that will be discussed both historically and contemporarily. These are context: (1) temporality; (2) inclusiveness; (3) stratification; and (4) commitment. It is hypothesized that the differential application of these variables determine the nature of the social exchange and the relative capacity a social order possesses to control dissidence. The need for an intellectual framework regarding macro theory is discussed in chapter one. This need bridges the social, scientific, and humanistic disciplines. Macro theory now exists as a collection of micro theories whose framework can be discerned by the type of questions it pursues. In general, these micro theories ask: (1) What is the range a society will permit concerning tolerable crime and/or social protests? and (2) What or where are the boundaries that balance freedom, societal constraints, and still allow for social creativity and change?

Generally, only people "marginal" to a discipline tend to evoke concern regarding these two major questions. It is also these individuals who attempt to explain both issues from a macro perspective. This entails a discussion of intervention capabilities that go beyond the use of brute force and the dynamic interplay between a social structure's initial attempts to integrate marginal people and the subsequent failure to maintain it as an objective.

To address this, aspects of cultural theories need to be utilized because they are akin to system theories that explain the features of a social setting in the realm of the functional needs of a system. These theories enable one to juxtapose a macro theory against the functionalist sociologist's perception, a perception that interprets social solidarity as being the presumed effects of the reinforcement of normative consensus. Although cultural and system theories fail to specify how the functional needs of a social order are connected to the consensual, there is in this framework the implied assumption that there is only one way to achieve the desired out come. However, this assumption fails to acknowledge that there is always more than one way to achieve a functional need. Therefore, this knowledge of alternatives negate the notion of an existence of a general normative consensus. Nevertheless, we are still forced to assess behavior alternatives in terms of legitimacy as specified by the nature of the social exchange. Theoretically, "legitimate" behavior distinguishable from "illegitimate" behavior is preferred because its function is to help structure and maintain social solidarity.

Nevertheless, functionalists contend that without deviance one would not know the boundaries of "normality." Nor could a society long endure without this type of behavior, construed to be safety valves, the purpose of which is to drain off excess energy generated by pressures to conform to institutional routines. The general use of deviance also functions at times to contain conflict. When the expression of some deviant behavior is repressed or not channeled into a legal form, it is then channeled into more illegitimate forms. As a consequence these forms may be manifested in ways (riots, rebellions, etc.) that constitute serious threat to the social order. Although deviance may be problematic, it does perform a functional role keeping the normative aspects of the society intact. The functionalist, theoretically, provide an unorthodox and incomplete schema when it comes to addressing the problems encountered in the attempt to maintain a ordered social system.

The perspective is incomplete due to a failure to recognize that the tendencies with in the normative order generate deviance and negative consequences accrue for those who are politically powerless. The negative ramifications occur when they attempt to change both their status and the system simultaneously. Despite the functional utility of deviance, the functionalist paradigm both advocates and accounts for social continuity by promoting system values over alternatives. It also promotes social stability over social change, which is underscored in the tacit acceptance of the elite definition of social order. It also suggests that tightly imposed social rules within a model of "engineered consent" are a necessary solution to social disorganization.

The concept of illegitimacy can and has been perceived to be instrumental to social solidarity.[1] For example, Erikson advanced the notion that societies derive ongoing benefits from the commission of criminal conduct. This perspective is an extension of Durkheim's perception, articulated in, the Division of Labor in Society. Durkheim argued that: crime (and by extension other forms of deviation) may actually perform a needed service to society by drawing people together in a common posture of anger and indignation. The deviant individual violates rules of conduct which the rest of the community holds in high respect; and when these people come together to express their out rage over the offense and to bear witness against the offender, they develop a tighter band of solidarity that existed earlier.[2]

These responses and their intensity, theoretically, provide cultural identity and uniqueness. With deference to Durkheim and Erikson, social solidarity in the United States is maintained, primarily, through the intertwining religious dogmas, abstract philosophies regarding order, notions of social exchange, and the responses to them rather than to criminal or deviant behavior. This perspective differs from that of Durkheim and Erikson who advanced from the general proposition that the failure to eliminate deviance promotes social solidarity to the specific conclusion that the form, for example, crimes, and how it occurs in a particular society can be explained by the contribution that these failures make in promoting consensus on shared beliefs and there by through this process provide feelings of social solidarity.

Another problem with Durkheim's and Erikson's conclusion is the failure to address how a social group forms its particular consensus around one set of shared beliefs rather than another. Durkheim and Erikson implicitly infer that there is an existence of a consensus, and that deviance is not only promoted but that it functions to manifest and reenforce it. There fore, erroneously, one is led to a conclusion that social institutions and their normative values reflect beliefs that are spontaneously shared by all. Even if we were to grant the proposition that all societies work to strengthen feelings of social solidarity, is it questionable whether we

could conclude that these feelings are spontaneously or even consistently shared?

That which is unquestioned is the existence of a general consensus regarding behavior that emanates from the carefully constructed social institutions through the
mechanisms of social exchange. There is a
reciprocal behavior expectation that is intended to reflect these institutions. In the
literature varied arguments are advanced
regarding these institutions and their ability
to make or reflect behavioral standards. These
institutions have been identified as being
ideological, economic, military, and political
(IEMP). These are more than institutions, they
are also overlapping power networks in a
social interaction or factors of a single
social totality.[3] They are also organizations
and institutional means to be used in the
attaining of goals.[4] These institutions determine what is "normative," what is the "social
structure," and which "social action" is
tolerable. These four interacting networks
define the political network whose purpose
primarily is to adjudicate disputes between
them. This adjudication is accomp-lished by
laying down rules that they deem collectively
to be normative. Mann emphasizes the interacting and intersecting nature of the four
power network by noting "the promiscuity of
organizations and functions."[5]

The promiscuity can be illustrated by
noting how the four networks fuse and borrow
from each other in complex ways. Despite the
scholarly efforts by Adam Smith, John Locke,
Emile Durkheim, Max Weber, Sigmund Freud, and
others the socially prescribed behavior, given
this configuration may not be, and often is
not, as Karl Marx contended, rational or
utilitarian. Rather, it may be more appropriate to characterize human behavior as being
irrational because "human nature" is ever

changing rather than being fixed. Given this, the failure to stamp out deviance, in this case crime, does not reinforce a consensus because one does not exist. Instead a process that attempts to exterminate any form of deviance can at best only achieve an artificial "consensus."

This process of extermination is generally agreed upon by the IEMP and it is this agreement that determines the "legitimate" consensus. This perception is utilized in this book because it provides a concept of social stability, the genesis of crime, and the contention that responses to it by IEMP are attempts to shore up general feelings of social solidarity. This orientation also enables the analysis of crime in general that attaches causation to disparities in the social order due to the nature of the social exchange. These disparities are characterized as striking disparities of wealth, power, and privileges.

These conditions are the results of human actions. Responses to these conditions are also human actions and have both subjective meanings and assessment. This subjectivity gives rise to the ideal type that will be used as the mechanism for theoretical generalization. [6] Briefly, there are two dimensions of the ideal type. First, it is a conceptual abstraction from reality that is sufficiently general cannot capture the whole of any actual phenomena. Second, it is a stylized construct that represents the perfect, and thus unreal it is not the average case; it is the pure one. As a pure case, the ideal type is an analytical yardstick against which we might measure actual actions and institutions or societies. This work refers to the ideal type concept to create generalized statements to help in the understanding of the intricate workings of social structure, social networking, social exchange, and social control. The ideal type must be juxtaposed to the concept of classes, which is also an ideal, to understand what they mean in combination and how they together converge in the contemporary social order to dictate behavior.

IEMP, class relations, and behavior are the essential components of social structure and solidarity. These, excepting behavior, had their genesis in the first few centuries after the Roman Empire collapsed. With the demise of the Empire private property developed in the context of a system of various small, weak states that struggled along in the territory previously dominated by the Roman state. This economic development was made possible by the "normative facilitation" provided by the Catholic Church and by predominance of military techniques that were used to render armored knights to an ascendancy over serfs and peasants.

Feudal lords did not need "states," defined primarily as territorial regulators whose function was to both protect private property and increase the exploitation of the producing classes. After the state supplanted the Church as the primary means of normative pacification, as late as 1505, the powers of the state were relatively few. Despite this, during the twelfth and thirteenth centuries for a number of reasons, markets grew within state boundaries and the need for state regulations increased. One illustration of the increased need for regulators can be gleaned by looking at the plight of the merchants. As they increased the scope of their activities they needed more protection from the bandits and petty warlords who impinged on their commercial activities.

The conquest of both the land and markets provided a commercial motivation that also triggered developments in the military network and cemented a relationship between private

property and the state. This was made possible
because the merchants, in their vested interest, encouraged and fostered the growth of the
state by lending it the necessary money to
help raise a large army.

The period from 1302 to 1312 contained a
series of dramatic battles that led to the
dismounting of the nobility and its need to
turn increasingly to the state to raise a
standing army to protect its land. From that
point forward, capitalism and the nation
state grew powerful together because they
needed, abetted, and aided each other. This
symbiotic relationship fits the Weberian
definition of the state. The state, in his
definition, is an organization that controls
the military and the police within given
geographical areas. Rather than being antithetical to each other, classes and states
have been closely intertwined and gradually,
the relationship between dominant classes and
the state became even closer and their interests began to merge. To paraphrase Marx, it is
fair to conclude that during the seventeenth
and eighteenth centuries, the state had become
an executive committee for managing the common
affairs of the capitalist class. This occurred
because the state lacked distributive power
over the classes that comprised civil society
and because the power flowed primarily from
economic power relations to the state.

To fully understand the relationship
between social solidarity and social control,
it is imperative that we note the group
labeled as being the dominant class and its
power. This groups' power is exercised rather
than processed and extended by those who are
dominated. Foucault states:

> Furthermore this power is exercised
> not simply as an obligation or a
> prohibition on those "who do not
> have it;" It invests them, is trans-

mitted by them and through them; it exerts pressure upon them, is trans- mitted by them, just as they them selves, in their struggle against it, resist the grip it has on them. This means that these relations go right down into the depth of soci- ety, that they are not localized in the relations between the state and its citizens or on the frontier between classes and that they do not merely reproduce at the level of individuals, bodies, gestures Al- though there is continuity (they are indeed articulated in this form through a whole series of complex mechanisms), there is neither analo- gy nor homology, but a specificity of mechanisms and modality. Lastly, they are not univocal; they define innumerable points of confrontation, focuses of instability, each of which has its own risks of conflict, of struggles, and of an at least temporary inversion of the power relations. The over throw of these "micro-powers" does not, then, obey the law of all or nothing; it is not acquired once and for all by a new control of the apparatuses nor by a new functioning or a destruction of the institutions. None of its local- ized episodes may be inscribed in history except by the effect that is induces on the entire network in which it is caught up.[7]

History suggests that it is a terrible thing to grow up feeling that you have no control over your own destiny and to many it is also unthinkable. Lack of control creates feelings of hopelessness and helplessness.

When one occupies this state, power appears to be and in reality is devoid of self. Rather than having the ability to control exogenous factors, one does that which is necessary to survive. In the contemporary United States, thousands of poor Blacks, Puerto Ricans, Mexicans, Indians, and Whites grow up with and endure this feeling. It is hypothesized that it is this sense of powerlessness that generates resentment which leads to "antisocial" actions for example, delinquency, crime, riots, or rebellion. therefore, a rational discussion of crime must begin by defining and operationalizing the concept of power and its application.

   Prior to beginning an analysis of the issue a discussion of the current state of criminological theories is necessary. Discussion of these theories is critical because they aid in identifying changing attitudes regarding social order, control, behavioral patterns, and the function of power. We do not live in a society in which moral issues are important aspects of the social order because they are used by individuals to fulfill their social obligations. Nor do the social institutions feel compelled to fulfill their social responsibilities. These obligations are not obligations to themselves, but rather to the individual. In social settings individuals feel an obligation to their fellowman because their fellowman feels an obligation to them. If we did live in this type of state social solidarity and control would be less problematic.

NOTES

   1. Kai Erikson, *Wayward Puritans* (New York: John Wiley, 1966): 4.
   2. Emile Durkheim, *The Rules of Sociological Methods*, trans. S. Solovay and J. Mueller, ed. George E. G. Catlin (Glencoe,

Ill.: The Free Press, 1950): 65.

3. Mann, Michael, *The Sources of Social Power* (New York: Cambridge University Press, 1986): 9,10, 518.

4. William G. Domhoff, *The Power Elite and the State: How Policy is Made in America* (New York: Walter De Gruyter Inc., 1990).

5. Mann, *Sources of Social Power*, op cit p. 17.

6. Weber describes the ideal types as: being formed by the one-sided accentuation of one or more points of view and by the synthesis of a great many diffused, discrete more or less present and occasionally absent concrete individual phenomena, which are arranged-- according to those one-sidely emphasized viewpoints into a unified analytical construct. See Max Weber, *The Methodology of the Social Sciences*, ed. and trans. Edward Shils and Harry Titch (Glencoe, II. Free Press, 1949): 90.

7. Michel Foucault, *Discipline and Punishment: The Birth of the Prison*, (New York: Vintage Books, 1979): 26 and 27.

Acknowledgement

No book today, including this one, conveys an adequate understanding of the changing dimensions of the social structure and its relationship to crime and delinquency. It is not that we lack good material as will be discussed in Chapter 1 rather it is the lack of or unwillingness of talented professors to guide those students who want to know more about the discipline without sampling every thing in the library on the subject and are able to see the discordance in the traditional theories used to explain behavior. This text attempts to provide some notion of the nexus between some of the issues as they exist in the social order and the occurrence of specific behaviors.

I gratefully acknowledge the numerous students whose eagerness to understand the differential occurrence and complexities of behavior provided the impetus to produce this manuscript. I owe special thanks to Mildred Bennett, Jim Strathman, Bill Rabeiga, and Walt Ellis, past professors who were always fair in their interactions with me. When I needed friends during my doctoral studies, they always aided me, and words could never convey my appreciation. I am also deeply indebted to my "brothers," Owen R. Owens, Majid

Razooladeh, Mohammed Al Bussqyes, Mike Mbanaso, and Abdullah Al Mutlaq, who were also colleagues. I thank my children, who are extremely special in their lack of involvement with the correctional system, an increasingly rare situation for blacks. I also love you deeply.

A special thanks to Purdue University for their financial support through a post-doctoral fellowship in 1992. This aid made it possible to devote a large block of uninterrupted time to this project. To that end I need and want to thank Clara Bell, Dean Knudsen, the administration, and others at that fine university for also letting me share a very memorable summer associating, teaching, and studying in Lafayette. Of course, this manuscript could not have resulted in a coherent form with out the special editorial skills of Catherine A. Lyons. Thank you very much for both your directions and patience.

Finally, I want to thank my colleagues, Jeff Schrink, Ed Grosskopf, Sheila Van Ness, Mark Hamm, Dave Skelton, Harry Marsh, Robert Huckabee, and Sherry Biddinger Gregg, at Indiana State University for letting me be a part of the team in one of the outstanding departments in the country. No department is complete without competent staff, and to this end I thank Peggy Strobel and Brenda Starkey. A very special thanks to Mani Mohapatra, Andre Hammonds, and Jim Conyers for always be available to sound ideas to. I also want to give special appreciation to Azonda Brogan, my graduate assistant, and Owen Williams for their willingness to help me with the mundane things in a timely fashion.

BLACKS
AND CRIME

1

Theorizing

Theories are free creations of the mind and they are open to execution or speculation by anyone. A careful reading of the criminological, delinquency, and criminal justice literature presents a condition that is tantamount to a system of apparent wisdom in the folly of hypothetical delusion. While this assessment will not sit well with the scholars in these areas, objectivity will force them to conclude that the fields of criminology, delinquency, and criminal justice have a paucity of scientific theories. While these scholars may argue to the contrary, they lack persuasion because a scientific theory is defined as a particularly controlled form of speculation.

Traditionally, while these scholars lack theories, they have consistently speculated regarding the etiology of various forms of deviant behavior and how to control them. The "classical" and "contemporary" literatures are replete with speculative explanations, some of which, with the passing of time, appear to be little more than pieces of science fiction. Despite these speculative explanations that use the ideographic technique, there is an

attempt by these scholars to provide profound
understanding. However, this is a task that
cannot be accomplished without resorting to
the use of scientific principles and theory.
Lacking this discipline, these speculations
are really metaphysical. Despite this, they
could be extraordinarily productive if used as
directives or regulative principles to guide
in the formulation of truly scientific theories.

Part of the problem revolves around the
perceived function of sociology of which
criminology is a subfield. Gibbons states:

> There a number of reasons for giving
> relatively little attention to the
> "why do they do it?" question. One
> is that it can be argued that the
> business of the sociologist qua
> sociologist should be with criminal-
> ity in the aggregate and with the
> social origins of law breaking,
> rather than with psychological,
> social-psychological, or biological
> hypotheses about the influences that
> lead specific individuals to engage
> in acts of criminality. Then, too,
> there is already in existence a
> rather sizeable body of theoretical
> and research work that centers on
> the "Why do they do it question."[1]

While, there is a plethora of why they do it
speculative research, one can argue that there
is a paucity of theoretical efforts.

When one sorts out the major lines of
criminological theorizing for example, premodern, conservative, mainstream, or radical-
marxist-critical, it is readily discernible
that each lack the elements of scientific
theory or a language for discussing the facts
that the theory is said to explain. Instead,

the orientations or speculations are burdened with a hazy combination of observation language that is used to describe events with an artificial calculus devoid of empirical content. For example, when various patterns of law breaking are "observed," for example, forcible rape, burglary, etc., and arguments are advanced that purport to account for them by using variations in sexual equality and/or variations in income inequality concepts, one can not logically conclude that these theoretical statements. They suggest a certain tentativeness when one moves from a particular incident of rape or burglary to the universality of these behaviors. In addition, these "theoretical" concepts are merely perception, because they fail to address or to explain the learning processes and spatio-temporal explanations that would account for individual preferences for one behavior or the other.[2]

The above criticisms are not unmindful of the fact that the construction of a corpus of theory in any field is fraught with numerous difficulties. Nevertheless, the elaboration of scientific theory requires the development of powerful, basic postulates or axiomatic statements from which empirically verifiable conclusions can be deduced. They cannot be poorly formulated or derivative. That is to say, criminological, delinquency, or criminal justice theories have to be more than the elaboration of economic, political, and/or psychological theories in a specific spatial context.

On the most superficial level, an appropriate methodological approach and the value of using such would seem obvious. Sweezy said, "from a scientific point of view, etc, question choosing between approaches can be answered quite simply. Which more accurately reflects the fundamental characteristics of social reality which is under analysis?"[3]

Nevertheless, theories regarding society must
be abstracted from a dynamic complexity while
working with relatively simple model of reality. Psychological theories in a specific
spatial context.[4]

Kuhn strongly argued that: "What scientists share is not sufficient to command
uniform assent about such matters as the
choice between competing theories." Different
researchers may place varying weights on
criteria like consistency and simplicity or
they may, on the other hand, judge the relative consistency of a given theory in different ways. These kinds of disagreements regarding values result from the differences in
language and perception. For example, economic
factors have been deemed to be a correlate of
both crime and delinquency.

However, the concepts, economic factors,
are value laden and to compound matters they
are operationalized in varying fashions in the
delinquency and crime research. When economic
factors or economic conditions are used as
variables, researchers must consider whether
they have meaning given the issues of stability or instability in regard to the three labor
force categories: employed, unemployed, or not
in the labor force. Operationalizing this
distinction would enhance the ability to
distinguish one of the dominant differences
between the poor and the nonpoor and to make
some predictions, using this factor, regarding
behavior. When one uses the differentiated
economic condition as a variable, one can then
factor in the randomness of work histories.
The findings can then more logically be correlated to the stability or instability of the
economic market and the effects that they have
on the behavior.

A scientific theory can be regarded as an
interpreted calculus or something that can, in
principle, be casted as such a calculus, for

example, deprivation leads to crime. Criminology, delinquency, and criminal justice have materials for these calculi, but a coherent calculus has failed to develop from any of this material because there has been a general and basic failure to make and /or accept the abstractions, for example, racism is a function of crime, from their subject matter.

In order to rationally discuss an abstraction, there needs to be observational and theoretical language. There is a critical difference between observational and theoretical language. Observation language describes empirical events directly, whereas theoretical language artificially creates calculi in a completely formal system. In such a system, observational languages, the terms, have analytic meaning but they are devoid of empirical content. While criminology, delinquency, and criminal justice researchers have the material to develop a formal calculus, comprised of theoretical language, they instead resort to some existing calculus or model, based on observational language, and use the existing elaboration of that model to extend it in some way to meet their particular needs.

The theoretical statements, albeit some what extended at times, of Lemert's professional theft; Sutherland's differential association; and Merton's anomie have the potential for theory development. However, it can be argued the efforts of Shaw, McKay, Thrasher, Miller, and others of this ilk, are little more than observational frameworks.

The major reason for the failure of Lemert, Sutherland, and Merton's efforts to develop into full blown theories is the omnipresent competing paradigms. Because the fields have this fixation on paradigms, the evaluative procedure depends upon the characteristics of the particular paradigm.[5] When paradigms enter, as they must, into a debate about paradigm choice, their role and the evaluative procedure becomes circular.[6] A good example would be, the main streamers and radical-marxist. These two groups use their own paradigm to argue, not for general theoretical truth but rather in the paradigm's defense. This paradigm defense results in tautological reasoning or circularity.

This circularity, which characterizes paradigms, is used to determine the evaluation procedure. This does not in itself make the conclusions wrong or ineffectual, but rather this entire process tends to generate too much useless baggage. For example, when the intellectual transition was made from premodern to modern criminology, the assimilation of all new paradigms should have served, in fact, demanded the destruction of the prior paradigms. If this action would have occurred, it in large measure would have negated the subsequent conflicts that exist between competing schools of scientific thought.

However, if we must save paradigms other than for historical reasons, it should be made clear that their range of application is restricted solely to historical reasons. In addition, it also must be made clear that the precision of historical observations are limited to the experimental evidence that previously existed if it lacks relevance to the contemporary issue of concern. There is a counter argument to this position that contends that an outdated paradigm can always be perceived as a special case of its up-to-date successor, which is used as a guide to derive the most recent paradigm. If this were not the case, the new paradigm would be so restricted that it could, at best, only restate that which is already known.

Although the paradigm's restatement functions with a certain utility of economy, this hardly enhances the guidance of further research through theory construction. For example, the differential social organization paradigm posits that social conditions influence the person and give rise to normative conflict. The theory suggests that this conflict becomes pronounced following the rise of modern capitalism, industrialism, and urbanization. These conditions, theoretically, led to changes in folkways, a commensurate rise in individualism, acquitiveness, and personal aspirations. These factors supposedly resulted in the weakening of the family, neighborhood, and community ties. From all of this we get a proposition regarding the genesis of deviant behaviors. It should be quite clear that these theoretical concepts could provide the basis for the development of a scientific theory that explains the occurrence of all deviances en toto. While there have been many arguments advanced against this paradigm, none of them have been based on the results of rigorous, controlled examination. Failure to perform this, simply stated but difficult to achieve, task has resulted in an inability to provide either motive or points of departure for additional theory construction.[7]

This paradigm contains many postulates and has the potentiality for the development of a rational calculus that would explain the correlation specifically between social disorganization and criminal or delinquent behavior. In its current state, it fails to achieve this. The paradigm does contain a theoretical language, although vague, but to be useful the factors must be translated into an observational language that would be appropriate for the calculus so that the factors could be empirically tested. The paradigm also has the potential for interpretation by text or correspondence rule, which would serve to link the abstract analytical statements with empirical subject matter. Without this text the domain

of the theory, as currently stated, can not be
accurately defined, for example, the notion of
modern capitalism. Therefore, without clarity
of definition, the texts are left to assess
the theorems in a state of improbability or
doubt. This assertion is true because the text
for a theory must be multifaceted.It also
needs to specify both a temporal and a spatial
domain. The concept of modern capitalism can
be, but has not been operationalized in these
domains.

Paradigms differ in substance because
they are not only directed by the nature of
the problem, but also by the science that
produced them. The particular science utilized
provides the source of methods, problem-field,
and the standards of solution that are accepted by the varying scientific communities at
any given time. As a result, the reception of
a new paradigm often necessitates a redefini-
tion of the science from which it is derived,
or there is further entrenchment to exclude
the new paradigm. This entrenchment presents
potential problems to new paradigms because
these suggest changes in the standards govern-
ing permissible problems, concepts, and explanations. One reason for excluding these new
paradigms are the threats they present in
transforming a science.

Shifts in the scientific community's
perception of its legitimate problems would be
less relevant if one could suppose that they
always occurred from methodologically lower to
higher ones. Generally, this is not the practice. Instead, these perceptual changes come
about because it is one or a few individuals
who are capable of seeing the world differently and possess the ability to make a perceptual transition seemingly possible by other
members in their profession. Generally these
are people so young or so new to the field
that they are not committed to prior practices. They are also less deeply committed to the

world view determined by the field's paradigms than most of their contemporaries. The problem of how and what these individuals can do to convert relevant subgroups or the entire profession to their "new" world view becomes extremely important and not always achievable.[8]

This does not suggest a conspiracy by theorists, but rather that scientists, being human, can not always admit their errors, even when confronted with strict proof. An excellent example is the failure to accept the fact that there is a direct correlation between race and those who receive the death penalty. However, a closer inspection reveals that error or proof is not the issue but rather the defense of traditional paradigms. One should remember that the willingness to embrace a new paradigm is a conversion experience, and one can not mandate this conversion. Resistance particularly comes from those who have had productive careers and whose production was or is based on a commitment to an older tradition. This obstinance is not a violation of scientific standards but rather an index of the field's scientific research at a given time. The resistance to change, in addition to personal reasons, is grounded in the belief that the older paradigms will ultimately provide a solution to the problems presented.

The aim of general theory, in both the natural and social sciences, are to unify a multitude of special hypothetical constructs that are formulated to deal with small groups of phenomena structured in a hypothetical-deductive system. This general characteristic of science is accomplished by placing a dependence upon the existing basic postulates that are used to structure a coherent theorem to develop a theoretical system.

In the social sciences, this has proven to be extremely difficult. This failure has resulted in the lack of construction of general theories. This inability has also presented obstacles to the development of powerful theories within the various disciplines. As a result, in the social sciences, we confront hypothetical constructs that can best be characterized as a chaos of vague postulates, fuzzy arguments, and often unwarranted conclusions.

It might well be argued that the most pressing concern of a criminologist and other social scientists should be one of imposing some order upon the chaos concerning the nature of man before attempting to undertake the problem of establishing the nature of the order with in which he functions, or the system it self. That is to say, it would do us no harm to spend considerably more research effort attempting to formalize some of the speculative traditional notions.

This discipline, which can accomplish the above, then would will be equipped to discuss the issues of how to control the problems of delinquency and crime. This is critical because there is a controversy that is focused around the public's willingness to continue to succumb to costly programs we advocate that fail. They fail despite promises to the contrary that they demonstrate preventive ability. The public is also confused by the methods favored by formulators of elitist paradigms; those with the most prestigious credentials (therefore, factors of power and status superseded the quality of content), and those that exist in the fields of criminology, sociology, and psychiatry.

Each of these fields was struggling in the 1920s to become an accepted profession and to expand its sphere of influence by demonstrating its usefulness. Prior to 1930, psychiatrists were firmly entrenched and suffered little interference from the other fields because they were either too young or poorly organized to be perceived as being capable of providing viable alternatives to solving the social problems. While psychiatry had a leg up, due to its association with the medical field, only a few of the psychiatric models were implemented because they too were limited to the same sort of environmental manipulation suggested by sociologists and criminologists. In short, they were applying a general medicalization approach that isolated the child, sought the particular cause of delinquency in the child's personal history, and then placed the child in a diadic relationship with a physician for psychotherapeutic treatment to prevent reoccurrence of the behavior.[9] This approach was deemed the most promising because children were seen as being malleable and if the early signs, which were believed to lead to serious problems in adults, were recognized and proper intervention techniques utilized, one would have the ideal preventive social intervention strategy. In the latter part of the 1930s, there were radical changes that were coupled with facets of the Progressive Reform Era for example, improvement in the welfare of children, isolation of young offenders from adults into separate institutions, the juvenile court's policy to provide nonpunative treatment, and the introduction of the probation system. All of these changes were structured to handle the educational needs and to reform the youth.[10] Because delinquency was perceived as an urgent problem, it provided the basis for the growing disciplines to apply new research methods to test their theories concerning human behavior. In addition, it provided a basis for obtaining legitimacy and to have an impact.[11]

Delinquency and criminal behavior are possible in a social order because life chances are not distributed evenly. Perhaps there cannot be such a condition. To paraphrase Aristotle, similars do not constitute a state.

This is not really profound, but it is relevant. In Aristotle's Politics, he elucidated on this perception and rendered pronouncements that many would find unacceptable today. For example, slaves were not part of the state because they were by nature "inferior men." Children, the son of free men at any rate, grew up to be citizens but were not citizens as children. Women differed somewhat from slaves, but nevertheless they were "by nature" inferior to men. Protests to these perceptions and conditions have taken the forms of crime and delinquency. It is clear that modern societies, in general, have a more generous concept of those who do and do not belong than Aristotle had, but the social order still remains problematic for many. How do we account for the current problematic conditions?

Each society varies in style, incidence, and level of social protest that can be attributed to persisting social and subcultural patterns of deprivation, patterns of coercive control, and supports that mitigates against social protest. Eckstein suggests that political disorientation (social protest) may give rise to the formation of new sets of orientations, establishing a predisposition toward violence (which is a threat to the social organization), that is inculcated by the experience of violence it self. He also contends that violence becomes a political style that is self-perpetuated unless itself disorients.[12]

Gurr states that:

> Reoccurrence of one riot, one rebellion, or one *coup d'etat* in a nation is not likely to create wide spread expectations about their repetition. The more frequently they occur, however, and the more closely spaced they are in time, the more

common people will expect them to be in the future.[13]

Gurr is quick to point out that expectations of violence do not necessarily lead to its normative justification, however there is an element of self fulfilling prophecy in the expectancies. He also implies that these expectancies may divert attention from remedying underlying causes to preparation for repetition. What aspects of self fulfilling prophecy and expectancies can account for crime, delinquency, urban riots, the assassinations of John F. and Robert Kennedy, Martin Luther King, Malcolm X, Richard M. Nixon's failed presidency, proliferation of drug trafficking, the Women's movement, expansion of urban gangs, and a host of other problems that confront this social order? If we were to analyze the riots in the urban areas for example, Harlem and Springfield, in the early part of the 1940s, would the violence in the South during the fifties, sixties, and seventies have anything in common with those earlier upheavals? Did the social conditions that begat one give rise to the others, or were they truly epiphenomenal occurrences unlikely to recur?

Perhaps crime, a form of social protest, is that which Mosca calls "mimetism."[14] This is the condition in which individuals get caught up in the passions, sentiments, and beliefs that prevail in the environment. This implies that those who submit have weak or conflicting normative structures and there fore are susceptible to accepting the norms of others. These individuals may be the ones who are perceived to be occupying an anomic state (normlessness). In this state, their behavior would be a function of their attitudes of expectancy. The concept, anomie, suggests tension. The behavior choice used to reduce

the tension is always contingent and balanced
between favorable benefits and unfavorable
costs. The benefit would be the reduction in
tension derived from some sense of deprivation, the cost is always the net level of
protest utilized to obtain the gain or the
minimization, in this case, of anomie.

To conclude, I will comment on a revised
paper presented by an ex-instructor to the
American Society of Criminology meeting in
1983. I do this for two reasons: 1) the address is a compact statement regarding the
social origin of crime, and 2) it lends considerable credence to the problems discussed
in this introduction. In fairness, the author
of the monograph agrees "that criminology is
still far from having a well-developed theory
or set of theories about social structure and
crime."[15]

While reasonable scholars can disagree in
regard to what the criminologist's task should
be in accounting for the criminalization
processes or explaining the patterns of law
breaking behavior, I contend like other critics, that it is this indecisiveness that
prevents the development of coherent calculi.
This indecisiveness is not totally the fault
of criminological theorists but rather the
failures are in a criminal process, which by
necessity must take into account the statutes.
This theory structuring process cannot use the
statutes, because of their vicissitude and
changing nature, not only in time, but locale,
to even begin to account for rates or patterns
of law breaking behavior. To suggest that an
analysis of the processes of political structure and how the criminal justice system
relates is an issue without direct connection
to criminal behavior, as some have advanced,
is without merit.[16] The attempts to make this
connection have been tendentious at best, but
nevertheless necessary if there is to be the

development of general theories. Therefore, a sufficient paradigm for the criminalization process would also have to account for the genesis of the criminal laws. This would enable us to hypothesize some theoretical assumptions about the inherent nature of those laws. This, of course, has been articulated in the philosophies of legal realism. It matters little whether operationalization of the laws are explaining historical or contemporary patterns of misconduct; theory construction using these variables could explain, at best, only the formulation of law in reference to specific tensions at a specific time. The theory, comprised of these variables, would not and cannot explain the genesis or function of the tension.

Similarly, an analysis of rates and patterns of law-breaking using fuzzy observational language, like variations in income in equality and/or variations in sexual inequality, permits only the construction of more paradigms where the proof becomes circular. The suggestion is, the use of factors, for example, economic, will not aid in constructing viable theories for expanding delinquency or criminality. Instead they will only yield findings to buttress the economist's arguments that criminal behavior has "utility" and is "rational" only. This explains why, in part, Cohen and Felson (1979); and Jackson (1984) can arrive at different conclusions after purportedly looking at the same behavior.

NOTES

1. Don Gibbons, "*Rethinking The Social Origin of Crime*" (Paper presented at the American Criminologists Society 1983): 1.

2. This analysis is based on Kuhn's discussion of paradigms and scientific revolutions. It is not based solely on his efforts, because unlike him I believe that there is transferability from the natural to the social sciences. See T.S. Kuhn, *"Logic of Discovery or Psychology of Research,"* in Imre Lakatos and Alan Musgrant, eds., *Criticism and the Growth of Knowledge* (Cambridge, England: Cambridge University Press, 1970).

3. Paul Sweezy, *"Toward a Critique of Economics,"* *Review of Radical Political Economics*, Spring 1980) 2.

4. Ibid. 186.

5. Kuhn said "translation Because as has often been remarked we have no access to a neutral linguistic means of reporting." Ibid. 268.

6. Kuhn suggested that translation may lead to persuasion or conversion.

7. E. Durkheim, *The Rules of the Sociological Method*, trans. Sarah A. Solovay and John H. Mueller, ed. George E. G. Catlin, (New York: The Free Press, 1965).

8. Nevertheless, in subsequent chapters this book will look at some issues, which although may not be "new" or world views, they will also not necessarily be in synch with prevailing thoughts.

9. See Peter Conrad and Joseph W. Schneider, *Deviance: From Badness to Sickness* (St. Louis: C. V. Mosby, 1980). Michael Foucault, *Madness and Civilization* (New York: Pantheon, 1965); Renee C. Fox, *"The Medicalization and Demedicalization of American Society"* Daedalus 106 (1977): 9-22.

10. See David Rothman, *Conscience and Convenience: The Asylum and its Alternatives in Progressive America* (Boston: Little Brown, 1980).

11. Prior to sociologists doing the Chicago Area Project in 1903, the only delinquent treatment programs were conducted by

innovative psychiatric clinics. In the early 1940s there was a collaboration by criminologists, social workers, and sociologists that resulted in the next major study, The Cambridge-Somerville Study. D. J. West and D.P. Farrington, eds. *"Who Becomes Delinquent?"* in *The Delinquent Way of Life* (London: Heinemann, 1977); D.J. West, *Present Conduct and Future Delinquency* (London: Heinemann 1969); also See Edwin Powers and Helen Witmer, *An Experimentation in the Prevention of Delinquency: The Cambridge-Somerville Youth Study* (New York: 1951); Edwin Schur, *Radical Nonintervention: Re-thinking the Delinquency Problem* (Englewood Cliffs, N.J.: Prentice-Hall, 1973).

    12. Harry Eckstein, *"On the Etiology of Internal Wars,"* *History and Theory* IV (1965): 150-51.

    13. Ted R. Gurr, *Why Men Rebel* (Princeton N. J.: Princeton University Press 1970): 169.

    14. Gaetano Mosca, *The Ruling Class*. Trans. Hannoah D. Kahn (New York: McGraw Hill, 1896, 1959): 184.

    15. Gibbons, *"Rethinking the Social Origin of Crime,"* 2.

    16. The current proliferation of child abuse cases is an example of this partnership.

2

Class, Family Structure, and Conflict

People have a strong sense of superiority regarding the existence of the nuclear family structures. This structure responds to social forces, which are more than figments of the sociological imagination. However, these social forces become visible, tangible, and above all practical only when they are expressed in political divisions and decisions.

The family is perceived as being the primary entity charged with upholding morality, preventing crime, maintaining order, and perpetuating civilization. In reality, the family is also boring, stifling, and intrusive. To its discredit, it has been identified as the unit that perpetuates oppression of women, abuses children, spreads neurosis, and prevents community. This suggest, that there is very little theoretical clarity to offer when analyzing the family.

Nevertheless, there are three general frameworks or orientations that have been proposed regarding the analysis of the family. One of these is by Shorter[1] who was influenced by Parsonian theory when he wrote the first comprehensive history of the family in Europe. He argued that the bourgeois family emerged as a nest of domesticity, as a private world

withdrawn from society, when the capitalist
economy liberated individuals from community
constraints. The capitalists eroded the collective authority of the village and other
corporate bodies and took over the intimate
affairs of the individual. Once capitalism
gave individuals the opportunity to escape
from parental restrictions many social changes
were imminent.

One reason for the perception and operationalization of class and family as a unit
can be tied to capitalism.[2] It is suggested
that the capitalistic system needs the family
to biologically reproduce the working class as
laborers for capitalistic production. This
suggests the division of classes. Even though
these laborers are individuals, it is essential to remember that the important unit of
society is not the individual, but rather the
family. Historically, the greatest function of
the family has been to generate the basic
elements that ultimately produced the state.[3]
Although the social order, in a psychological
sense, is ultimately based upon the social
instinct, expressed primarily in and through
the family, the wider and more highly developed forms of social organization, as exemplified by the state and society, are based upon
the Aristotelian principle of the distribution
of functions and the combination of efforts.

The dynamic changes in the structure of
the family can be traced to changing social
and cultural trends. For example, the growing
problem of unemployment not only has impacted
the family but it has also changed the social
composition of neighborhoods and communities.
It is instructional to look at the family from
a historical perspective to discern its function and attempt to apply that concept to the
contemporary familial structure. The literature shows that from the fifteenth to the
seventeenth centuries, the interpersonal

relationship between the members of a family were both cool and indifferent. There was little tolerance, and the slightest provocation between the spouses led to casual physical and verbal violence. As a result, the trial courts were clogged with cases of domestic assault and battery.

Despite this, it is significant to note that the one large scale study of crime conducted in medieval England in the early fourteenth century, shows that violence was more frequently directly outside the family than within. Only eight percent of the homicides, for example, were within the family, compared to over fifty percent in contemporary England. Even more striking is the fact that the family was more a unit for the perpetration of crime a third of all group crimes were by family members than a focus for crime. It is tempting to reiterate the family that slayed together, stayed together.

In addition, brutal and unprovoked assaults by idle youths who formed gangs from respectable families, such as the Mohawks, were a frequent occurrence on eighteenth century London streets. While romantic love and sexual intrigue was certainly the subject of the sixteenth and early seventeenth century poetry and of many Shakespearean plays, it was a reality that only existed in one very restricted social group, the one in which it had existed since the twelfth century, the house holds of the princes and the great nobles. In the other familial structures, if the husband could find sexual gratification through casual liaisons it was both expected and accepted. In any case, the expectation of felicity from marriage was pragmatically low because the marriage was no more than a union to increase the reproductive and nurturance functions. Perhaps all that can be said with confidence about the kin family is that there was at all social levels a general psychological atmo-

sphere of distance, manipulation, and deference, and that children, except for the rich,
were perceived to be economic drains. Family
relationships were characterized by inter-
changeability, so that the substitution of
another wife or another child was easy, and by
conformity to external rules of conduct. In
essence, these families were institutions that
lacked firm boundaries that the state had to
provide.

While the modern state provided those
firm boundaries, it was also a natural enemy
to the values of the clan and kinship. This is
attributed to the fact that the families
occupying this social and political level were
perceived to be a direct threat to the state's
own claim to prior loyalty. In the modern
state, there was a fundamental shift in human
values and in the social arrangements that
went with them. This is exemplified in the
period between 1560-1640, which has been
described as a fundamental shift from a "lin-
eage society," characterized by bounded hori-
zons and particularized modes of thought, to
the universalistic standard of values of a
"civil society. The reason for this change can
be traced to the Reformation, its powerful
drive for the Christianization of society and
its claim to overriding moral allegiance
through the preaching of the "word." This
period marks the emphasis on the nuclear
family. This shift of emphasis toward the
nuclear family was given powerful support by
Reformation theology and practice. For example, the medieval Catholic ideal of chastity
that was a legal obligation for priests,
monks, and nuns, and also perceived to be an
ideal state for all members of the community
to aspire to, was replaced by the idea of
conjugal affection. At that time, the marriage
state became the ethical norm for the virtuous
Christian.

The purpose of this union was no more

than what Milton described contemptuously, referring to the Pauline view, as the pre- scribed satisfaction of an irrational heat and the promiscuous draining of a carnal rage. Puritan preacher William Perkins described marriage as being a rage in itself far more excellent than the condition of a single life. This clearly was in contrast to the contempo- rary Catholic view of Cardinal Bellarmine, who perceived that marriage was a thing humane and that virginity was angelical. In other words, marriage is no more than an unfortunate neces- sity to cope with human frailty. This sancti- fication of marriage by matrimony was a con- stant theme of Protestant sermons during the sixteenth century, and they were directed to all classes in the society. This sentiment is also found in both the Puritan and Anglican moral theology of the early seventeenth centu- ry from William Gouge to Jeremy Taylor.

However, it was Archbishop Crammer, in England who first officially added, to chasti- ty and sanctification, a third reason for marriage, the avoidance of fornication and the procreation of legitimate children. The motive of mutual society, help, and comfort were added to his Prayer Book in 1549. He surmised that the one ought to have the other, both in prosperity and in adversity. Together, these defeated all efforts to legalize divorce. Remarriage was precluded even by an innocent party to the adultery or desertion of the wife. This stance was novel because marriage due to these circumstances was recognized by most Reformed churches abroad.

It is important to remember that the distinctive family lifestyles that have devel- oped as a result of historical and contempo- rary social processes must be assessed in realms of the family activities that can be identified. Contemporarily, these activities, euphemistically, have been denoted as being family values. Baker's article, "Rhetoric begs

questions: Which family's values?," point out
the problems in attempting to define the
family and the values that are supposed to be
inherent within them.[4] Baker said:

> The political types, Republicans in
> the 1992 presidential race were not
> talking about family values. They
> were talking about "family values,"
> an empty political phrase meaning
> "good,swell wholesomeness."
>   Family values, with quotation
> marks stripped away, are something
> else. When talking family values,
> let's remember the Jarrett family
> for she had a real-life model in the
> dreadful Ma Barker. In the *God fa-
> ther* trilogy, the Corleone family is
> tightly knit, intensely loyal and in
> fact a private government at bloody
> war with the public government and
> the very politicians who extol "fam-
> ily values."
>   In *Bonnie and Clyde*, people
> choose devotion to family over the
> rightful demands of the state. In
> *the Grapes of Wrath*, the Joad family
> survives in spite of government
> hostility and endures because the
> Joads believe their first obligation
> is to family rather than law. Im-
> plicit in the politician's call for
> "family values" is a summon for
> people to shape up start living
> their messy lives the way government
> wants those live lived.
>   What could be more loathsome
> than a government supervising the
> moral elevation of the family? To
> ascribe nobility to such structures
> is absurd, for each operates under
> its own rules and morality. "Family

values"? That just gas that politicians run on.

The primary problems with developing a theory of the family are the attempts to shift from the conflicts, discontinuities, and antagonism that are exemplified in the family structures and replace them with a perception of them being harmonious and self-regulating mechanism. This latter perception suggests the possibility of a consensus of comprehensive values. At the same time, it denotes the individualism which characterizes the structure. The family can only partially be perceived as the institution that functions to show the individual members the meaning of the world, how the individual attains ego strengths, and how they achieve the spiritual values that enables them to live in his world. The danger of this orientation is the tendency to skew the theory of the life cycle of the family from a critical analysis of the structure toward a search for organic unity of individuals. To be more specific I refer to Erikson who stated:

> We are speaking of goals and values and of the energy put at their disposal by child-training systems. Such values persist because the cultural ethos continues to consider the "natural" and does not admit of alternatives. They persist because they have become an essential part of an individual's sense of identity, which he must preserve as a core of sanity and efficiency. But values do not persist unless they work, economically psychologically and spiritually; and I urge that to this end they must continue to be anchored, generation after generation, in early child training; while child training, to remain consistent, must

be embedded in a system of continued
economic and cultural synthesis.[5]

Poster in response states:

There are no concepts for compre-
hending psychologically the wider
world, institutional patterns or
interpersonal relations. One still
does not grasp directly what goes on
between people, but only what happens to them. Thus for each stage in
the life cycle, society somehow
provides an appropriate institution:
religion for the stage of trust, law
and order for the stage of autonomy,
the economy for the stage of industry, and so forth. But the economic
system, for example, is important
for the first stage as the second:
impoverished peasant families cannot
provide sustenance for their babies,
so they die of malnutrition or become deformed or are destroyed by
their parents.[6]

Families do not live in a vacuum, but
within a community and the larger society.
Family actions and interactions are patterned
by family roles, with obviously idiosyncratic
variations which grow out of family histories.
Therefore, family life is embedded in a complex culture, each member holding beliefs,
images, expectations, evaluations, and other
ideological patterns that concern themselves,
other family members, and the world in which
they live.[7]

There are discrepancies between the
"ideal" and the "real" aspects of that which
constitutes husband, wife, mother, and father
roles. There are also differences in the
public versus private roles, and how they are

manifested in these domains. Similarly, there
are distinctions in regard to normative behavior for the children. Gan's study of Italians
in the West End of Boston describes the significance of the peer group as a socialization
mechanism for children: Before or soon after
they start going to school, boys and girls
form cliques or gangs. In these cliques, which
are sexually segregated, they play together
and learn the lore of childhood. The clique
influence is so strong, in fact that both
parents and school officials complain that
their values have difficulty competing with
those being taught in the peer group. The
sexually segregated clique maintains its hold
on the individual until late adolescence or
early adulthood.[8]

This socialization process is in stark
contrast to the Puerto Ricans' whose preference for association and beliefs are established in the warm interpersonal relationships
within their kinship group. Because most individual needs are met inside the family, there
has been little necessity to establish numerous interpersonal relations with persons other
than kin.[9] This process differs still from
those that are practiced by Korean and other
Asian families. Some of these families cling
to the traditional socialization practice
while others adhere to the more democratic
method of socialization that emphasizes mutual
respect between the children and parents.[10]

Many studies have conveyed a negative
image of the Black mother because she is
perceived to deviate from the middle-class
modes of child rearing. The fact remains that
these mothers have fulfilled their function of
socializing their children into the multiple
roles they must perform in this society. They
prepare the children to not only take on the
appropriate sex and age roles but also a
racial role. Black children must be socialized

to deal with the prosaic realities of White
racism that they encounter daily. This socialization requires the utilization of techniques
that are alien to middle-class White mothers.
There is also a strong suggestion that the
middle-class socialization patterns may not be
that desirable for the psychological growth of
the Black child. Instead the "casual" upbring-
ing of the Black child may produce a much
healthier personality than to imbue them with
the status anxieties that has been associated
with some of the rigid White middle-class
child rearing practices.[11]

If one wants to understand what families
are, how they work, how they transform individuals into not always comfortable models of
their class and society, one needs to focus on
the relation between child rearing patterns,
psychic development, family patterns, and the
social system in which they develop and are
played out. This orientation is crucial if one
is to use Parson's definition of the family,
because he defined the structure of the family
in relation to its basic function of socialization. A brief discussion of his orientation
is in order because it is the one that predominates in this culture. Parson reasoned that
only two structures are essential to the
family; a hierarchy of generations and a
differentiation of socializing agents into
"instrumental" and "expressive" figures.[12] He
postulated that all families contain these
features, and that the nuclear family manifests them particularly well. Here Parson has
elevated parental domination of children as
well as contemporary sex roles into inviolable
principles. In Parson's conceptualization, the
husband alone can provide the instrumental
role model and only the wife can provide the
expressive role model.

When confronted with anomalous anthropological evidence in which either the role

models do not conform to the nuclear family or
the immediate parents are not the primary
socializers, Parson and other advocates of his
position employ two strategies. First, when
confronted by cases like Margaret Mead's, who
has shown that women can be instrumental role
models, they deny the validity of the demonstration. Alternately, they argue that such
data bespeaks a society at a low level of
"differentiation" or "modernization" (definition utilized to describe Black families).
Secondly, when confronted with a pre-industri-
al community that is dominated by kinship,
Parson found that beneath the primary socializing group, which happened not to resemble a
nuclear family, the family mechanisms of to
day's middle-class family.[13] In this way,
kinship structures were explained as being the
precursor of the nuclear family prior to
differentiation. From this perspective, Parson
thought that he had proven the universalness
of the nuclear family, when in fact he denied
the intelligibility of the nonindustrial
society and the varying familial configurations. This is a condition that still prevails
in contemporary society.

NOTES

1. Edward Shorter, *The Making of the
Modern Family* (New York: (no publisher name
given) 1976). Peter Laslett offered another
thesis that contends that there was no extended family from the sixteenth century on ward.
On the contrary, the family unit was fairly
stable in size, consisting of the conjugal
unit with a small number of children. This led
him to question the use of the family as suitable object for historical investigation since
it seemed impervious to change (due to the

high mortality rate of the progeny). This factor affected the sentimentality and morality of that unit. See Peter Laslett, *The World We Have Lost* (New York: (no publisher given) 1965). The last orientation is in Aries' which he contends that the separation of the workplace from the home initiated new forms of intimacy, especially between parents and children. See Phillipe Aries, *Centuries of Childhood: A Social History of Family Life*, trans. R. Baldick, (New York: (no publisher name given) 1965).

2. The concepts of family and capitalism are that which has been called historicism in that the concepts are hypothesized for analysis. Instead of using them to identify aspects and elements of real societies, they are confused with reality itself. Instead, for example, there never was such a thing as a capitalist society or economy, but only societies and economics that displayed traits as capitalist to a greater or lesser extent. The same concept should be applied to family. See K. R. Popper, *The Poverty of Historicism* 2d ed.(London: Routledge and Kegan Paul: 1960).

3. Comte stated that society can no more be decomposed into individuals than a geometric surface can be resolved into lines, or a line into points. The simplest association, that is, the family, sometimes reduced to its original couple, constitutes the true unit of society. From it flow the more complex groups, such as classes and cities Cf. F.H. Giddings, *Principles of Sociology* (1896): 511-13.

4. Russell Baker, "Rhetoric Begs Question: Which Family Values?" Observer Column, New York Times Service, July 10, 1992.

5. Erik Erikson, "The Imposition of Sexual Morality," in *Sex-Pol Essays*, ed. Lee Baxandall (New York: (no publisher name given) 1972): 248.

6. Mark Poster, *Critical Theory of the Family* (London: Pluto Press, 1978): 71.

7. Helena Z. Lopata, "The Polish American Family," in *Ethnic Families in America: Patterns and Variations*, ed. Charles Mindel, Robert W. Habenstein, and Roosevelt Wright, Jr. (New York: Elsevier, 1988): 18.

8. Herbert Gan, *The Urban Villager* (Glencoe, Il: Free Press, 1962): 38.

9. See: Anthony J. Lauri, "Respeto, Relajo and Interpersonal Relations in Puerto Rico," *Anthropological Quarterly* 37 (1964): 53-67.

10. See: Bok-Lim Kim, *The Asian-American: Changing Patterns, Changing Needs* (N. J.: (no publisher name given), The Association of Korean Christian Scholars in North America): 1978.

11. See: Arnold Green, *"The Middle-Class Male Child and Neurosis,"* American Sociological Review* 11 (February 1946): 31-41; Andrew Billingsly, *Black Families in White American* (Englewood Cliffs, N. J.: Prentice-Hall, 1968).

12. Talcott Parsons et al., *Family Socialization and Interaction Process* (Glencoe, Ill.: Free Press, 1955): 45-47.

13. Talcott Parsons et al., *Social Structure and Personality* (New York: Free Press, 1964): 44n.

3

Class and Race

In *The Chaos of the Living City*, Tilly explored the proposition that instead of urbanization "the structure of the community" led
to collective violence such as the bread
riots, industrial strikes, and revolutions.[1]
This was a refutation of the "disorganization
hypothesis" that suggested that those on the
margin of urban existence for example, the
under class, blacks, etc., are most likely to
engage in urban protest.[2] Although this paradigm no longer commands the respect it once
did in sociology, it still has its adherents.
For example, the Cone Commission Report used
this hypothesis to explain the Watts Riots in
Los Angeles. After an exhaustive study the
report concluded that the rioters were primarily persons marginal to the urban experience
and society, that is, recent migrants, the
unemployed, and the poorly educated conclusion
seemingly lacking in merit.[3]

It is well established that criminogenic
conditions such as poverty, family instability, slum residence, and migration, conditions
that the Chicago School sociologists operationalized to construct their disorganization
hypothesis, are indeed important factors to be
considered when assessing crime. However,
separately these are dimensions and as such

they are also viable and logical responses to
these contexts. As dimensions, they serve to
differentiate among groups and those with
which the group interacts. These dimensions
occur because individuals develop insurgent
values to the varying social contexts. These
insurgent values constitute varying contexts
that conflict with the institutionalized
values of maintaining order. This value is
operationalized to suppress non-normative
dimensions. A context comprised of insurgent
values must assess the social structures to
determine how it should function to address
counter values contrary to its interest. A
discussion of crime in terms of insurgent
value is meaningless. It is also meaningless
to suggest that a response to a perceived
suppressive context is more prevalent in one
racial group than another.

In order to rationally discuss the origin
of crime, the use of social exchange theory is
advocated. Social exchange theory is concerned
with how the structure of rewards and costs
relationships affect patterns of interactions.
In its most common form, the theory applies to
social interactions that meet the following
conditions: (1) actors are dependent on one
another for outcomes they value; (2) actors
behave in ways that increase outcomes they
positively value and decrease outcomes they
negatively value; and (3) actors engage in
recurring exchanges with specific partners
over time.[4] A fundamental prediction of the
theory is that the frequency and distribution
of exchange in the relation varies with the
amount and distribution of power. The greater
the average power in the relation, the greater
the exchange. The greater the imbalance in
power, the more asymmetrical the distribution
of exchange. Theorists have proposed two
different processes that can be used to evalu-
ate out comes relative to their expectation.

One outcome is cognitive, that is an evaluation which compares the actual to expected results. The other is normative or moral, a process which the individual uses to compare the results to "justice." Justice in this sense means equity, equality, or need.

Criminal and delinquent behaviors are contexts, and when they occur it is generally in response to the prevailing context of the social exchange. It is this context that is conducive to its expression. Stated differently, the social exchange configuration gives rise to all behavior, and this behavior is a response to the normative values currently being adhered to. Crime is the emergence of insurgent values in response to the configuration. The emerging values and normative values provide the potential for conflict and characterize the prevailing social condition. Failure to look at behavior in conflict or exchange terms is to provide no basis for the origin of contrary social behavior. This type of reasoning is valid because it has been demonstrated, for example, that when Whites confront similar social context as Blacks in the urban areas, the crime and delinquency rates are also similar. This similarity can be explained in terms of the prevailing nature of the social exchange system, the normative values and their true instrumental function. The crime rates for the two groups will decline in direct relation to the diminishing need for insurgent values in an attempt to balance the exchange. As this occurs, there is a lessening of conflict and a change in the individual and group context.

In addition to delinquents and criminals, heretics, vagrants, and other types of marginally integrated individuals, prominently mentioned in the influential efforts by Chicago School sociologists, are examples of individuals who possess insurgent values, dimensions, and contexts in the urban areas. These

are individuals who experience social isolation because they are perceived to represent a
context of considerable concern to the social
order. Social exchange determines the behavioral responses to the conflict values of
these individuals because in the broader
community, the actors behave in ways that increase outcomes they positively value, and
they respond by labelling, conceptualizing,
and stigmatizing. As a result, these individuals come to be perceived as social misfits due
to their conflictive dimensions and context.
However, it should be remembered, these individuals do not create the conflict, rather
they present a conflict to the social order.
Although, the contexts of the varying groups
in the social order are not comparable, due to
the social exchange configuration, behavioral
expectations are comparable.

Perhaps a less sanguine but no less per-
suasive argument regarding behavioral expectations is one which contends that the social
exchange conditions experienced by Whites,
regardless of differentiation, and Blacks have
been comparable. Therefore, there is a general
belief that behavioral expectations for the
groups should be similar. However, an expectation of commonality for dissimilar groups
would be inane. Ironically, social exchange
becomes a case of expecting the victim to
assimilate and practice the attitudes and
behavior of the oppressor.

The abuser-depressor configuration, an
aspect of social exchange, can be utilized to
characterize the difference in dimensions and
contexts that exist between Whites and Blacks
in general. Theoretically, even if a commonality existed in terms of political, social, and
economic conditions, one should expect differential behaviors that would be attributable to
differential histories of abuse, oppression,
and deprivation. If we could factor out differential historical experiences, one would

still expect different performance rates due
to the different contexts and dimensions
Blacks occupy within the social structure.
These contexts and dimensions are perceived to
be conflictive, because like the vagrant and
heretic, their presence creates a conflict. In
terms of social exchange, the conflict centers
around differential values regarding race.
This differentiation is an essential aspect of
racism and as such it is one of the dimensions
differentially comprising the contexts of
Blacks and Whites.

The dimensions and context can be assessed in terms of the laws and its enforcement apparatus. The function of the latter is
to regulate the recurring exchanges. A cogent
example of how recurring exchanges function to
devise an outcome that is valued through
differential enforcement and incarceration
rates can be seen in Moses's study. His controlled investigation analyzed matched sets of
contiguous White and Black neighborhoods in
Baltimore. These matched sets were partially
equated to selected socioeconomic factors of
the inhabitants and assessed in terms of
differential arrest rates.

The two neighborhoods had similar dimensions as respect to the populations' racial
homogeneity, dominance of lower occupational
and education levels, and mean size of the
household. However, there were variances in
the percentage of home owners-Whites home
owners exceeding Blacks homeowners 7 to 1 in
one matched neighborhood, and 10 to 1 in the
other. The results revealed that Blacks exceeded Whites in arrest rates for felonies by
a ratio of 6 to 1. How would one account for
this disparity despite seemingly similar
dimensions between the four groups? Moses
suggested that the disparity could be attributed to racial proscriptions accentuated by
the burden of socio-economic status.[5] In other

words, race was a critical factor in determining who was arrested. Despite this, and
other studies supporting Mose's interpretation
of his findings, there is a persistent belief
that race is not a correlate of crime. Social
exchange theory would confirm that race is a
direct correlate of crime and delinquency because it is a crucial determining factor that
is used to decide who is arrested, charged,
and sanctioned.

The issues of race, arrest, and the
definition of crime has been researched by
many sociologists. However, a review of their
works make it difficult to discern whether
they were structuring and/or validating social
exchange configurations and the existing
policies. Generally, they spent little effort
in analyzing why the dimensions and contexts
that emanated from it gave rise to delinquent
and criminal behaviors.

Sellin was one of the exceptions. He
utilized social exchange to assess the dimensions and contexts to the social order when he
wrote:

> Nothing points to a conclusion that
> the Negro's real criminality is
> lower or as low as the whites. The
> American Negro lacks education and
> earthly goods. He has had very lit-
> tle political experience and indus-
> trial training. His contact with
> city life has been unfortunate, for
> it has forced him into the most
> dilapidated and various areas of our
> great cities. Like a shadow over his
> whole existence lies the oppressive
> race prejudice of his white neig-
> hbor, restricting his activities,
> and thwarting his ambitions. It
> would be extraordinary, indeed, if
> this group were to prove more law
> abiding than the white, which enjoys

more fully the advantages of a civilization that the Negro has helped to create. The assumption that the Negro presents the higher rate of real criminality is, therefore, no indictment of the Negro race. The responsibility lies where power, authority, and discrimination has its source, the dominant white group. To that group the existence of a high rate of crime among Negroes is a challenge which cannot be brushed aside by platitudes about "race inferiority," "inherent depravity," or other similar generalizations. The only way to meet it is by a conscientious and determined search for the causes in general among Negroes in particular.[6]

Sellin correlated social interaction to social structure in an attempt to derive an understanding of the correlation between dimensions, contexts, and behavior. In addition to social exchange, the urban social structure refers to those factors that organize the city for example, size, density, and heterogeneity of human population.[7] These factors have been deemed to give rise to pathologies in this form of social order. How ever, it is not the social order per se, but rather the nature of the social exchange that gives rise to the pathologies. They may be construed to be reactions to the conditions of urbanization. However, there is no credible evidence to support the contention that the urban area is inherently more pathological than other forms of social orders. While it is common knowledge that pathologies, like crimes, are not spatially specific, it is possible that due to the density greater opportunities are provided for riots, rebel-

lions, social disorder, and social movements
to occur. It may not necessarily be density
but rather a greater ability to net work with
a critical mass of people who share similar
contexts that lead to these behaviors. Like a
tautology, the factors of urbanization are
attributed to the culturally differentiated
populations and the rise of varying forms of
deviance. However, social exchange theory
reveals that it is not the heterogeneity of
the population, but rather it is the heterogeneity of the economic classes which provide
the conditions for differential behavior.
Therefore, Hauser's effort to extend Wirth's
social disorganization hypothesis was wrong
when he contended that racial conflict, emanating from these pathologies, was a specific
social problem attributed solely to urbanization. He stated:

> At present rapid urbanization in the
> United States involves the absorp-
> tion of new streams of immigrants
> with difficult problems of adjust-
> ment to urban life. The difficulty
> of intergroup relation especially
> that of the white-Negro relation are
> particularly trouble some; and they
> are being greatly aggravated by the
> high rate of immigration and by
> rapid urban growth.[8]

The tension in race relations could not
then nor now be attributed to urbanization.
Rather this tension was and is a consequence
of social exchange that both created and
fostered racism and economic competition. Nor
was rapid immigration problematic, as is often
suggested, until racism and competition were
factored in. Racism, competition, and insurgent values were the factors that gave rise to
and provided impetus to differentiate the

population.

Wirth and others from the Chicago School examined a class and caste configuration in an attempt to understand the social arrangement. Clearly that which they found was both a racist and racialist social order. The social arrangement was racist because it was premised on a concept of individual deficiency. Deficiency theories place the blame on the racial group and the individuals in that group for the conditions they confront in the social structure. Blacks like the Poles, Irish, and particularly immigrants from Southern Europe, or the most recent immigrants, were perceived to be problematic to the social order because they were deemed to be biologically inferior. Therefore, it was reasoned, their biological deficient traits rendered them incapable of handling the strains and rigors presented by the urban area. They were also deemed to be incapable of participating in a symmetrical distribution of exchange. However, Park, Wirth, Burgess, Small, and others failed to realize or acknowledge that these individual's failure were not the result of biological determinants, but rather their failure was intrinsically ties to the cultural determinants for example, political power and values regarding prejudice, hate, and the general failure by the social order to rationally confront poverty conditions prevailing in the urban area.

To reiterate, urbanism did not give rise to behavioral pathologies, rather it was the structure of the urban area. Blacks were not, as Hause contended troublesome. Instead it was their presence that was troublesome for those attempting to relegate them to the bottom of the class and caste configuration. Therefore, in the social exchange matrix, these people confronted both race and social inequality. These two factors were utilized to impoverish and to keep them poor. Those in the classes

and caste above them operationalized social
exchange elements to increase the outcomes
they valued. Normatively, they contended that
their social status, values, and attitudes
were similar to those that the Blacks held.
Given this variance in normative expectation,
one would expect the emergence of insurgent
values and attitudes evolving around the sense
of equity.

In response, Blacks assumed many forms or
types of dimensions and contexts, and there
fore they cannot be defined as Eysenck attempted to do in terms of correlated traits.[9]
Blacks are no more a type of group than
Whites. This is because a group of traits may
not be correlated to biological acts or action
tendencies to explain an individual or group.
Biological traits do not determine behavior,
rather it is how the social order reacts to
those traits that determines behavior. Although Eysenck advanced this proposition in
terms of offenders, it has been used to describe groups. He advocated the correlation
between traits despite the Glueck's conclusion
that their typological investigation failed to
yield a positive correlation between the
assumption of a "delinquent personality" and
body type, personality traits, and socio-
cultural factors. They also added there was no
consistent combination of physique, character,
temperament, and environment that can account
for this designation.[10] Despite this, Seelig
advance an explanation that seems to drive the
general perception that there is a difference
between types and classes. This has also been
applied to groups. He saw "types" as being
distinct from class with the latter being
mutually exclusive and the former lacking this
characteristic. Using both, he developed eight
categories to differentiate between individuals who committed criminal behavior. One of
his categories, number eight, was comprised of

individuals who lacked social discipline.[11] It is this class that predominates the public's concern and serves as the basis for the construction of public policy. Why do these individuals lack social discipline? Why should they comply to social expectations when it is clearly not in their best interest? Social exchange theory directs the analysis.

Emanating from the lack of social discipline and why individuals should be disciplined when it is not in their best interest is the source of contentment and antagonism. The nature of and amount of social discipline determines the characteristics of the social order, and social exchange determines the differential values regarding these characteristics. This configuration gives rise to both the form and rate of crime and delinquency. Therefore, crime and delinquency are a function of, or more precisely, a response to antagonism generated by operationalization of social exchange.

Fundamental to an understanding of the history of crime in the United States, it becomes necessary to consider the paraphrases of Karl Marx and Herman Melville who asked in so many terms, how could White men repress or "mutilate" themselves, become "less" than they "were," and construct a culture of "self-renunciation" and "alienation"? How did their process of domination produce a rage in and about themselves so intense it overwhelmed even rationality itself?[12] The process that enabled these White individuals to arrive at this point has its genesis in antiquity.[13] It was fixed in a process of domination which produced the rage so intense that it overwhelmed rationality itself.[14] This irrationality is still manifested in contemporary society and has, as usual, been expressed through forms of racism.[15]

In response to Marx and Melville, they

got there by maintaining fetishes regarding
social exchange and production to the inurement of the relevance regarding that which
they produced. In the process, they divorced
themselves from judgments regarding the distinction that Galbraith made between the
satisfaction of needs which are absolute to
those which only serve to make them feel
superior to their fellow.[16] A superiority that
skewed the social exchange system in their
favor.

Contemporarily, Welsing argued that
Whites bear responsibility for what ever
disorders exists in the urban area and the
ghetto. He said, "Racism is a behavior system
that is organized because White people are a
minority on the planet. The Black male is
threat to White genetic annihilation. And so
he is profoundly attacked in this society."[17]
The attacks are most prominent in the media
which overwhelming emphasizes the pathology of
black behaviors, drugs, gangs, crime, violence, poverty, and illiteracy almost to the
exclusion of reporting on normative factors
that occur in these areas.

Social exchange is exhibited in the
differential press coverage, collective irrationality, and the process of dominance that
has led to the development of a caste system
in addition to one of class. This system is
one in which Blacks are situated on the bottom. Historically, this class and caste system
gave rise to a perception by Whites in the
social exchange paradigm that Blacks were and
are no more than "child/ savages," the Indians
"pure savages," and the Chinese were "hea-
thens." These perceptions were more than mere
stereotypes. These were images carefully and
consistently promoted by the wider culture and
policy makers. The perception was pregnant
with implications because it served to create
a social order in which the classes would con-

stitute caste divisions. Once this social order was functional, with the inclusion of the factor race, it was instrumental in constructing a society in which white reigned supreme over black, red, and yellow in the exchange system.

Herbert Spencer, was instrumental in the attempt to validate this racist perspective with his bastardization of Darwin's theory of evolution. To Spencer, who created the philosophy of Social Darwinism, a ideology which was both antisocial and anti-Darwin, the social order was comprised of the "survival of the fittest." This meant that the suffering by the poor was nature's mechanism for assuring the survival of the fittest--just as the wealth of the rich was nature's means for assuring the propagation of superior types. He and racialist William Graham Sumner strenuously opposed any law or action designed to protect the poor from slum living conditions, from dangerous working conditions, and from the perils of not having enough money to pay for medical and hospital care when needed. To Sumner, poverty belonged to the struggle for existence and we are all born, he believed, into that struggle. He felt that the economists who seemed to be terrified that distress and misery still remained on earth and who felt that this continuum of social injustice bears harshly on the weak were all guilty of very fuzzy and unscientific thinking. It mattered little to Spencer, Sumner, Malthus, Ross, and Banfield the color of the individuals who comprised either the pauper class or the slums. Their survival had to result, they contended, from an act of providence rather than a social program.

Class and caste generated an isolation or segregation of entire groups into spatial settings. This isolation created distance from others in the social setting. Park felt that this separation was a natural process, and that the social forces of economic competition

generated by division of labor were forces
that helped to foster this social distance. He
contended that individual groups in the segregated areas are there due to earlier processes
of competition. Once in existence, he felt,
poor people will naturally migrate to specific
areas to the exclusion of all others. He also
felt that some of these areas were "natural"
areas for the expression of crime and vice,
regardless of the characteristics of the
nationality living there.[18]

The only thing natural about the areas
were the stigmas and reactions to them. These
were the "natural areas" in which each racial
or immigrant group was forced to situate.
These were the slums, and perceptions that
they were disorganized were in comparison to
those urban settings not similarly situated.
Despite Park's conclusion that as individuals
in the slums were assimilated into the broader
social setting the pathologies do not follow
them, a horde of policy makers contend other
wise. They fail to under stand that the characteristics of the social exchange gives rise
to poverty, deprivation, and the social condition that accounts for the "pathological" behavior. These characteristics also determine
the dimensions and contexts by clarifying the
relationship between capital and labor.

Mechanically, the exchange system in the
United States has always been manifested in
the structure of a social system in which the
ruling class stratified to provide a continual
access to an "industrial and agrarian reserve
army." This "army" functioned to alleviate the
ruling class' continual concern with trade
unions, strikes, or social revolution. In the
aristocracy, evolving principles were used to
construct a social configuration that enabled
the affluent to criticize all attempts to out
law slavery on the basis that slavery prevented the conflict between labor and capital.

Exercising economic acumen, they correctly reasoned that this type of conflict must inevitably exist in populous and crowded communities where wages were the regulator between the classes. However, in the aristocracy, the asymmetrical distribution of exchange accomplished the same end.

The utilization of slavery, rationalized in part by the prevention of conflict, contrasted to agrarian societies in which labor was White and free. In those settings, workers had certain political rights that could be used to help control a domination threat to the asymmetrical arrangements. However, in a slave society where labor was Black and in bondage, the culture-makers "capitalist", could exercise dominion over the "working class." This was achieved through the denial of rights to assemble, vote, or bear arms. In addition, labor could be punished for insubordination and all work-related infractions. It was in every sense a system structured to maximize cognitive outcomes. It was also a system in which slave labor was perceived to be a form of social control that would ensure tranquility, order, and a distorted perception of normative social exchange. This condition can be contrasted to the exploited and miserable conditions endured by White workers living and working in free societies. The slavers contended this form of labor was preferable and normative because slavery made the workers "comfortable", "docile", "submissive," and "happy."[19]

It is impossible to chronicle the extent of acts of violence this perception initiated in the attempts to maintain the system. However, the few statistics gathered and preserved by Whites reveal that in the period after emancipation and prior to 1894, more than ten thousand Blacks were killed in cold blood without the formality of judicial pro-

cess or legal execution. Historical records
reveal that this behavior occurred with almost
absolute immunity for those who chose to kill
Blacks; during this time, only three White men
were tried, convicted, and executed for these
types of crimes.

The occurrence and response to this behavior enables one to make an assessment about
the characteristics of the social exchange,
the public's conscience, the social system,
the routine entrenched brutality, and the per-
vasiveness of White crime. Social exchange was
utilized to provide the rationale for the
criminal behavior that centered around the
perceived emergency to its projected out comes
which the South felt it confronted. These
emergency responses were deemed counter acts,
or exchanges, to 1) impending race riots; 2)
the franchise; 3) maintenance of the purity of
White women; and 4) the planned insurrection.
No insurrection nor riot by Black people ever
occurred nor was one Black ever convicted for
violently protesting their oppressive state.
Despite this, the killings were justified in
the mind of White Southerners. As an aside, it
is instructional to also note, that during
these so called insurrection and riots, not
one White man or woman was even injured let
alone killed.

This criminal behavior occurred in a
social system, capitalistic, where greater
emphasis was placed on property than on human
rights. This orientation impelled those of
means to form interest groups and to influence
the formation of laws to protect those interests. These economic interests were instrumental in the racial oppression. However, justification for this form of domination was both
dependent and independent of economic considerations.

These interest groups, capitalist elites,
utilized economic factors that represented the
basic elements necessary for class configura-

tions. The concept "Class" is one of the most widely used and thoroughly contested terms in the social sciences. While there is little agreement among sociologists regarding the meaning of the term, it resonates with political meaning for some, but for others it means no more than an individual's position on a scale which correlates factors, for example, year of education, income occupation, etc.

However, Weber perceived class as being multidimensional. In this schema it is comprised and weighted in combination using a variety of position effects, for example, property, income, occupation, authority, education, and/or prestige. Although the concept of Class is both objective and subjective as well in its dimensions, it is important to note that the dimensions can be realized separately in the realms of production and/ or consumption. Although production and property relations are important, neither are the only criterion nor determinant of class position. Therefore, the Weberian schema of class is not a static one. Like Weber's, the Marxist perspective is also a dynamic one. In this framework classes are defined in realms of their relationship to the other classes within a given system of production. In a capitalist system the social relations of production form the material basis of class, rather than market relations or relations of exchange. Marx contended that as such these social classes stood in contradictory and antagonistic relationship with one another.[20]

A minimalist assessment of class perceives the class structure as serving to shape broad constraints on action and change. This perspective differs from those that analyzes the division within classes or between sectors, the relationship between work and community, or the role that the state and ideology play in shaping the collective organization of

classes.[21] In short, this book sees class as
being a potent and systematic determinant of
individual action and social development. As
such, this perspective is consistent with the
notions of social context, dimension, and con-
structional theory because it refers to the
divisions between sectors, groups, and within
classes.

In the mid 1960s, urbanologists and analysts began to discuss a new dimension to the
urban crisis. This discussion centered around
the large sub population of lower-income
families and individuals whose behavior contrasted sharply with the general population's.
Despite a high rate of poverty in the urban
areas, which was apparently acceptable policy
wise, throughout the first half of the twentieth century it has now become an issue of concern. This despite President Bush's assertion
that class is "for European democracies or
something else--it isn't for the United States
of America. We are not going to be divided by
class."[22]

This myth of classlessness has a history
that can be traced first to the framers of the
Constitution who refused to impose land and
property qualifications for federal office.
More recently by millions of Americans who are
two paychecks, if not less, away from insol-
vency. However, these individuals protest
strenuously against the concept of class
stratification.[23] However, a casual perusal of
the individuals who are unemployed, not to
mention under employed and those who have
given up on looking, teenage pregnancies, out-
of-wedlock births, female-headed families,
welfare dependency, and those increasingly
involved in serious crime are perceived to be
individuals who have failed primarily to
achieve or hold on to their "middle-class"
position. The rates of these occurrences have
reached catastrophic proportions. These condi-

tions have occurred because of the unequal distribution of privileges and bounties that are attributed to stratification. These inequities have created additional hazards, in every sector of life, for those not situated in the preferred middle or upper class. A cogent example of these inequities is the federal housing donation of close to $40 billion awarded every year to millions earning more than $50,000 annually. The "donation" takes the form of tax abatements, for example, the mortgage interest and property tax exemptions and the capital gains deferral on housing sales.

How did so many Americans get to this point of misperception regarding class? We can initiate the analysis by looking at the urban area beginning in the early or mid 1960s. While urban analysts hardly provided an adequate explanation of changes in the social organization of inner-city communities, they did forcefully and candidly discuss the rise of social dislocations among the inner city Blacks. There was a fixation on these people despite the exodus from the urban area to the hinterlands and the problems that this movement created. The fixation was on the symptom of the lower-class urban or ghettoized Blacks who were unable to participate in this exodus. To explain this phenomenon, the characteristics ascribed to these people for example, low aspirations, poor education, family instability, high rates of illegitimacy, chronic unemployment, escalating crime, proliferating drug addictions and alcoholism, and high morbidity and mortality rates were explored and re-explored. In addition, there was the omnipresent specter, but never discussed as the etiology for these symptoms, of the blackening of the cities and the ascribed inferior racial status. Rarely discussed were the burdens of despair and loathing that these individuals confronted daily that may help to account for the rigidization of their underclass status.

Those who discussed these conditions and experiences of inequality closely tied their discussions to the structure of inequality. This was an attempt to explain how the economic and social situations into which many disadvantaged Blacks are born produced modes of adaptation and behavior that were centered around norms and patterns that supposedly took the form of a self-perpetuating pathology.

A more prevalent perspective was the conservative one that crystallized around a set of arguments that dealt with the importance of different group values and competitive resources to account for the experiences of the disadvantaged underclass. When reference was made to the economic or political structure, it was in terms of the adverse effects that various government programs had on individuals or group behavior and initiative. Somehow it was felt that donations to one class fostered initiative while donations to another class had a deleterious effect.

The major problem with the conservative explanations is its racial orientation. How ever, these explanations have become, if not always been, just as apropos for explaining urban White--under and lower class behaviors. To illustrate, one merely has to look at the homeless rate and idleness due to unemployment that must be attributed primarily by the killing off of one industry after another by corporate America. The ramifications of the lack of employment has created a condition that has given rise to and enables us to focus on the maladies to see if in fact they are indigenous to the values and predispositions of Black individuals. What we find is, that these conditions are linked to the structure of inequality and that these specific behaviors are responses to it. To illustrate, I cite the National Center for Health Statistics that reveals that the rate for unmarried Black

women was 89 births per 1,000, compared to 27
for Whites. But the White rate grew fifty one
percent from 1980, while the Black rate rose
seven percent over the same period. Some of
this growth can be attributed to class "slippage" or the downward movement of individuals
from the middle to lower classes. Despite
this, and the previously mentioned problems,
there are individuals and policy makers who
staunchly refuse to address any of these
issues. Instead, they continue to utter the
conservative perspective and claim that we are
"one."

This contention lacks credibility when we
consider that there are 23 million Black
Americans and one-third of them live below the
poverty line, which qualifies them for inclusion into the underclass.[24] Despite the fact
that nearly one in ten U.S. citizens have a
Hispanic heritage and that behind only Asians,
Hispanics are the fastest growing segment of
the nation no learned individual can argue
that "their" problems are not multiplying
almost as fast as their barrios. Census data
reveals that during the past decade, the
nation's Hispanic population has grown by
fifty three percent from 14.6 million in 1980
to 22.4 million in 1990. But the majority of
these Hispanics have not, and show no likeli-
hood of being, assimilated into the U.S. main
stream nor escaping their underclass status.
This inertia can not be attributed to their
resisting of societal strains to pull them
from this condition.

There have been very specific reasons for
the conservatives to address all of these
issues in racial terms. Primarily discussions
of this type tend to shift the focus of the
analysts away from classes and a discussion of
the consequences of racism, racial isolation,
and economic subordination to the perceived
internal "pathological" differences within the

Black community. More over, since the problems
are defined in racial terms, very little discussion is devoted to either the problems
created by economic shifts and their impact on
the Black community or to the need for economic reform or to social exchange. This has enabled the conservatives to effectively divert
attention from the appropriate solutions to
the dreadful economic conditions of not only
the poor Blacks but the Whites as well and
makes it difficult for both the blacks and the
lower class whites to see how their fates are
inextricably tied to the structure of the
American economy.[25]

The conservatives have acknowledged that
a growing number of inner city residents do
get locked into a culture of poverty but that
government programs are not the solution to
their plight. They cite a study conducted by
the Michigan Panel Study of Income Dynamics
(PSID) which tracked the actual experiences of
the poor who received welfare assistance in a
longitudinal fashion. What they found from a
series of initial studies based on the (PSID)
data was that only a very small percentage of
those in poverty and on welfare were long-term
cases. For example, one study contends that
only three percent of the population was poor
throughout a ten-year time span, and another
study reported that only 2.2 percent of the
population was poor eight of the ten years
(1968-1978) covered in the research. These
studies were cited to refute the notion of a
permanent underclass.

However, more valid and recent studies
based on the (PSID) data seriously challenges
these findings. Specifically, these studies
revealed that the previous (PSID) research on
spells of poverty and welfare dependency observed over a fixed time frame--say eight or
ten years, underestimated the length of
spells, because some individuals who appear to

have short episodic spells of poverty or welfare receipt are actually beginning or ending
long spells.

After correction for this problem, a new
study was necessitated to identify spells of
poverty and welfare receipt; they then calculated the exit probabilities by year to estimate the duration of spells. This revised
methodology found that although most people
who become poor during some point in their
lives experience poverty for only one or two
years, a substantial subpopulation remain in
poverty for a very long time. Indeed, these
long term poor constitute about sixty percent
of those in poverty at any given point in time
and are in a poverty spell at a given point in
time. The study also found that the average
child who became impoverished due to familial
status changes and had to live in a female-
headed household endured a spell of poverty
lasting almost twelve years. It was also reported, on the average, approximately twenty
percent of the poverty spells began at birth.
When these spells occur at birth they tend to
last at least ten years. In contrast, the
Black child appears to confront a poverty
spell that will exceed three decades. These
spells of poverty were similar for those
receiving welfare receipts.

While conservatives lack alternatives but
to accept the data that supports the existence
of a under class that exhibits the problems of
long-term poverty and welfare dependency, they
fail to associate the genesis of social dislocation in the inner-city urban areas as being
primarily a condition attributed to racism.
They also fail to, or refuse to, under stand
how a cycle of pathology that characterized
not only the ghettoes, but also the inner-city
urban "non-ghetto" area can be comprehended in
realms of racial oppression and its manifestations. They persistently refuse to accept the
argument that there is a conscious refusal by

Whites to accept Blacks as equal human beings, despite a history replete with examples, and their willful, systematic effort to deny Blacks equal opportunity. This has led to a complex set of issues that must be analyzed from a race specific thesis because it was race that provided the etiology for the conditions. Rather than intellectual honesty, they point to the deepening economic class divisions between the have and have nots in the Black community to refute the racism thesis. They contend that you could not have this class cleavage in the Black community if racism was invoked as equally and vigorously across class boundaries as the liberals suggest in the Black community. Nor can one account for the rapid deterioration in the inner-city in the post-civil rights period compared to the period that immediately preceded the notable civil rights victories. The conservatives put the question more pointedly, even if racism continues to be a factor in the social and economic progress of some Blacks, can it be used to explain the sharp increase in inner-city social dislocation since 1970? In response, they contend that the proponents of the contemporary racism thesis fail to distinguish between the past and present factors and effects of racism on the different segments of the Black population. It is quixotic how they, the conservatives, can fail to recognize that the effects of historic racism are directly correlated with contemporary racism, and that they both have had an insidious impact on the economic class position of Blacks and modern economic trends confronting them. Surely, they must realize that policy programs are based, although not necessarily acted upon, utilizing the premise of racism, and that these have given rise to the deepening social dislocation, unemployment, etc. These conditions to cite Michael Harrington are:

the result of the psychological
state of mind of white America, a
kind of deliberate, and racist, ill
will. it is a relatively simple part
of the problem for there is an economic structure of racism that will
persist even if every white who
hated blacks goes through a total
conversion (racism is not seen as a
state of mind but as) an occupational hierarchy rooted in history and
institutionalized in the labor market.[26]

Conservatives argue with this conclusion
and state that America and worldwide economies
have little to do with race. This seems in-
credulous considering the Third World countries and the hue of their population.

NOTES

1. Charles Tilly, "Revolution and Collective Violence" in Fred I. Greenstein and Nel-
son W. Polsby, eds. *Handbook of Political
Science* (Reading: Mass.: Addison-Wesley,
1972); Charles Tilley, *From Mobilization to
Revolution* (Reading: Mass.: Addison-Wesley,
1978): 86.
2. This orientation can be traced back to
the Chicago School of sociologist e.g., Burgess, Park, and Ogburn, who contended that
social disorganization as well as collective
behavior, social movements, and protests were
linked.
3. An analysis of the 1965 Watts Riot and
the 1992 Los Angeles (Rodney King) riot reveals that if you define the middle class as
white collar and skilled blue collar or if
educational achievement is the determinant or
if every one above the poverty line is middle

class or higher, only one out of six American
Blacks was in the middle class in 1965, compared to four out of six in 1992. This alone
suggests that the Cone Commission was in
error, because this was not the profile of the
typical rioter in 1992.

4. Traditionally, exchange theories were
restricted to the exchange of positive (reward) outcomes.

5. E. Moses, "Differentials in Crime
Rates between Negroes and Whites based on
Comparisons of Four Socio-Economically Equated
Areas," *American Sociological Review* 12 (Au-
gust 1947): 441-520.

6. T. Sellin, "The Negro Criminal, A
Statistical Note," *The Annals of the American
Academy of Political and Social Science* 140
(1928): 64.

7. Louis Wirth, "Urbanism as a Way of
Life" in Paul K. Hatt and Albert Reiss, eds.,
Cities and Society (New York: The Free Press
of Glencoe, 1957): 50.

8. Philip Hauser, "The Social, Economic
and Technological Problems of Rapid Urbanization," in Bert F. Hoselitz and Wilbert E.
Moore, eds., *Industrialization and Society*
(The Hague: Mouton for UNESCO, 1966): 213.

9. H. J. Eysenck, *The Structure of Human
Personality*, 2d ed. (London and New York: Free
Press, 1960): 10ff.

10. Sheldon Glueck and Eleanor Glueck,
Physique and Delinquency (New York: Harper
Row, 1956), 15 ff.

11. Seelig, Ernst, *Lehrbuch de Krim-
inologie*, (Graz: (no publisher name given),
1950).

12. Robert T. Takaki, *Iron Cages: Race
and Culture in 19th Century America* (Seattle:
University of Washington Press, 1979): XVII.

13. James A. Chambers, *Philosophy, Slavery and Socio-Economic Disorder* (Langley Park,
Maryland: IASS Publishers, 1993).

14. In *Philosophy, Slavery and Socio-*

Economic Disorder, I argued that the desire to accumulate resulted in a retardation of asceticism and a rise in self-renunciation. In the process these individuals repressed many of their human needs and the sense of wholesomeness. Also see Norman O. Brown, *Life Against Death: The Psychoanalytical Meaning of History* (University Press of New England: Middletown, Conn. 1985); and Sigmund Freud, *Civilization and its Discontents* (Garden City, New York: n.d.). which are contain historical and deeper analysis that reflects this condition.

    15. See J. K. Galbraith, *Affluent Society* (Boston, Mass.: Dutton, 1969): 18.

    16. Frances Welsing, "Town Meeting," Ted Koppel, *Nightline*, (n.d.) 1989, ABC.

    17. See R. E. Park and E. Burgess, *Introduction to the Science of Sociology* (Chicago: University of Chicago Press, 1921); R. E. Park, E. Burgess and R. D. McKenzie, *The City* (Chicago, Ill.: Chicago University Press, 1925).

    18. Dahrendorf said: "Those who wrote and sang about the new world of the proletariat apparently know little about the real views of working people. Contrary to abstract belief, they tend to be intolerant rather than tolerant, Nationalists, rather than internationalist, hostile to libertarians, and protective rather than freedom-loving and open." Ralf Dahrendorf, *Modern Social Conflict: An Essay on the Politics of Liberty* (Berkeley: University of California Press, 1990): 75.

    19. The differences between Weberian and Marxist perspectives have been narrowing because both approaches focus on the problems of proletarianization, the role of credentials, and culture in creating and maintaining class boundaries, and the independent role played by bureaucracies in structuring the middle class. Both also view status not as a passive attribute but as one means by which fractions of a class actively organize to

protect their relative standing from challenges.

20. The concept of class structure is only one element in a broader theoretical enterprise that can be called class analysis. Other elements include class formation (the formation of class into collectively organized actors), class struggle (the practices of actors for the realization of class interest), and class consciousness (the actors' understanding of their class interest).

21. Benjamin DeMott, "Myths About Class Hurt Public Policy." *New York Times*, Oct. 16, 1990. Op-Ed page.

22. This protest is inconsistent with the perception that most Americans consider themselves to be middle class. These individuals also acknowledge the existence of lower--and upper--class people.

23. Nearly 36 million Americans are trapped in poverty. The 1991 federal poverty lines were $13,924 for a family of four and $6,932 for a single person. Blacks make up 32.7 percent of this total, Hispanics 28.7 percent and whites 10.7 percent. The total national population living in poverty is 14.2% percent.

24. There are more poor whites in America than blacks or Hispanics. However, they are not depicted for various reasons. They are found in the White ghettos in the urban trailer parks, lower-class neighborhoods, suburban areas, and rural towns. The Census Bureau's 1992 figures reveal that there are a total of 35.7 million people living in poverty. This was an increase of 2.1 million from 1991. Of the 2.1 million who fell below the poverty line, 1.4 million were White and only 405,000 were Black. (Another 330,000 were Hispanics). The underclass welfare queens are White, not the stereotyped Black, women. Andrew Hacker asks in *Two Nations*, why do Whites think of Black poverty as being pathological, a natural

outgrowth of history and culture, while they view White poverty as too atypical to deserve much attention? The proportion of White single mothers (37.9 percent in 1990) who live in poverty exceeds that for the Black population on the whole (29.3 percent). It is clear that the poor and "working poor" are realities that cross lines of race and ambition.

26. Michael Harrington, *The Other America: Poverty in the United States* (New York: Macmillan, 1962).

4

Contemporary U.S. Society

Given the contexts, discussed in the previous chapters, that are predicated on temporality, inclusiveness, stratification, and commitment, we can now turn our attention to the Black family and its dimensions. This unit is crucial for analysis because the prevailing contention is, that this is a nonfunctioning entity and provides the etiology for all types of social pathologies for example, morbidity, mortality, delinquency, and crime. This differentiated function assertion has found its way in to the literature despite the fact that this entity cannot be treated monolithically. Casual observation reveals that these units, in the main, occupy different contexts due to the application of traditional values regarding social exchange, historical differential treatment, and the degree of their social integration into the broader culture. Historically, these factors and their application have always enabled one to make differentiations regarding family compositions and the behaviors that they give rise to. Therefore, prior to discussing the Black family, we must assess families in general in that these factors apply to familial structures across the social setting. How a family unit perceives its attributes determines the personal-

ity these varying structures assume. These
perceptions may be shared in a consensual
fashion or be differentiated by each family
member. Nevertheless, they are manifested in
attitudes and when combined with perceptions,
they deter mine the nature of the symbiotic
relationship that the unit has with the social
order in which the family is situated. Because
the Black family, like the majority of families in the United States, has been analyzed
from its socialization function to the complete inurement of its economic and political
functions, one cannot totally understand the
resulting behavior. Historically, families
have been perceived to be organizations that
should be based on close kinship ties and a
clearly demarcated division of labor between
the primary breadwinner (male) and the primary
childbearer (female and spouse). These are two
distinct but specific roles that coincide with
the ideology regarding that which we generally
describe as the structure and function of the
family. When these characteristics are applied
to Black families, the literature, in the
main, contends that these units lack those
divisions and therefore are abnormal. This
contention is persistent despite the fact that
less than one-half of the family units in the
United States meet these criteria.

In the late nineteenth and first quarter
of the twentieth centuries, industrialization
contributed significantly to the developing
ethos regarding the family. This occurred
concurrently when the weavers of the perceptions failed to fully perceive that the existence of advantages derived from one's position in the industrial system had an effect on
that structure, its function, roles, and
destiny. Those structures that failed to, or
were unable to, adhere to this perception were
disadvantaged in their ability to attain those
rudiments that were necessary to function in
the specified familial fashion. This disadvan-

tage was popularly perceived as resulting from these individuals' personal ineptness or misbehavior. These individualistic determinants were significant because they had become the core tenets resulting from the U.S.'s culture of inequality. This culture fashioned these subjective attitudes, and therefore the behaviors which germinate from them. Using this inequality paradigm, the social order condition is perceived to be determined by the differentials in the individual's productive exertion. This presumption meant and means that the individual could logically be held accountable for the presence or absence of their well-being.

This perspective has led to deficiency explanations that correlate the absence of productive effort and morality to success. Deficiency explanations, simply stated, contend that those individuals possessing inadequate personality structures, self-defeating images, subscribing to lower-class subcultural view, are members of a social structure where there is an absence of strong paternal models of conventional masculine competence. Due to these conditions, they are suffering from a general state of amorality and are therefore socially deficient.

Such an argument provides broad support for the nuclear familial structure, but it fails to consider or understand that there is equal support for progressive or alternative configurations. This support for the nuclear structure also negates a sense of altruism which that exist if indeed the family, in its many complexities, is to be the remedy for the inferred pathologies or inequalities that exist in the social order. It is not only too simplistic, but unrealistic to think of the family unit solely in terms of the demarcation between the primary breadwinner and the primary child bearer because this is not contemporary reality. The perception must be expanded

to include those arrangements where there are
personal relationships in which people make
long-term emotional and financial commitments
to each other, and those which provide ongoing
love and intimacy but are not nuclear in
structure. In addition, to totally understand
the contemporary family, there simply has to
be some movement from the notion that only
those structures that meet the test of hege-
monic heterosexism can in fact only be families.

Using this as a backdrop we can discuss
not only the Black family, but the changing
nature of families in general. Historically,
we know that the worldviews and value systems
regarding the family have manifested them
selves. This manifestation is related to each
other in terms of legal arrangements, structure, custom, power, and how they are treated
and used by each other. In addition, the world
view and values of the families are concerned
with primarily how they regard them selves in
relation to God and to the varying levels of
social organization. Collectively, all of
these factors were critically important in
forming the conception of the nuclear family
and its relationship to the state. Therefore,
the microcosm of the family was used to open a
window to the wider landscape of cultural
change.[1]

The issue of family dominated the 1992
presidential campaign with coded terms, which
when reduced to the base level, meant that the
nuclear structure was being threatened because
women were not staying home and being responsible for the day-to-day care of their young.
Due to this behavior, the socialization value
of this unit was no longer effective, but
still apropos to the well-being of this
society. Those females, who were forced into
the job market, were perceived to be behaving
in a fashion deemed to be in violation of the
code words, worldview, and broader social

values. Therefore, their behavior was perceived to be antithetical both to the culturally defined family and traditional values surrounding that unit. The behavior was antithetical because, on its face, it did not lend support to that which underlined the perceived nuclear family structure. Violation of the code words, which engendered these values some how magically, had come to account for all pathologies and the gradation of severity that existed in the social order. Which was to suggest that all of the social pathologies would disappear if the family structure once again became intact nuclearly and assumed its primarily role. This orientation was consistent with the Kerner Reports that cited familial pathologies as being the primary reason for the social disord in the 1960s.[2]

While it is true that in the thirty years since the Kerner Report much has changed to help families, in general it has not occurred without conservative opposition. To a large extent, the government overrode this opposition to help these families by initiating federal programs for employment training, educational subsidy, housing assistance, and welfare reforms. To help a large group of people in addition to Blacks, the courts and Congress expanded the contracted civil rights protection. Employment opportunities were also expanded and contracted to cover all prior alienated groups. These measures resulted in raising the income and educational levels for some Whites, Blacks, Chicanos, Indians, and women and enabled them to wield some political clout at all levels of the government. While these actions were aimed initially at strengthening the Black family, it is clear that they were not the sole benefactor.

In fact, the benefits received by the Black community paled in comparison to those given to ethnic Whites. Nevertheless, this group is the most articulate in opposition to

programs, of which they were greatest beneficiary, they deemed to give an advantage to
Blacks. The largesse comprised of social
security benefits, medicaid, medicare, subsi-
dized home mortgages, educational subsidies,
unemployment benefits, food stamps, aid to
dependent children, and other benefits that
they received make those benefits given to
Blacks minuscule in comparison. Despite the
disbursement ratio and totals of these benefits, these ethnic individuals still perceive
themselves as being victimized. By whom?
Certainly it is not by the blacks. They are
victimized because changes in the economic
structure have in fact threatened their social
solidarity in every area and necessitated that
they receive these government programs. Programs, incidentally, they rail negatively
about but could not exist without. Owing to
changes in the economic structure, they are
now confronting behavioral problems, pathologies, in their family unit. Behaviors that
involve sexuality, marriage, child bearing,
illegitimate parenting, crime, and delinquency.

Given these pathologies, there are essential questions that must now be asked regarding their worldview and values. Their previous
worldview is indefensible because from a moral
position their children are involved, as Black
and other minority youths are, in drug abuse,
sexual promiscuity, and other forms of social
deviance. They are also indolent and without
self discipline, disrespectful of traditional
authority, unreliable, untruthful, and un-
faithful. In their communities, like Black
ones, the family, the church, and other institutions appear to be broken. To exacerbate
the problem, these ethnic Whites like the
Blacks are finding themselves increasingly
trapped in the inner city with out hopes of
escape. They are also beginning to realize
that they are quickly being absorbed into the

under class. Not only are the inner-city whites confronting this slippage, but there are those on the periphery of the core area and in rural settings confronting the same conditions. Can the family, as it is commonly believed, provide explanations for these pathologies that are existing in these communities?

In a recently published report, "The Index of Leading Cultural Indicators," by William J. Bennett,[3] he reported that the number of babies born to unmarried White women recently passed the number born to Black women. If one factored in the disparity in the number of abortion, achieved by the two groups, the net figures would reveal a significantly larger amount of immoralities by White women in comparison to Black women. This behavior, as stated by President Johnson in 1965, was the chief threat to the well being of Black America. At that time, fifty one percent of the Black teenage mothers were single, and 27.9 percent of all Black children were born out of wedlock. Remarkedly, twenty-seven years later, the situation for Whites is similar to that of Blacks in 1965. In 1990, fifty five percent of White teenage mothers were single, and twenty one percent of their children were born out of wed lock. In 1991, 707,502 babies were born to single White women representing twenty two percent of white births. The elite wisdom holds that this phenomena cuts across social classes. However, the Census Bureaus' study of fertility showed that birth to single women with college degrees was only six percent. The greatest proportion of these single mothers, forty eight percent, had only a high school education or less.

These numbers are dominated by Whites. Assessing the numbers by race, women with college degrees had four percent of the white illegitimate babies, while White women with a high school education or less had eighty two

percent of these type of births. For White
women below the poverty line forty four percent of the births were illegitimate compared
to six percent for women above the poverty
line. Can the policy makers and the racists
attribute this behavior to a specific race and
its character flaws? To persist in doing so
would be illogical because they must explain
why in 1960, there were 82,500 births (2.3
percent) to unmarried White mothers and 138,
744 (about 23 percent) to unmarried Black
mothers; and why in 1990, it was 647,276 (21
percent) White and 472,660 (65.2 percent)
Black. To be fair and ideologically consistent, the change in behavior has to be explained in terms of those factors that have
previously been used to account for the differential occurrence in the rates for Black
women. To account for the differentials using
racial traits would be as nonsensical now as
it was then.

Nevertheless, all types of social pathologies have been trending upward along with the
rate of illegitimacy. For example, Bennett's
report contends that the rate of violent crime
has leapt from 16.1 per 100,000 population in
1960 to 73.2 in 1990. Consistency in methodology mandates that we correlate the rates of
White illegitimacy to this rise in the violent
crime rate. However, this would be irrational.
Therefore, it becomes rational to conclude
that any discussion of crime must forego the
variables used to account for its occurrence
in terms of race and racial traits unless it
is done society wide. A more rational approach
would be to look at the social system and the
varying contexts to account for this behavior
and other behaviors deemed to be pathological.

Having said this, how does the above
pertain to the Black family that is deemed to
be pathological? Much of what we know about
black families has been biased by placing an
emphasis on women and children. This has been

balanced by the corresponding neglect of the
Black males. These units have been depicted as
being female-based or female-centered households and their dependent children. The adult
male, if not simply characterized as absent,
is depicted as a somewhat shadowy figure who
drifts in and out of the lives of family
members. Curiously, these males are really no
different from the Poles, Lithuanians, Hungarians, Irish, and other ethnic groups that
make up the lower-middle class or the so
called "silent majority."[4] A casual perusal of
the literature and the latest statistics on
illegitimacy suggests that their family units
must also be deemed to be as pathological
because their males statistically are behaving
in the same fashion.

However, these and other statistics regarding the family, crime, and delinquency do
not reveal the whole story. In the United
States, there is a revival of interest in
primordial attachment. This is a response to
the apparent resurgence of self-conscious
ethnic identity, not only among Blacks, but
among Latinos and many White ethnic groups.
This primordial attachment has its roots in
the decades of the early community settlement.
It was in the community, where the majority of
individuals spent their lives among extended
kin. From this spatial setting some sense of
status and class mobility was derived. Historically, these communities were replete with
racism that was operationalized to prevent the
loss of neighborhood. A loss of community was
perceived to signal the potential disruption
of close ties, security, and a loss of those
ethnic institutions that characterized the
neighborhood or community. Therefore, racism
was instrumental, like segregation.

A community is characterized by five
major functions that have locality or spatial
relevance. These relevances are: (1) produc-
tion--distribution--consumption, which con-

cerns the availability of goods and services essential to daily living in the immediate locality (and includes all social institutions found in the community); (2) socialization, which refers to the transmission of the basic values and behavioral patterns to the individual members of the system; (3) social control, which is the structural arrangement for influencing or coercing members toward behavioral conformity; (4) social participation, which refers to those structures that facilitate incorporation in its life; and (5) mutual support, which describes the process of care and exchanges for help among members of the group especially in time of stress.

If we go back thirty years to the National Advisory Commission on Civil Disorder, more popularly know as the Kerner Commission, you will remember that the commission concluded that White racism was the cause of the urban riots. The members concluded that "Our nation is now moving toward two societies, one black one white--separate and unequal."[5] As previously stated, much has changed in the intervening years, yet the problems of our inner cities seem as intractable as ever. In fact, our society appears to be developing into three units rather than the two to which the Kerner Commission averred. One of these units now includes those ethnic White "minorities" who previously felt themselves immune from the factors which bedeviled Black Americans. These individuals and their communities now feel the tensions that gave rise to the spate of violence in the summer of 1967, which left the nation in a state of crisis.

The factors that generated these tensions were alienation and hopelessness, inferior education, limited economic opportunity, and the prevailing attitudes of indifference. The major differences in that which these ethnic Whites are forced to confront today compared to that which the Blacks faced in the sixties, and prior to that time, are the consequences of racial isolation, hostility because they were Black, and that White society never fully understood that it was fully implicated in and responsible for the conditions confronting Blacks. They were fully implicated because White institutions created the conditions, White institutions maintained them, and tragically White institutions still condone them to a large extent.

Despite these historical and contemporary differences, working-class White ethnic males see injustices everywhere, and now cast themselves in the role of victim in the same fashion that Black males legitimately have in the past. However, there are some important differences in conditions that we must discuss. These White ethnic males some how have arrived, erroneously, at the conclusion that the political system only cares for the Blacks and that the recent gains that blacks have garnered only serve to prove their point. As a result of this misperception, these individuals spend an exorbitant amount of their time complaining how they have been victimized by rising taxes, reduction in personal services, the necessity of having to work a second job, and that their wives have to enter the job market on either a full, or part-time basis. They fail to realize that these conditions do and have always existed for Black males. They also fail to factor in, as previously stated, the amount of aid they receive.[6]

Failing to acknowledge these factors, these individuals now feel justified in revolting against all that they previously stood for, except the double standards of which they were the beneficiary. However, they have seemingly conveniently forgotten the double standards that were part of a conspiracy that gave them a considerable head start and some security regarding the American dream, while at the same time relegating Black males to a

condition of unparalleled and continual despair. These ethnic White males are in revolt
because they are becoming more and more like
those individuals they despise, despite the
largesse they previously enjoyed; more and
more like those individuals depicted in
Howell's *Hard Living on Clay Street*. They are
also very similar to those in Liebow's *Tally's
Corner*. They are behaving like Prospero toward
Calaban. It is this commonality in behavior
that shows that the pathologies historically
used to describe the Black family are not prevalent characteristics solely of that group,
but traits that can, and should, be used to
describe a growing number of White families.

　　Historically, in early modern English
society, like the contemporary United States,
the social order was comprised of a number of
very distinct status groups and classes. Then
like today, these different social strata
resulted in less suppression of family patterns and values by acknowledging and making
provisions for a widening number of quite
different configurations.[7]

　　These family configurations and their
prevalence were previously determined by
economic conditions. The level of poverty,
like other aspects of class inequality, had a
lot to do with not only the structures but the
functioning of differentiated family units.
Today, there is a singular sociological emphasis on the Black families, to the exclusion of
White families, and the use of statistics have
been operationalized to provide a distorted
reality. Sociologist Andrew Hacker, in a recent book on U.S. race relations, *Two Nations*,
argues that if Black families are disinte-
grating, White families suffer the same fate.
He cites as evidence data that show that in
1950, 17.2 percent of Blacks households were
headed by single females. In 1990, 17.3 White
house holds were headed by single females, and
the rate continues to climb.[8] Murray wrote an

article entitled "The Coming White Underclass" and in it he detailed the problems of white illegitimate births. He said:

> Illegitimacy is the single most important social problem of our time--more important than crime, drugs, poverty, illiteracy, welfare, or homelessness because it drives everything else. This brings us to the emergence of a white underclass. In raw numbers, European-American whites are the ethnic group with the most people in poverty, most illegitimate children, most women on welfare, most unemployed men, and most arrest for serious crimes. And yet Whites have not had an "under class" as such, because the whites who might qualify have been scattered among the working class. Instead, whites have had "white trash" concentrated in a few streets on the outskirts of town.[9]

Perhaps the politicians are unaware of these statistics and conditions. Perhaps they are aware of them and to redirect responsibility they appeal to ethnic White s by saying provocatively that these are troubling times to be a White male in America.[10] This irresponsible rhetoric enables these individuals to believe that they are indeed being discriminated against. This discrimination is seen in the forms of acts such as affirmative action, women's rights, equal opportunity hiring, and placement goals and quotas. These are controversial topics embellished through the use of acrid terms for example, reverse discrimination and blatant ignorance. While this is a sad ploy that ignores history, it also distorts the truth and masks the real nature of the problems facing a growing number

of people in this country. The real problem is
virtually one hundred percent of all good jobs
are kept from women and people of color. The
verbiage of reverse discrimination presented
as a fact is both dishonest and statistically
indefensible. Legislation formulated to end
public and private policies that conspires to
exclude women, Blacks, Asians, Latinos, and
Native Americans and mandate substandard
existences cannot logically be perceived as a
form of reverse discrimination. Failure to
address these issues openly and honestly is
the condition that makes it a troubling time
to be a White ethnic or White male in America.
However, it is now a troubling time to be a
poor anything in America because of the current economic conditions.

Why is it troubling? Because this condition underscores that which is really troubling in America: (1) One in every four young
Black males is in jail, on probation, or on
parole, and the number one cause of death for
that group is homicide (2) Native Americans
have the highest prep school drop out rate in
the nation (3) Unemployment for Latino males
is expected to become the highest in the
nation, at the same time Latinos become the
largest U.S. ethnic group (4) Women in many
parts of this nation still do not receive
equal pay for doing the same work as their
male counterparts (5) The wealth of the nation
continues to be concentrated in the hands of a
few; and to maximize profits, the wealthy are
shipping jobs and industrial capabilities out
of this country. The last fact reveals that it
is not women or people of color taking over
anything. It is a matter of fewer jobs that
pay living wages being introduced into a
marketplace, at the same time twenty five
percent of the population has demanded their
share of the action.

What are the actual conditions existing
in the United States? Despite the economic

conditions, and contrary to stereotype, only one in ten poor U.S. child is urban, Black and living with a mother on welfare. Nevertheless, the perception that child poverty is mostly the problem of poor, Black urban families on welfare is so entrenched that few Americans and criminologists can deal with the true facts. Similarity there is a reluctance to believe that most poor families are employed. The data reveals that in 1989 nearly two in three families considered to be poor included at least one worker. In addition, two of every five Black children lived in families in which the father was present.

The statistical data also reveal that poor families are not large but are rather small. In addition, almost two-thirds of all poor families with children live in an urban area, but the fastest growing poverty problem is occurring in the suburbs, where a fourth of all poor children now live. This is not to suggest that ghetto areas do not exist and that the issues regarding deprivation are diminishing in these areas.

The Joint Center for Political and Economic Studies, focusing on Black families, stated that half of the nation's Black children live in poverty and that the youngest were the worst off. The center also reported that Black children under three tend to live in families headed by women in their 20s who have never married and have few marriage or job prospects. Cynthia Rexroat, a sociologist at Clemson claims that youngest children are even more likely to be at risk than are the older ones. She contends, that of all Black children, 46.5 percent lived in poverty in 1984. In addition, in 1984 those families headed by never married females that contained children under the age of three had a poverty rate of eighty seven percent. This figure represents an eleven percent increase from 1979. More significantly, two thirds of this group was comprised of women in their 20s.

The Director of the Center for Afro-American Studies at U.C.L.A. Belinda Tucker, contends that sociological projections indicate that thirty percent of Black women born in the early 1950s will never marry. This does not mean that they do not value marriage, rather that there are limited prospects correlated to limited employment opportunities that account for much of the decline in marriage. The increase in homicide and crime rates also adds to the problem.

Using data from the 1980 census, Rexroat concluded that the average Black child who lives with a never married mother will spend fifteen years in poverty. This poverty is caused in part by discrimination, racism, decline in the quality of education, and the failure to translate the education that they received into employment opportunities that would enable them to move out of poverty.[11] All of these conditions suggest the presence of a growing under class. We can attribute the solidarity and growth of this class to many factors, but a crucial one has to be the demise of the Rust Belt over the past thirty five years. The eclipse of the industrial sector by the service sector has had a strong influence on the development of this class. In addition, many contend that the economic policies of the Reagan and Bush Administrations have served to exacerbate these conditions.[12]

From a policy perspective, that which happens out side the family is much affected by the perception, not necessarily the reality, of the family and the level of privileges that it enjoys. For example, the number of Black single-parent households are in large part a direct result of the policies that created the joblessness suffered by Black males. These individuals are jobless because of the racism, discrimination, and deindustrialization that has occurred in the urban areas where they were heavily concentrated. Partially due to racism, they were unable to follow those plants that moved to the suburbs. Therefore, racism explains in part why there are a large number of Black males and families peculiarly vulnerable to the changes in the economic structure. These changes manifested them selves in White flight, substandard schools, school failures, single-parent house holds, crime, and general disencouragement. Illegal activities, like drug dealing or the fencing of stolen property, are often the most readily available means by which adult males and adolescents from these communities can earn income. This income is critical because it helps the families meet their needs and support some of their basic requirements. One result of this activity, driven by need and an inability to engage in licit activities is that these individuals routinely become in-volved in the criminological enterprise rather than the world of work, which is closed to them.

Finally, while the median income of Whites is roughly twice that of Blacks, the disparity in wealth is much greater. This dis-parity is attributed partly to racism because wealth reflects decades of differences in earnings, investment, and the inheritance of property.[13] There are various factions that take pride in the fact that the median income for all households in 1988 was $35,750. However, when this figure is disaggregated, the elation evaporates because the median income for Whites was $42,280, $4,170 for Blacks, and $5,520 for Hispanic households. Predictably, the census bureau found that married couples were much wealthier than households Blacks and Crime headed by women or men who had no spouse present. They also re-ported that the median income for households headed by women was $13,570 compared to

$13,050 for households of males with no spouse present.

The statistics also reveal that in 1988, there was in increase in the number of individuals slipping into poverty despite holding a job. The figures reveal that 21 million persons over the age of 14 lived below the poverty line in 1988, but that 8.4 million of these individuals worked at least on a part time job and that 2 million worked full time, year round. These figures represent an increase of twenty seven percent when compared to the 1978 data, a full forty six percent increase of the full time working poor. At the same time, the total population of those mired in poverty increased by twenty four percent. This data does not coincide with the conventional wisdom prevalent in this society in regard to poor people.[14]

NOTES

1. Philosophers like Fourier and Marx denounced bourgeois marriages as being a form of prostitution. This was premised on the fact that financial considerations were upper most in the minds of middle-class men. They degraded affairs of sentiments by mixing them with economic considerations. This perspective is an abomination of the bourgeois theorists and other contemporary writers who accuse these two of wanting to abolish the family and substitute in its stead a configuration to accommodate perversions and promiscuity. Engels suggests that the important stages in family history occurred in the age of savagery when group marriages predominated. Only during the barbarism stage did a form of pairing become common. The pivotal stage occurred with the onset of "civilization," which ushered in changes in property relations which led to modern monogamy or "individual sex-love." This

he concluded was the greatest moral advance.

2. See *The National Advisory Commission on Civil Disorders Report* (New York: E. P. Dutton, 1968): 13-14.; L. Rainwater and W. Yance, *The Moynihan Report and the Politics of Controversy* (Cambridge, Mass.: MIT Press, 1967).

3. See Todd Gitlin and Nanci Hollander, *Uptown: Poor Whites in Chicago* (New York: Harper and Row, 1970); Louise H. Kapp, *The White Majority: Between Poverty and Affluence* (New York: Vintage Books, 1970); Joseph T. Howell, *Hard Living On Clay Street* (New York: Anchor, 1972).

4. Roland Warren, *The Community in America* (Chicago: University of Chicago Press, 1972): 10-11.

5. Ibid.

6. Historically, these government programs have been rife with racism which favors Whites. For example, the Farmers Home Administration program, which makes loans to help save family farms, gave Black farmers on the average $21,000 less than they gave whites. See J. Dixon and T. Bovee, "Blacks get smaller average loans from programs to aid family farm." *The Associated Press*, February 21, 1993.

7. Lawrence Stone, *The Family, Sex and Marriage in England 1500-1800* (New York: Harper & Row Publishers, New York, 1979): 21-22.

8. *U.S.A. Today's National News Network*, September 4, 1992, 5-A.

9. Charles Murray, "The Coming Under class" *The Wall Street Journal*, Oct. 29, 1993, A-13.

10. Sally Jacob, "White Men Feel Besieged in Diverse Society." Oregonian. December 4, 1992, A-4.

11. While there have been great strides toward closing the gap between Blacks and Whites with respect to education, employment,

and therefore economic resources and stability, at the same time there is a growing segment of the Black population that is becoming increasingly mired in poverty.

12. During this period manufacturing jobs were cut almost in half in these areas, affecting upward of six-tenths of the workers in this employment sector. This deindustrialization, not the growth of welfare, accounts for the joblessness and the concomitant effects on the families in these areas.

13. In the Census Bureau's survey, twenty nine percent of Black house holds reported that they had any wealth, meaning that they did not own any assets or that their liabilities exceeded their assets. By contrast only nine percent of all White house holds and twelve percent of Hispanic house holds reported this condition.

14. K. M. Neckerman, K. M., R. Aponte, and W. J. Wilson, "Family Structure, Black Unemployment and American Social Policy," in *The Politics of Social Policy*, ed. M. Weir, A. S. Orloff, and T. Skocpol, (Princeton, New Jersey: Princeton University Press, 1988): 64; H. G. Gutman, *The Black Family in Slavery and Freedom, 1750-1925* (New york: Pantheon, 1976).

5

Race and Attack on EEOC

When the United States experiences a recession, Black American have a depression. This
contention is one that has long been used to
characterize the plight and conditions of
Black people in this country. Ironically, this
contention appears to contain considerable
credence. To illustrate, the statistics reveal
that during the 1990-91 recession, blacks were
the only racial group to suffer a net loss of
jobs. This loss occurred despite the fact that
the factors used to explain this phenomena
down sizing, restructuring, and relocation of
plants did not impact Whites, Asians, Hispanics and women. In fact these groups showed a
net gain during this cycle.

The Wall Street Journal surveyed the
employment records of 35,242 companies,
approximately one-third of the national work
force, that file reports with the Equal Employment Opportunity Commission. There were
many causative factors used to account for
this employment condition but the salient ones
are: 1) racial discrimination both unconscious
and deliberate; 2) subjective assessment of
Black's compatibility with the other employees; 3) general notions that Blacks are incompetent; and 4) lacking seniority they had to

be the first laid off. While these factors
suggest disparate treatment of Black workers,
there are those who hesitate to see them as
being a function of racism. Rather the job
losses have been attributed to the changing
patterns of corporations, which are manifested
in take overs by other corporations, corporate
owned outlets to franchisees, reorganization
of corporations that, by necessity, excluded
the clerical and support jobs which Blacks
primarily held, and the de-emphasis of the
EEOC to bring class action suits in favor of
individual discrimination claims.

Whatever the reason, Black workers lost
59,479 jobs in the period spanning July 1990
through March 1991.[1] Those especially hard hit
were Blacks in blue-collar jobs.[2] George
Fraser, publisher of a Black professional
directory, contends that this job performance
is due to subconscious, deep seated racism.
Clarence Page, a Pulitzer Prize syndicated
columnist for the Chicago Tribune, wrote,
"When a major employment agency in New York
City called legal secretary Linda Scott to
offer her a job, the employment agent also
asked her if she was black."[3] The rest of the
conversation was taped and played on WCBS-TV
in New York and rebroadcasted later on 60
Minutes. The tape was a disjointed and horrible example of psychobabble. To cite:

> To me, you know, it makes no dif-
> ference, but if we (send) a resume
> to a company and they're not inter-
> ested in seeing black people, they
> tell us. As soon as they give us the
> job order, they say they want 'AA,'
> which means all-American, you know,
> white, blond hair, blue eyes. OK? I
> mean, believe me, to me it doesn't
> matter. I've dated, you know black
> women, you know, I, uh, have friends

that are black. You know, to me it
doesn't matter. I go to church where
most of the parishioners are black.
OK? So, you know, it doesn't matter
to me, I'm not prejudice.[4]

Thirty years after the passage of the
Civil Rights Act, millions of minorities are
still being discriminated against in the job
market.

CRITICS OF AFFIRMATIVE ACTION

When the issues of equity and equal
opportunity are discussed in realm of employment, they are subverted by the issue of
diversity, not affirmative action. The recent
recession clearly illustrates the notion that
as a nation, there is a shift in the strategy
regarding the justifying and extension of
equal opportunity. This shift is away from the
emphasis to remedy past discrimination through
affirmative action to assertive action to
enhance diversity. This concept of diversity
is one that articulates a policy of having a
Cabinet and a government that reflects the
diversity of America. By taking assertive actions to achieve this goal, affirmative action
has lost ground. While it can logically be
argued that the concept of diversity is also
an attempt at achieving equal opportunity
there are distinct differences between the
two. Diversity is currently accepted as being
a more positive concept than affirmative action because it has the goal of achieving a
government that includes women as well as men
and it reflects the multi-racial, multi-eth-
nic, and multicultural character of the nation. As such, it is a ideology that openly
cannot be defamed as the idealogue of affirmative action.

In contrast the strategy of affirmative

action advanced by President Lyndon Johnson in the 1960s evokes a relatively negative response from many segments of the majority population. This perception is due to the fact that many Whites saw affirmative action as being a capitulation to the Black Power Movement and other elements in the Civil Rights Movement. Opponents of affirmative action deem it to be inherently discriminatory even though it was meant to provide opportunities for the population who had been the focus of past discrimination. This meant that many individuals in the White population perceived affirmative action as a policy structured to deny them opportunities while giving an unfair advantage to minorities.

A lot of the problems surrounding the concept of affirmative action results from the erroneous use of what really are noninterchangeable terms: equal employment opportunity, nondiscrimination, and affirmative action. Critics fail to understand that these terms have distinct meanings, implications and applications. The most inclusive of these terms is equal employment opportunity. It can only occur when employees and applicants are assessed on individual abilities without regard to race, sex, or ethnic background. Nondiscrimination and affirmative action then become subsets of the concept, equal employment opportunity. Nondiscrimination means that no employee or applicant for employment or admission to a professional school or educational institution can be subjected to different treatment based on race, color, religion, sex, physical traits, mental characteristic, or national origin. Affirmative action requires that special action be taken to ensure that groups previously excluded from employment or admission be included in those activities to overcome past discrimination.

The enabling legislation for equal employment opportunities and affirmative action are found in: 1) **Executive Order** 11246 as amended by **Executive Order** 11375;[5] 2) **Executive Order** 11478 (34 F.R., 60-62 August 10, 1969) as amended by **Executive Order** 12106 (44 F.R. 1053, December 30, 1978);[6] 3) **Title VII** of the **Civil Rights Act** of 1964, as amended by the **Equal Employment Opportunity Act** of 1972;[7] 4) The **Equal Pay Act** of 1963;[8] 5) **Age Discrimination in Employment Act** of 1963;[9] 6) The **State and Local Government Assistance Action** of 1972;[10] and 7) Section 503 of the **Rehabilitation Act** of 1973.[11]

Glazer, while emphasizing his preference for the law, proceeds to articulate his distaste for affirmative action and discrimination, If any concrete connection with the Negro condition is made, it cannot be that this and that qualified black has been denied a job or admission--for the evidence is now all too clear that the qualified (and a good number of the unqualified, too) get jobs and admissions. The concrete connection with an individual's personal fate that is likely to be made tends to be this form: If more Blacks were given these jobs, perhaps less would be on the streets, or drug addicts, or killing unoffending shop keepers. It is one thing to be asked to fight discrimination against the competent, hardworking, and law-abiding; it is quite another to be asked to fight discrimination against the less competent or incompetent and criminally inclined. The statistical emphasis leads to the latter. Undoubtedly even those of lesser competence and criminal inclination must be incorporated into society, but one wonders whether this burden should be placed on laws against discrimination on account of race, color, religion, or national origin.[12]

This type of rhetoric characterizes the polemics on this issue in the White community. It is verbiage based on half truths that are

expanded to provide a mythical perspective of
the real world. Glazer is fully aware that the
neither the statistical nor cases (epiphenome-
na) data support his contention that those
Blacks who are qualified are incorporated
willingly into the work force or are admitted
to public and private institutions based solely on their merits. Glazer certainly was aware
of **Griggs v. Duke Power Co.**, [401 U.S. 424
(1971)]. The Court ruled on this case that
while some employment practices or procedures
may be neutral on the surface or in intent,
they cannot be maintained if they operate to
freeze the status quo of prior discriminatory
practices. Glazer knew that the employment
practices were too broad and general testing
devices, as well as the affinity for using
degrees as fixed measures of capability, were
discriminatory in nature and practice. If
Glazer was unaware of this case, surely he was
aware of **Albermarle Paper Co. v. Moody**, [422
U.S. 405 (1975)], decided the year he wrote
his manuscript, that the Court ruled that if a
test was to be used it had to be job related.
He was fully aware that this was not the
practice statistically or by case when administered to Black applicants; in this case, the
court held that under the due process rights
of the Fifth Amendment, the use of written
personnel tests by the police departments
could be sustained despite the fact that four
times as many Blacks failed the test as
Whites.

To further confuse matters, in **U.S. v.
Chicago**, [(573, F.2 d 416 (1978)], the Court
ruled that the Chicago police department had
violated Title VII because the test that was
used excluded a disproportionate percentage of
minority applicants for invalid reasons. The
case of **U.S. v. City of Syracuse**, [(80-Cv-53.
(1980)], resulted in the signing of a consent
degree whereby the police and fire departments
were mandated to recruit and set five year

affirmative goals to overcome the past effects of civil service testing. The Court further clarified the Moody ruling in **Washington v. Davis**, [(426 U.S. 229 (1976)], when it stated that the Grigg standard cannot be applied unless the case is brought on the Title VII grounds. This meant that even though the tests were having an adverse impact, they were not necessarily illegal.

In total disregard of these cases, Glazer writes that some "make it believe that there is such a deeply ingrained prejudice in Whites, leading to discrimination against blacks and other minorities, that it can be assumed prejudice is the operative cause in any case of differential treatment, rather than concerns about qualification. The ordinary public opinion surveys do show a substantial decline in prejudice, but certainly no one who believes in the persistence of an in grained and deeply based prejudice which will make itself felt in every situation will accept such admittedly crude and broad-brush evidence. There is no answer to the argument that every case of differential treatment must be based on prejudice since we are all prejudice. Clearly, the decisions of the anti-discrimination agencies are the least charitable possible. But they have support in liberal opinion, which consistently insists on the guilt for racist actions of each and every one of us.[13]

It is quite difficult to argue with Glazer because he argues tautologically for his proof residing in the causes and the causes residing in the proof. For example, he discussed the ethics of putting Black criminals to work and concluded that it was an issue that should not be entertained by law. He advanced this unprofound perspective to demonstrate that Blacks who are non-criminal do not confront problems when they attempt to

join the work force, but Black criminals do.
Therefore, any disparity regarding Blacks in
the work force can be attributed to their
differential involvement in the criminal
enterprises. What Glazer fails to remember, or
realize, is the fact that the majority of
Black males in the urban areas have been
arrested but that the arrest does not necessarily make them a criminal.

More significantly, there is no direct
nor positive correlation between arrest and
job skill. If that was the case, a lot of
individuals in the Nixon, Reagan, and Bush
administrations would be unfit to hold jobs.
This also holds true for those in the democratic administrations. The incidence of
arrest does not render one incapable of functioning satisfactorily when they are included
in the job market. This knowledge can be
readily gained by reading *Tally's Corner* or
Hard Living on Clay Street. In the latter work
he will discern, much to his surprise, White
individuals who are marginally skilled and
possess arrest records, but nevertheless they
have been easily incorporated into the work
force. If we use criminal past as a factor to
determine whether one should be included in
the work force, then more White males than
Black males should be excluded premised on the
differential in the total number of offenses
committed. Another factor that seemed to elude
Glazer is the direct correlation between unemployment and the commission of offenses.

Affirmative action is premised on the
contention that some groups have been discriminated against and suffer disadvantage due to
past injustices. Injustices that emanate from
that which Glazer identified--prejudice. There
fore, advocates of affirmative action reason
that special compensatory action and assistance is required to enable these affected
groups to compete on an equal basis for jobs
and education. These remedies fly in the face

of the mythologies perpetuated by the majority, which is based on the erroneous assumption that everyone has an equal chance to succeed, that every group has experienced hard ships, and that determination and hard work should be the catalyst to overcome disadvantages.

Linda Scotts' and million of other similar cases were not supposed to occur according to Reagan's free market theory of racial justice. This ill advised theory, like supply side economics, contended that companies would be so eager to find the best possible candidate for jobs in the increasingly enlightened and technical age, they would hire the most qualified regardless of race, creed, color, or gender. Therefore, the only discrimination this nation needed to be concerned with was that described by Glazer, reverse discrimination--reverse discrimination perpetrated against White males resulting from quotas and timetables.

Given this fantasy, under Reagan the EEOC, under Reagan shifted from the interest of the candidate to the employer who discriminated. They were in a position to ignore the law because cases had to be decided on a case by case basis rather than on class. Stripped of previous procedures that enabled the employee to meet with the employer to address a grievance, cases were more difficult to pursue due to the necessity of having to hire legal counsel. Given this environment, the number of complainants who were told they had "no cause" rose from 28.5 percent under Carter to fifty four percent under Reagan. Those who were successful in pursuing their case to an affirmative conclusion fell from approximately one-third to less than fourteen percent. Ironically, Clarence Thomas, U.S. Supreme Court Justice, was Reagan's EEOC director.

According to Perkins, despite this data Reagan's Era was a good one. He states:

It should be remembered that when
Ronald Reagan inherited the White
House, America was mired in its
worst economic crisis since the
Great Depression. The unemployment
rate topped 10 percent, inflation
exceeded 13 percent, and interest
rates were in excess of 21 percent.
By the time Reagan had left office,
inflation had been pared to less
than 4 percent and the interest rate
to just over 9 percent. But perhaps
the biggest economic accomplishment
of the Reagan era was the creation
of a record 20 million jobs.[14]

When chided that these jobs were of the
low wage variety, Perkins responded by stating, "the Bureau of Labor Statistics show that
82 percent of the jobs created during the Reagan era were high-paying, high-skilled posi-
tion--managerial, professional, technical and
the like."[15]

This is more than sheer fantasy; the contention is ludicrous. The Labor Department reported that in September 1992, the nation's
jobless rate remained stuck at 6.7 percent as
factory jobs fell to the lowest level since
the mid-1960s. However, it also reported that
this decline in manufacturing jobs were off
set by an increase in service sector and low-
skilled jobs that were either low-paying or
part-time. The biggest gain in the creation of
jobs was in the government sector, but this
was a statistical blip because a large percentage of this gain was attributed to summer
jobs rather than a sign of any real improvement in the job market.

In addition, one of the biggest gains in
the private sector came from an increase of
jobs in restaurants and bars. The September
1992 jobless report showed that there were

1.75 million people who had been unemployed
for six months or more, an increase of eighty
four percent. These job losses occurred in the
manufacturing sector (18,000), and in middle
management (11,000). Horwitz captures the
plight of managers in his article, "Not Home
Alone: Jobless Male Managers Proliferate In
Suburbs, Causing Subtle Malaise."[16] He describes the sense of alienation and useless-
ness that these individuals encounter after
losing their jobs.

Sadly, a lot of these individuals do not
define themselves in realm of who they are but
rather where they work. This has a profound
effect on economic status, and it radically
structures political beliefs. Similar to those
individuals in the urban ghettos, they have
become socially, economically, and politically
isolated. However, one of the major differences is in the length of unemployment.

Despite the arguments regarding affirmative action and civil rights, Blacks have become further entrenched in poverty. This can
be due to the unwillingness of the government
and the private sector to provide equal access
to the job market. There is constant lamenting
by Whites and some Blacks regarding a perception that the government is unfairly handing
out welfare payments to these unworthy individuals. This has spurred individuals like
Perkins, who is Black, to write:

> The reason the government has so
> miserably failed to get the better
> of poverty is that, contrary to the
> aims enunciated by (Pres.) Johnson,
> the present welfare system does not
> attempt to cure or prevent poverty.
> It concentrates almost exclusively
> on the symptoms. Since the poor
> don't have much money, the govern-
> ment gives them cash. Since they

can't afford health insurance, the
government provides them medical
coverage. Since we don't want the
poor to miss any meals, we offer
them food stamps. And since many of
the poor are between jobs, the government puts them through training
programs. While these and other programs may ameliorate poverty on the
margins, they don't get to the root
cause of poverty: the breakdown of
the American family. Since the War
on Poverty was launched, we have
witnessed an explosion in single
parent families and out-of-wedlock
births. Government welfare spending
surely has had something to do with
this.[17]

Perkins has long been a riddle, if not a
joke, due to his propensity to blame the
victim or agency that attempts to alleviate
their conditions. His writings do not capture
the reality of poor people. In addition, he
buttresses the racist strategy and perspective
which contend that Blacks lack ambition,
Blacks deserve what they get, Blacks are the
largest recipients of government handouts, and
a willingness by a large number of my students
to cite his distorted assessments as validating the governments' inaction. To these students, Perkins positively validates the mis-
perceptions that they have always nurtured.
They have yet to analyze columnists and their
motives. Perkin's motive is simple, he chooses
to remain a part of the media elite and this
cannot be accomplished by tweaking the nose of
the masses. When he discusses groups other
than Blacks he merely deletes and inserts poor
people where Black has been removed. In the
interest of helping my students to understand,
I urge Mr. Perkins to explain how the break

down of the family, Black or White, has resulted in 36.9 million people being firmly
entrenched in poverty in 1992. Robert Greenstein, executive director of the Center of
Budget and Policy Priorities, cited eroding
wages, shrinking state assistance, in addition
to the increase of single-parent families as
major concerns. The Census Bureau contends
that work was not an answer to the persistent
problem of poverty because approximately forty
percent of poor Americans older than 16, or
9.4 million, worked at least some of the time
in 1992. Research shows that the continual
shift from higher-paying, more secure manufacturing jobs to lower paying service jobs
accounts for much of the stubborn persistence
of poverty.[18] This is at considerable variance
with that which Perkins reports.

Perkins' oblique suggestion that government subsidies create a condition in that the
family disintegrates can be quickly dashed by
analyzing the largesse which these people
receive. "In determining the official poverty
rate, a family of four with an income of
$14,335, the government includes cash assist-
ance, such as Social Security payments and Aid
for Families with Dependent Children.[19] Perhaps
Perkins feels that the changing demographic,
which reveals that one-sixth of all households
are headed by women and that they account for
52.4% of poor families in 1992, would be
changed if the family was nucleated in structure. If so, the statistics do not buttress
his contention, because the decline in the
male's wage will continue due to the changing
nature of the corporate structure and its
activities to maximize profits. This has already been reflected in male's wages (which
remained unchanged from 1991).

These conditions exacerbate urban conditions by enlarging the unemployed and underemployed totals and at the same time shrinking

the already inadequate tax base. These individuals confront a hostile conservatism in
their attempts to ameliorate the conditions,
and Blacks must contend with the specter of
affirmative action. Marable contends that
"racism is out of control," moving forward on
a "green light."[20] It is doing so with a so-
phistication that leaves the victims blaming
themselves. Although the victim recognizes
racism when it impacts them, it is difficult
to define the term other than in realms of
discrimination. It is dynamic and omnipresent
in the United States and it is enjoying a resurgence. In 1966 the Harris Group conducted a
poll and found that sixty six percent of all
Whites felt that blacks have less ambition
than most other people and that an even higher, seventy one percent felt that most Blacks
ask for more than they are ready for.[21] Harris'
data in 1987 reveals that "evidence of real
progress in rooting out prejudice and discrimination is difficult to find people may now be
far more aware of discrimination against
minorities and women, but the underlying,
basic disparities have barely budged."[22]

Pickney presented a litany of oppressive
incidents in his "The Myth of Black Progress."
He cited oppressive acts for example, the re-
segregation of schools in Little Rock to the
murder of a five-year old Black child by a
White police officer in California.[23] While
these types of events were occurring with
alarming frequency, Blacks and Whites were
publishing books and articles proclaiming that
this country no longer confronted a race
issue. This conclusion was drawn despite
governmental data to the contrary and the
vivid escalation of anti-Black feeling by conservatives.

Through most of the decade of the 1960s,
there was reason for America's black citizens
to suspect that their liberation from oppres-

sion was underway and that those citizens
opposed to equality for blacks were in a small
minority. And it appeared that government
agencies supported their aspirations. But as
is so characteristic of American society, the
national mood shifted radically, and through a
variety of actions at all levels, blacks found
themselves with fewer allies in their quest
for equality. Public support for black progress virtually disappeared, and blacks were
once again being blamed for their plight in a
society where racism has historically been an
integral part of all of its institutions and
has served to maintain and protect white
privilege.[24]

Despite the data, Glazer writes:

> There is another justification for
> the statistical approach which may
> be easier to deal with in open dis-
> cussion: This is the justification
> from "institutional" causes. A ref-
> erence to "institutional forms of
> exclusion and discrimination" occurs
> in an official document of the Of-
> fice for Civil Rights of HEW. We
> also know the term as "institutional
> racism." This term has not been sub-
> jected to the analysis it deserves.
> It is obviously something devised in
> the absence of clear evidence of
> discrimination and prejudice. It
> suggests that without intent, a
> group may be victimized.

He then leaps to some flight of fantasy
by further stating:

> Racism, in common understanding
> means an attitude of superiority,
> disdain, or prejudice toward another
> person because he is of another

race, and a philosophy or ideology
that justifies such attitudes on the
basis of the inferiority--genetic,
cultural, moral, or intellectual--of
a race. The rise of the popularity
of the term "institutional racism"
points to one happy development,
namely that racism pure and simple
is less often found or expressed.
But the rise of this term has less
happy consequences in that it tends
to assume that all cases of differential representation in an institution demonstrates "institutional
racism.[25]

The concept of institutional racism was
well documented by Carmichael and Hamilton in
"Black Power: The Politics of Liberation in
America." They stated:

Colonial subjects have their political decisions made for them by the
colonial masters, and those decisions are handed down directly or
through a process of "in direct
rule." Politically, decisions which
affect black lives have always been
made by white people--the "white
power structure." There is some
dislike for this phrase because it
tends to ignore or over simplify the
fact that there are many centers of
power, many different forces making
decision. Those who raise that objection point to the pluralistic
character of the body politic. They
frequently overlook the fact that
the American pluralism quickly becomes a monolithic structure on
issues of race. When faced with
demands from black people, the mul-

ti-faction whites unite and present a common front the white groups tend to view their interests in a particularly united, solidified way when confronted with blacks making demands which are seen as threatening to vested interests. The whites react in united groups to protect interests they perceive to be theirs--interests possessed to the exclusion of those who, for varying reasons, are outside the group.[26]

Given these two explanations, Glazer is well aware of the full meaning of the concept "institutional racism." He also understands that it is comprised of collective racism and prejudices, and that it functions to perpetuate the interest of the White group. This is graphically illustrated in the opposition to affirmative action, equal employment, and non-discrimination legislation.

Due to these changing conditions, there is an enhancement of the salutogenic aspects in the urban areas. These conditions do not occur, as Perkins suggests, because poor men have been marginalized or because they have been deprived of their self-esteem by a paternalistic government who feel obligated to provide the basic amenities of life. These have been provided over the objection of individuals like Perkins and Glazer and others who fail to see that there is a direct correlation between the inability of minority and White men to find gainful employment and the surge in female-headed one parent families. It is not true, as Perkins claims, that a single mother can never escape poverty as long as she depends on government largesse. A woman can supersede this status with out a supporting husband if the Equal Pay Act of 1963 was fully enforced. Nor does she need a supporting husband working with her to raise her children, because many women are opting to raise their children without the presence of a male figure. It matters little if the government programs do not sanction the marriage by the mother receiving Aid to Dependent Children to the children's father by severing the subsidies if the father can not find employment which would could be used to support the progeny.

However, this is not that which dooms the poor mother and her children to a state of poverty, rather it is an indifferent conservative element that fosters frontal assault on the affirmative action programs, equal employment opportunities and equal pay provisions. It is their mean spiritedness that quickly cites data, for example, that between 1945 and 1965, when the government spent comparatively little on welfare programs, the poverty rare declined from roughly thirty percent to fifteen percent. But between 1965 and 1993, when welfare spending mushroomed, the poverty rate remained more or less constant at fifteen percent. Perkins says," The costly lesson of the War on Poverty is this: It matters not how much money the government spends fighting poverty."[27] A problem with this type of reasoning can be illustrated in the U. S. war on drugs.

Despite the pronouncements and the money allocated, as we all know, there has been no war on drugs, similarly there has been no war waged on poverty. In addition, Mr. Perkins fails to realize that a lion's share of the dollars allocated to fight poverty, as in the war on drugs, ended up in the pockets of individuals who too would most likely be impoverished or drug users if not for the public dole. Some of these have made careers administering and abusing the programs. In addition, their salaries and benefits consume a large

portion of the amount allocated to ameliorate
the misery of poor people. Also, there are
individuals who appear to have all the trappings of middle class status but have no
difficulty availing themselves of head start
programs, free lunch programs, food stamps,
and medical benefits. It is incorrect to
assert that all of the resources allocated to
help those in dire straits receive the emolu-
ments as intended. Once again it appears to be
fashionable to blame the victims for the administration, abuses, and failure of the programs.

If the government would have spent the
$5.1 trillion dollars, which Perkins cites, on
fighting racism and opposition to affirmative
action, equal employment opportunities, and
equal pay legislation, perhaps it would not
have had to address a massive poverty problem.
The insanity of it all is not the size of the
welfare system, but rather a system that contains individuals who still feel that they are
privileged and scuttle everything that they
deem not to be in their best interest. If a
portion of the money allocated to the Pentagon
to engage in questionable endeavors had been
targeted to enhance families in the urban area
perhaps there would no longer exist a need for
housing programs, which financial agencies are
the biggest beneficiaries of; welfare programs
and supplement health care which benefitted
the private not for-profit and profit sectors.

True, Mr Perkins there has been insanity.
But your suggestion that if we had given every
poor family a check for $5,500 in 1992, the
poverty problem would have been surmounted is
even more insane. I state this in light of the
fact that the household, as you defined it
would be constituted by a family income for
Whites of $32,368; $18,660 for Blacks; $38,153
for Asians, and $22,848 for Hispanics. Your
paltry check for $5,500 would not equal the

mean income for the bottom fifth of American households, which was $7,328 in 1992.

While the family may not be the criminogenic element in the salutogenic aspects of the Black community, its very survival is at stake and the family as we know it society wide is in trouble. This can be attributed to the fact that in 1992 more than 20,000 people in this country were shot to death. There is no need, here, to engage in polemics regarding gun control; however, the majority of the individuals who died from this method were children. The courts have taken a stand off approach to this behavior because a large percentage of the victims are Black and they appear to be unconcerned about Black on Black violence. Violence has only become a general concern since it is perceived to be impacting first, tourism and, secondly, White youths. While the public decries this violence, which generally occurs as a by-product of gang behavior, there is a general reluctance for them to understand that gang behavior is an escape from pathologies that exist in the gang member's life, for example, alcoholic or drug-infected parent(s), rampant poverty, lack of legitimate opportunities, and a fatalistic out look on life. Can we logically blame the parents of these youths who them selves were nurtured in similar kinds of environments? Can we realistically absolve individuals like Perkins and Glazer from sharing a large portion of the responsibility due to the fact that they are a major part of the problem?

While this is not a treatise condemning Perkins, it is difficult not to refer to his efforts because they attempt to present an image that there is little wrong with the social structure. Instead he perceives that there is plenty wrong with individuals, mainly Blacks, who have failed to be socialized in a fashion which he deems to be commensurate with the broader social expectation.

In Perkin's defense, he is not only ap-
pealing to the masses' perspective and the
conservative ideology, he is also a strong
advocate of Wilson's[28] contention that race is
declining as a significant factor in the social structure. This is a haughty contention by
Wilson, and thoroughly embraced by the conservative element; but the behavior that has
occurred in the 1980s, and the direction provided by the Reagan and Bush administrations,
strongly suggest that race does count. Race
does and always will matter in the Western
world.

NOTES

1. *The Wall Street Journal* reported that
during the same period, Hispanics gained
60,040 and Whites 71,144 jobs. 13 Oct. (1993):
A-10.
2. Blacks lost one-third of the 180,210
blue-collar jobs during the recession. The
service industry added 53,548 jobs during this
period, but the records reveal that Blacks
lost 16,630 jobs in this sector. Ibid. *Wall
Street Journal*.
3. Clarence Page, "Employment Discrimination Pervasive." Chicago Tribune. (October
5, 1990), A-13.
4. Ibid. "Employment Discrimination
Pervasive."
5. This order prohibited discrimination
in employment by all employers who held federal contracts and required affirmative action
programs by all federal contractors and sub-
contractors. This meant that firms with contracts worth more than $50,000 and involving
fifty or more employees had to develop and
implement written programs of affirmative
action. This order was to be monitored and

enforced by the Department of Labor's Office of Contract Compliance Program.

6. This order required federal agencies to develop equal opportunity programs including affirmative action plans. The EEOC issued guidelines for development and implementation of the affirmative action plan for minorities and women. These guidelines covered the same aspects of the personnel process spelled out in *Section 41, CRF 60-2* of the *Executive Order 11246*. In essence, it required that the employer make a "good faith effort." To do so, their plan had to be developed using the following minimum guidelines:

A.   Developing a data base for all job classifications.
B.   Identify all areas of underutilization. This term is used for the purpose of setting numerical goals and timetables under the executive orders. It was established by reviewing all job categories and determining which of them had fewer women and minorities than are proportionally available in the relevant work force.
C.   Analyze all employment practices for possible practices that are having an adverse impact on women and minorities.
D.   Identify problems and develop programs of change that affirms commitment to affirmative action.
E.   Appoint an individual to be responsible for the implementation of the program.
F.   Develop numerical goals and time tables to overcome any underutilization identified.

7. Forbids discrimination on the basis of race, color, national origin, religion, or sex in any term, condition, or privilege of employment by unions and by employers. The Act

covered all private employers who had *fifteen* or more employees. It was *amended* on March 24, 1972 to cover all public and private educational whether or not they received any federal funds, state and local governments, and all public or private Equal Employment Opportunity Commissions. The legal principles for this Act are found in the *Fifth and Fourteenth Amendments* to the *Constitution*.

8. This is the first sex discrimination legislation enacted requiring equal pay against equal work regardless of sex. Differential in pay based on seniority, merit, or any factor other than sex are permissible.

9. Bans discrimination against persons at least 40 but less than 65 years of age, and applies to any organization with twenty or more employees.

10. This act was amended in 1976 and 1980 in *Public Law 93-112*. More commonly known as Revenue Sharing, it requires that there be an absence of discrimination by state and local governments on the basis of race, ethnicity, origin, religion, and sex.

11. Prohibits discrimination against the handicapped if an agency has a federal contract of $2,000 or more. This would only apply if the physically or mentally handicapped applicant or employee was qualified for the job.

12. Nathan Glazer, *Affirmative Discrimination: Ethnic Inequality and Public Policy* (New York: Basic Books. Inc., 1975): 67-68.

13. Ibid. 68.

14. Joseph Perkins, "From Here In The Clinton Era, Reagan Era Looks Good," *Newspaper Enterprise Association*, 5, Feb. (1993), A-12.

15. Ibid.

16. Joseph Perkins, "America's 30-Year-Old War On Poverty A Sham Battle," *Chicago Tribune-Star*, 7 Oct. 1993, A-8.

17. Demetra Nightingale, "Reflection on Poverty Issues," (Urban Institute, Washington

106   **BLACKS AND CRIME**

D.C., 1992).

18. Paulette Thomas, "Poverty Spread in 1992 to Total of 36.9 Million," *The Wall Street Journal*, 5 Oct. 1993, A-2.

19. Manning Marable, *How Capitalism Underdeveloped Black America* (Boston: South End Press, 1983): 243 -249.

20. Louis Harris, *Inside America: Public Opinion Expert Looks at* (New York: Vintage Books, 1987): 187.

21. Ibid. 190.

22. Alphonso Pickney, *The Myth Of Black Progress* (New York: Cambridge University Press, 1986).

23. Ibid. 1.

24. Glazer, *Affirmative Discrimination*, 69.

25. Ibid.

26. Stokely Carmichael and Charles Hamilton, *Black Power: The Politics of Liberation In America* (New York: Vantage Books, 1967): 6-7. Carmichael and Hamilton cite Robin Williams, Jr. who stated:" In a very basic sense, race relations" are the direct outgrowth of the long wave of European expansion, beginning with the discovery of America. Because of their more highly developed technology and economic and political organization, the Europeans were able by military force or by economic and political penetration to secure control over colonies, territories, protectorates and other possessions and spheres of influence around the world. In a way, the resulting so-called race relations had very little to do with "race" -initially it was an historical accident that the people encountered in the European expansion differed in shared physical characteristics of an obvious kind. But once the racial ideology had been formed and widely disseminated, they constituted a powerful means of justifying political hegemony and economic control. See Robin M. Williams, Jr.,"Prejudice and Society," in *The*

American Negro Reference Book, ed. John P. Davis (Englewood Cliffs, N. J.: Prentice-Hall, 1966): 727-729.

27. Perkins, "*America's 30-Year-Old War On Poverty A Sham Battle.*" Chicago Tribune Star, September, 12, 1992, A-11.

28. W.J. Wilson, *The Declining Significance of Race* Chicago, Ill.: University of Chicago Press, 1980).

6

Pathologies

Family units deemed to be problematic to the production of capital and stratification are perceived to be threatening to the social structure. Utilizing this orientation, historically, the Black family has been perceived to be problem-oriented. Problem-oriented because they are perceived to deviate from normative expectations. Arbitrarily this deviation has been designated as pathological. Such a designation ignores the possibility that despite a deviation from the normative structure, the unit may be instrumental in aiding its members to meet the needs of the group.[1] Therefore, forms of familial structure deviating from the norm cannot be construed, in the narrow sense, to be pathological.

The Black family must be assessed in terms of the context in which it developed. This can be done by looking at the institution during varying times, for example, the pre-slavery era, the slave era, the period immediately after manumission, and the changing contemporary patterns of social factors that impinge on the unit. The familial configurations that emerge are responses to the differential social factors they have confronted or been forced to endure.

It has been stated that, "a true view of the world must be casted in the particular-- e.g., the dramatic mode. To understand an experience the event must be framed in both a historical and dramatic mold rather than in an abstract and mathematical one. This is why, it is said that, Plato was a wiser man than Aristotle. Plato never built his house in a static sense, instead he used myth to present a dramatic interpretation. However, to Aristotle the world was something which could be represented by an intellectual photograph, by an architect's metaphysics. Only drama catches things 'as they really are.'"[2]

Fifty years ago Myrdal used the dramatic or an abstraction when he described the "black problem" as being not only America's greatest failure, but an incomparable opportunity for greatness.[3] He perceived the Blacks as presenting both a problem and an opportunity. However, Myrdal failed to realize that America was not confronting this dilemma because there was a lack of acceptance by Whites that Blacks and the other minorities were their equal as human beings.[4] Given this orientation, a dilemma is precluded.

It was felt that their mere presence necessitated brutal suppression. This suppression was inflicted on blacks, Hispanics, Indians, and Orientals. Behavioral responses of this nature reflexed the barbarity orchestrated in response to the paranoid state experienced by the oppressors. Paranoic because if these individuals lacked qualities of humanness, they then were to be feared and controlled. This paranoic state permeates all interactions and perspectives. Contemporarily this paranoia is directly related to the attitude Whites hold regarding crime and ethnicity. Historically, the systematic attacks and virulent hatred thrust on these

minorities emanated primarily from the failure
to understand the extent of humanness and
cultural bias. To comprehend the number and
type of crimes committed against these minorities necessitates an understanding of the
social order in which they took place.

This behavior occurred within a capitalistic society where greater emphasis was
placed on property rights than on human
rights. It was exacerbated by a culture in
which profits and individual value were measured by one's ability to amass acquisitions.
This orientation impelled those of similar
means to form interest groups that could
impact the formation of laws and the adjudication of them. These laws were designed to
function in a manner that protected those
interests to the inurement of all others.[5]

Although these interests were primarily
economic, they help to differentiate the
social structure as discussed in chapter two.
A major part of this differentiation emphasized racial aggression and racial oppression.
When the formal institution of slavery ended,
the South still deemed it in their best interest, as capitalist societies do, to maintain a
servile work force. In response, a more
specialized organization for dealing with the
recalcitrant Blacks was developed--the Ku Klux
Klan. Lynchings, murder, whippings, and tor-
ture, instruments utilized to maintain the
sense of differential social entitlement, were
indiscriminately applied with the force of
law. There were many sources of oppression,
but the dominant one in the United States was,
and still, is economic.[6] In fact, the labor
violence of the nineteenth and early twentieth
centuries was in reality ethnic conflicts in
which upper-class capitalists, the managers
and owners, were pitted against the unskilled
immigrant labor force, comprised of Irish,
Italians, Slavs, Jews, and other Eastern and

Southern Europeans.

Historically, the first crimes occurring in America were committed by White individuals against Indians and Blacks. The crimes involved the calculated strategy to bring about their total dehumanization. It was a strategy and process fostered by an oppressive system. Oppressive because the system condoned it by making it permissible to engage in violence with almost no restrictions. The violence had both latent and manifest functions, which was to destroy the family group, kinship ties, attain subservience, and kill the spirit. The necessary mental capability to exercise this violence was achieved because the tormentors first psychologically, and later, sociologically factored out the victims' humanity. This mental state was validated through the use of crude empirical social science "facts," customs, and laws. The bestial violent assaults resulted in the tormentors' ability to employ various fanciful behavior and character traits. These behaviors and traits were ascribed to their victims to justify their racist thinking and behavior.[7]

Historically, it is quite clear that every aspect in the development of this social system, whether it was in law, religion, education, politics, commerce, the family, and most certainly in all human intercourse between Blacks and Whites for two hundred years, was a further refinement of the doctrine that the slave and Indian were not men nor were they real humans. This deductive reasoning was possible, in part, because the people enslaved were reduced to a state of utter wretchedness. This wretchedness gave rise to numbness, shock, and despair owing primarily to a series of experiences that took two out of every three lives of persons originally captured for sale. Given conditions they confronted, the Blacks did indeed appear to be less human. How ever, during their experience, the concentration camp inmates also appeared to be less human than their Nazi tormentors.

When a person is defined in terms of certain assumptions regarding dignity, bearing, pride, courage, and conditions in which people are shackled between decks as little as eighteen inches apart, one cannot help but conclude that slaves were not men because men are not treated in this fashion. If the slaves were not men, this means they were inferior to men, and therefore enslaving them could be justified. If slavery was justified, it needed to be defended, and the best way to accomplish this was to make sure that slaves did not become men.

Habits nurtured for generations are not easily set aside. The elements of racism in our laws have created both a psychosis and a state of ambivalence for the White populace.[8] The psychosis experienced and acted upon by this nation has fostered a split personality. This pathology has been addressed by the usage of White fratricide and attempted genocide.[9]

This behavior was not only pathological, it was criminal. Was this criminal behavior conditioned by tensions confronting the White familial structures, or can we attribute it to the context that these individuals were occupying? Our theoretical elements, temporality, inclusiveness, stratification and commitment, suggest that it was not the family per se but rather those exogenous social factors, centered around profit making, that impinged upon the family structure. It can also be attributed to the criminalistic tendencies of individuals like Rush who, on July 4, 1792, presented a paper before a special meeting of the American Philosophical Society, entitled "Observations intended to favor a supposition that the black color (as it is called) of the Negroes is derived from the Leprosy." Based on his

medical analysis, he prescribed an interim
separation of the races in order to achieve a
greater good for both races. Rush claimed,
"like lepers, Negroes had remarkedly strong
venereal desires." Commenting on the infec-
tious quality of leprosy, he explained that it
was no longer as contagious, but there were
some cases in which something like a contagious quality had appeared and it was possible
for whites to be infected. "A white woman in
North Carolina not only acquired a dark color,
but several features of a negro, by marrying
and living with a black husband. A similar in-
stance in the change of the color and features
of a woman in Buck's county in Pennsylvania
has been observed and from a similar cause. In
both these cases, the women borne children by
their black husbands."[10]

Dr. Rush failed to mention whether there
were instances of White men acquiring Negroid
features from their cohabitation with black
women. This is a cogent example of the paranoia, pathology, and ambivalence. Nevertheless, Rush's efforts called for a demise in
the criminality by his White brethren against
Blacks, but he urged a greater solidification
of the existing social context. He suggested
the following to deal with these lepers:

> 1. That all claims of superi-
> ority of the whites over the blacks,
> on account of their color, are foun-
> ded alike in ignorance and inhumani-
> ty. If the color of the negro be the
> effect of a disease, instead of
> inviting us to tyrannise (sic) over
> them, it should entitle them to a
> double portion of our humanity, for
> disease all over the world has al-
> ways been the signal for immediate
> and universal compassion.
> 2. The facts and principles

which have been delivered, should teach white people the necessity of keeping up that prejudice against such connections with them [Negroes], as would tend to infect posterity with any portion of their disorder. This may be done upon the grounds I have mentioned without offering violence to humanity, or calling in question the sameness of descent, or natural equality of man kind.[11]

His suggestion also urged White civility to enhance social solidarity.

By the time Western "civilization" had been accomplished, the American Indian had long since lost their property and human rights. They were doomed to survive in poverty-ridden, germ-infested, famine-cursed concentration camps called reservations. This was of little consequence or concern to the capitalists because the coming railroads and sewers, having been built by the Chinese coolies and the Irish peasants, coupled with the defeat of the slavocracy, the ethnic groups had new value to the free market. In addition, they added to the group of seasoned contributors used to generate the wealth and comfort. But they also became targets to hate. These hordes of Chinese, Irish, Poles, Hungarians, Italians, and Blacks were newcomers to the urban area, and they were willing and anxious to work. However, they were also perceived to be a problem by the wealthy and not so wealthy Whites.

They were perceived to be a problem because they inhabited the slums and exhibited poverty, disease, and filth. There were also the behavioral pathologies. These were the urban conditions they confronted and endured and for the elite, the seminal question was,

what to do with them? One solution was to
attempt to have the states enact laws for
compulsory sterilization of the "socially
inadequates." Therefore, a movement was initiated to sterilize the "hereditary paupers,
criminals, feebleminded, tuberculous, shift-
less, and ne-er-do-wells."

Misguided as they may had been, in 1897
the Michigan State Legislature introduced a
bill to sterilize people identified as being
of "bad heredity." It was soundly defeated.
Nevertheless, there were zealous individuals
who continued to press the crusade. For example, in 1899, without the benefit of enabling
legislation, Dr. Harry Sharp, physician at the
Indiana State Reformatory at Jeffersonville,
began to perform vasectomies on young inmates
he deemed to be either hereditary criminal or
otherwise genetically defective.[12]

In 1905, The Pennsylvania Commonwealth's
Senate passed "an act for the prevention of
idiocy." This act declared: "Whereas, heredity
plays a most important part in the transmission of idiocy and imbecility," be it decreed
that it should henceforth "be compulsory for
each and every institution in the state,
entrusted exclusively or especially with the
care of idiots and imbecile children," to
appoint on its staff one skilled surgeon
"whose duty it shall be, in conjunction with
the chief physician of the institution, to
examine the mental and physical condition of
the inmate." If, upon this examination, the
surgeon and the house doctor found that the
"procreation [of the inmate] is inadvisable,
and there is no probability of improvement in
the mental and physical condition of the
inmate, it shall be lawful for the surgeon to
perform such operation for the prevention of
procreation as shall be decided safest and
most effective."[13] The governor returned the
bill with the following observation, "the

plainest and safest method of preventing procreation would be to cut the heads off the inmates, and such authority is given by the bill to this staff of scientific experts." In his veto address he said: "[it] inflicts cruelty upon a helpless class in a community which that state has undertaken to protect violates the principles of ethic furthermore (it is) illogical in its thought. Idiocy will not be prevented by the prevention of procreation among these inmates. This mental condition is due to causes many of which are entirely beyond our knowledge."[14]

Despite this wisdom, in 1907, The Indiana State Legislature passed, and the governor approved, "an act to prevent procreation of confirmed criminals, idiots, imbeciles, and rapists." They reasoned that "heredity played a most important part in the transmission of crime, idiocy, and imbecility." This contention could be traced to Eugenists especially Galton, Pearson, Hall, Davenport, who advocated eugenics to control the urban horde.[15]

When in 1909, the state of Washington passed its bill to prevent procreation by feebleminded, insane, epileptic, habitual criminals, moral degenerates, and sexual perverts who may be inmates in the state institutions, it joined California and Connecticut which passed similar bills that year. These four states were soon joined by the majority of the forty-eight states in passing equally Draconian laws. This type of legislation occurred at the behest of the Eugenics' Record Office. In 1912, Woodrow Wilson, governor of New Jersey, signed into law a similar bill, but the State Supreme Court found it to be unconstitutional. This was echoed by the high courts of some of the other states. In other states, like Idaho, Vermont, and Nebraska, the governors vetoed such bills as being unfair, unjust, unwarranted, and inexcusable

discrimination that could not be tolerated. In
addition, these bills were in violation of
Section 9, Article 1, of the *Bill of Rights*,
as well as being paganistic in nature. These
were gelding measures, and they were intended
to victimize marginalized people who were the
least menace to society because they were
institutionalized.

In Oregon, a sterilization bill was
passed by the legislature and signed into law
by the governor in 1911. However, it was re-
pealed by a popular referendum in 1913. In
1921, the second sterilization bill to be
passed in the twentieth century by a Pennsylvania legislature was vetoed by the governor.
However, by World War II, laws providing for
the compulsory sterilization of the poor, the
helpless, and the misdiagnosed were on the
books in thirty states and Puerto Rico. Some
of this legislation was influence by former
President Theodore Roosevelt, an old advocate
of racial superiority, who on January 14, 1913
wrote a letter to the *Van Wagenen Committee*,
the *Committee to Study and to Report on the
Best Practical Means of Cutting off the Defective Germ-Plasm in the American Population*.
This committee was set up by the *American
Breeder's Association's Eugenic Section*, and
its report said in part:

> As you say, it is obvious that if in
> the future racial qualities are to
> be improved, the improving must be
> wrought mainly by favoring the fe-
> cundity of the worthy types and
> frowning on the fecundity of the
> unworthy types. At present, we do
> just the reverse. There is no check
> to the fecundity of those who are
> subnormal, both intellectually and
> morally, while the provident and
> thrifty, tend to develop a cold
> selfishness, which makes them refuse

to breed at all.[16]

By "proving" that the lower and middling classes were subhuman creatures who persisted in wallowing in the joys of gin, sex, and in squandering all of their "capital" without a thought "of the future," Malthus thereby initiated societal aggression against the poor by using "science." This "war" was waged against humanitarian concepts such as child labor, lower wages, unsafe working conditions, over crowded and filth-ridden slum housing, and compulsory illiteracy. This one-sided battle emerged in the consciousness of the educated and affluent classes as being perfectly proper and a natural approach to their own social and human condition. These individuals did not feel any responsibility to the men, women, and children who dug the coal, manned the factories, and produced the foods and fibers on which their own expanding wealth was based.

These sadistic insensitivities were applied to everyone. For example, the Italians were deemed to be a menace because they were perceived to be content living on stale beer and bread, and because fruit and other food which would be rejected as unfit by most other races furnished a diet upon which the Italians seemed to thrive. In the case of the Jews, the privileged felt that it would have been much better for them to stay home and be raped, lynched, shot, slashed, beaten, pillaged, their homes burned to the ground and their children tortured by drunken Cossacks first, then if any of them survived such actual persecution, they then had a right to emigrate to Australia. Thus was the racial effect on immigration. These foreigner's biggest problem was the belief that they were replacing the biological strain of the elite, not reinforcing it. From this perception emanated their wretched conditions.

To further justify the continuation of the inhuman treatment of the working poor, it was first necessary, in Christian England and subsequently in the United States, to deprive them of their right to be considered as fully human as their employers, their landlords, and their rulers. This human right Malthus helped tear from the realms of civil society using his pseudo laws of population, production, and the limits of agricultural growth. Despite its acclaim, the sole function of Malthus' *Essay on Population* was to preserve the status quo of low wages, child labor, and the absence of education and health care for the White, Anglo-Saxon, Protestant families who worked for wages on the land, in the factories, and in the mines.

In conscious pursuit of these objectives, Malthus succeeded beyond his wildest dreams. His harsh judgments of the poor and the middling classes as being subraces of the population, and his strictures against coddling these sub-humans with such spoiling mechanisms as higher wages, free education, healthier housing, the right to vote, and remedies for the prevention of ravaging diseases are still shared by many powerful governmental agencies. They remain the basis for forging insights and the value judgments of far too many individuals who design policies regarding health, education, and welfare. These antihuman homilies, based on unscientific and anti-cultural data, did more than the thoughts of Paine, Jefferson, Bentham, and Pasteur to set the stage for "civilization" in the western world.

The attempts to stop the breeding were meant to resolve perceived conflicts in the social order regarding the right or ideal type. When we look at this conflict from a legal, rather than a moral, perspective, we must use a conflict model. The conflict-consensus model considers law as a weapon of social conflict and an instrument of oppression employed by the ruling classes for their own benefit. When diverse groups encounter conflict, they compete to have their interests protected and perpetuated through the formalization of laws that express those interests. Quinney argues that rather than the law being a device to control interests, it is an expression of interest. He goes on to say:

> Society is characterized by diversity, conflict, coercion, and change, rather than by consensus and stability. Second, law is a result of the operation of interests, rather than an instrument that functions outside of particular interests. Though law may control interests, it is in the first place created by interests of specific persons and groups; it is seldom the product of the whole society. Law is made by men, representing special interests, who have the power to translate their interests into public policy. Unlike the pluralistic conception of politics, law does not represent a compromise of the interest at the expense of others.[17]

Contrary to popular wisdom, law is the states' coercive weapon is used to structure and maintain the social and economic order. It is not concerned with achieving either justice or fairness except in the most oblique manner.[18] Instead, it is concerned with policy formation and policy enforcement. These policies reinforce the prevailing values, and despite moderate alterations they have continuity. The criminal codes specifically refer to the seminal values engendered in this social order since its inception. The vagrancy

laws for example, have served to force laborers, free or not, to accept employment at a
low wage in order to ensure first the landown-
er and later the industrialists an adequate
supply of labor at an affordable price. Moderate alterations to the core part of the law
were made to protect commercial interests and
to ensure safe transportation of commercial
commodities. These laws clearly were used to
enhance the affluent.

Jonathan H. Turner points out the: "linkages between law and society are often left
implied; changes in the relative importance of
these linkages are frequently not discussed;
and there is a tendency to place too heavy an
emphasis on a single variable and there by
ignore the multiplicity of institutional
influences on legal development.[19]

Despite Turner's statement, there are
many examples of interest groups, a single
variable, whose influence in lawmaking is
plentiful. The single purpose of or the con-
texture of law regulating behaviors for example, alcohol use, sexual conduct, abortion,
pure food and drugs, etc., are all well documented examples of single interest group
policies. Friedman stated:

> The "public opinion" that affects
> the law is like the economic power
> which makes the market. This is so
> in two essential regards; Some peo-
> ple, but only some, take enough
> interest in any particular commodity
> to make their weight felt; second,
> there are some people who have more
> power and wealth than others. At one
> end of the spectrum stand such fig-
> ures as the president of the United
> States and General Motors; at the
> other, migrants, laborers, babies,
> and prisoners at San Quentin. They

(the lawmakers) know that 100
wealthy powerful constituents pas-
sionately opposed to socialized
medicine outweigh thousands of poor,
weak constituents.[20]

In this book, one issue of concern is the
differential application of the law to minorities, specifically Blacks. Here it is important to note that the concept minority is a
characterization of a fragment of American
society and a perception about the intercon-
nections with diverse social problems. The
concept is powerful because it also calls
attention to the conjunction between the
character of individuals and the impersonal
social forces that include the larger economic
and political order. For example, the perception of Blacks evokes adjectives like dis-
agreeable, disreputable, dangerous, disrup-
tive, dark, evil, hedonistic, nihilistic,
aggressive, and many other uncomplimentary
terms. When one uses these terms for identification, the user fails to consider the laws,
social policies, and history that have combined to make these people so designated what
they are. It is also important to remember
that these individuals are problems to the
social order, not because they are troubled as
a group, but rather because they are troubling
to someone else. Their behavior in the social
system like in the legal arena when it is
delinquent or criminal, where the behavior is
ultimately assessed is based on the conclusion
reached by the assessors that the responsibility for the behavior resides in the individual
and not the social order. In addition to
determining responsibility, the legal system
must also devise methods to control them. One
way to exercise control over these individual
types, even if they have not committed an
offense, is to define their behavior as being

consistent with characteristic(s) that are
either mental or pathological in nature. These
behaviors are labeled disorders, and they can
cover activities ranging from running away, to
aggressiveness, to incorrigibility, to promiscuity, to murder. However, there is a reluctance to realize that these adjectives denote
behaviors and not statuses. Furthermore, for
these behaviors to have meaning it must be
correlated to the characteristics of the
social order, as homicide rates are correlated
to the prevalence of guns.

There has been a historical attempt to
differentiate between terror, terrorism,
force, and violence, all behaviors used to
structure and change social orders. Terror
represented the use of force to maintain the
present social and political system. Force and
violence seek to alter individual and collective behavior through coercion, intimidation,
and fear. The trait of this extraordinary
violence is the indiscriminate, random nature
of the violent act. Officially, the state has
used terror to attack and to intimidate specific individuals or groups who threaten the
existence of the state. In summation, violence
is also the manufacturing, labeling, and
spread of fear by legitimate authority or its
designated official agent, that is, the police, military, etc.

In *Politics Among Nations*, Morgenthau defined political power as "the psychological
control over the minds of men."[21] This control
includes the attempt by the oppressor to have
his definitions, his historical descriptions,
accepted by the oppressed. Carroll understood
this when he said:

When I used a word, Humpty said in a
rather scornful tone, it means just
what I choose it to mean--neither
more nor less. The question is said

Alice, Whether you can make words mean so many different things. The question is, said Humpty Dumpty, which is to be master--that's all.[22]

Wilson, like Clark and Moynihan, emphasized that family deterioration, as revealed in the urban Black's rising rates of broken marriages, female-headed homes, out-of-wedlock births, and welfare dependency, was one of the central problems of the Black lower class.[23] Wilson contend that: "Although the official poverty figures show that whites constitute a majority of the poor population, even in urban areas, many of the social dislocations related to poverty (e.g., crime, out-of-wedlock births, female-headed families, and welfare dependency) reflect a sharply uneven distribution by race."[24]

This assessment is consistent with Hammond's concept of the underclass;[25] but both are inconsistent with Bennett's report that reveals that those factors used to describe the Black underclass apply to Whites who also occupy the lower social strata. These statistical factors will be discussed further in the next chapter. We need to analyze this from a statistical perspective, but we must not for get the historical antecedents. Neckerman said: "It is particularly useful to consider black families in historical perspective because recent research has challenged assumptions about the influence of slavery on the character of the black family."[26]

NOTES

1. A. Billingsley, *Black Families in White America* (Englewood Cliffs, N. J.: Prentice-Hall, 1968).

2. Clyde Kluckhon, "Foreword" *In The*

World's Rim Hartley B. Alexander (Lincoln: University of Nebraska Press, 1967).

   3. G. Myrdal, *An American Dilemma* (New York: Harper and Row, 1964).

   4. In *Black Power: The Politics of Liberation in America* (New York: Vintage, 1967) Carmichael and Hamilton wrote: "there is no 'American dilemma' because black people in this country form a colony, and it is not in the interest of the colonial power to liberate them. Yet they stand as colonial subjects in relation to the white society. Thus institutional racism has another name: colonialism." p. 5.

   5. New entitlement concepts emerged that may not have had the binding force of the law but were nevertheless social obstacles to those who did not share this interest. These entitlement perceptions created inequalities that restricted full social, economic, and political participation.

   6. Opposition to slavery was primarily an economic phenomenon supported by powerful industrial or manufacturing interests. These interests were pitted against the equally powerful agrarian interest of the South, and the political compromise was a sort of balance of power decision reflected in a number of legislative decisions for example, the *Missouri Compromise*.

   7. Scheri cited an excerpt from a lecture on "The Urban Crisis" in a seminar on "A Black Looks at White America," Detroit, October 15, 1968. Also found in George W. Crockett, Jr., "Racism in the Law," in *Science and Society*, 33 (Spring 1969): 78-91.

   8. Sacred pledges contained in the Declaration of Independence and the Constitution embodying democratic principles, the ideas of brotherhood of all men and equality, have in practice been used to segregate and alienate because of differences in ethnicity and skin color.

9. So entrenched was racism and this psychosis in American Law and behavior a Civil War had to be fought in an attempt to obtain some sanity.

10. Benjamin Rush, *Transactions of the American Philosophical Society* 4 (1799): 294.

11. Ibid. 295-296.

12. Francis Galton,"Hereditary Improvement," *Fraser Magazine*, January 1873, 118.

13. Ibid. 118.

14. Allan Chase, *The Legacy of Malthus: The Social Costs of New Scientific Racism* (Champaign. Ill.: University of Illinois Press, 1980): 125.

15. Ibid. 126.

16. Ibid. 127. Discussions regarding the poor and the correlation of various undesirable consequences such as sickness, vagrancy, crime and hopeless despair go back into antiquity. Cf. Walter D. Wilcox, "History of Statistics," *Encyclopedia of the Social Sciences* 14, (date unknown): 356; Thomas R. Malthus, *Essay on Principles of Population as it Affects the Future Improvement of Society* (London: No publisher acknowledged 1798).

17. Richard Quinney, *The Social Reality of Crime* (Boston: Little Brown, 1970): 35.

18. The imagery of law and justice obscures the way by which the judicial process yields distinctly unequal opportunities and results. In the pursuit of justice prosecutors, defense attorneys, jurors, as well as judges are influenced by their attitudes and personal interests. These actors in the judicial system make subjective and discretionary decisions that determine the outcome of cases.

19. H.J Turner, *Patterns of Social Organization, a Survey of Social Institutions* (New York: McGraw-Hill, 1972): 3.

20. Lawrence M. Friedman, *The Legal System, a Social Science Perspective* (New York: Russell Sage Foundation, 1975): 163-164.

21. H. Morgenthau, *Politics Among Nations* (New York: Alfred A. Knopf. 1966): 29.

22. L. Carroll, *Through the Looking Glass* (New York: Doubleday Books, Inc., 1987): 196.

23. W.J. Wilson, *The Truly Disadvantaged: The Inner City, The Underclass, and Public Policy* (Chicago: The University of Chicago Press, 1987): 21.

24. Ibid. 173.

25. Andre D. Hammonds, "The Black Underclass: Conflicting Perspectives," *The Western Journal Of Black Studies* 13 (1989): 217-222.

26. K.M. Neckerman, R. Aponte, and W. J. Wilson, "Family Structure, Black Unemployment, and American Social Policy." in *The Politics of Social Policy* ed. M. Weir, A. S. Orloff, and T. Skocpol, (Princeton, N. J., Princeton University Press, 1988); H. G. Gutman, *The Black Family in Slavery and Freedom, 1750-1925* (New York: Pantheon 1976).

7

Delinquent and Criminal Behavior

SOCIOGENIC PERSPECTIVE

Scientists at Nijmegen University Hospital in
the Netherlands reported that they found that
five violent men from the same family shared a
genetic mutation by which their bodies did not
produce monoamine oxidase, an enzyme that
deactivates brain chemicals that induce aggression. In 1992, more than 23,000 people in
the United States were shot to death. Some
argue it is the fault of people rather than
the guns. Gang members are in gangs because
they are attempting to escape from dirty
houses, alcoholic parents, and crying and
dirty siblings running all over the place. The
Center on Hunger, Poverty and Nutrition Policy
at Tufts University estimated that in 1991,
eighteen percent of U.S. children under the
age of 18 experienced hunger. Arson, assault,
manslaughter, murder, possession and distribution of illegal drugs, rape, robbery, and
sexual abuse are the reasons why so many
youths are now incarcerated. Nationwide, more
and more children are committing violent
crimes. The U.S. Dept. of Justice reported
that crime of all kinds committed by women

increased 16.4 percent from 1987-1991, while crime for men during that period increased 33.6 percent. UNICEF reports that ninety percent of all murderers of young people, ages 15-24, in the industrialized world live in the United States. There are 15.3 homicides per 100,000 in this age group. Can the theories used to explain delinquency and crime be used to explain these behaviors?

In Homer's, the *Iliad*, Thersites was depicted as being one of the ugliest Greeks and a crude and defiled defamer. Caliban was Shakespeare's deformed servant who was contrasted with Prospero to draw parallels between that which is good and beautiful and that which is bad and evil. These individuals were perceived to have sick minds, which generally resulted from evil sources. Who can we use today to draw parallels from? Are they individuals who are intricately involved in Abscam, Watergate, BCCI, the Keating Five, the Ku Klux Klan, the Fourth Reich Skin Heads, the American Front, the Aryan Resistance League, the Northern Hammerskins, the Old Glory Hammerskins, the Northwest United Skins, and a host of other groups? Is it the family and the nature of the social order?

The sociogenic perspective of criminal and delinquent behavior is centered on two analytically distinct problems: 1) the forms, types and the rates of their occurrence in a society, and 2) the causative explanation for the differential patterns of its occurrence. In order to arrive at plausible explanations for these distinct problems, sociologists first analyze the nature of the macro-system (social order) and then the micro-relationships of the individuals and how these play out in the broader society. Forms of behavior, conforming and nonconforming, are then explained through the interactive associations that occur in the individuals' macro and/or micro-relationships.

Hirschi provided a succinct and clear analysis of the sociogenic perspectives which are utilized to account for delinquent behavior, when he stated that: Three fundamental perspectives on delinquency and deviant behavior dominate the current scene. According to strain or motivational theories, legitimate desires that conformity cannot satisfy forces a person into deviance. According to control or bond theories, a person is free to commit delinquent acts because his ties to the conventional order have somehow been broken. According to cultural deviance theories, the deviant conforms to a set of standards not accepted by a larger or more powerful society.[1]

SOCIAL STATUS

The majority of criminal and delinquency theories tend to focus upon the social system's characteristics, the formation of conduct norms, assessment of individual behavior, and the sanctioning process. Barron[2] for example, contended that much delinquent behavior can be explained as a clash of values in a pluralistic society-impersonality, individualism, disrespect for law and order, exploitiveness, and other ingredients central to the American way of life. Explanations for criminal behavior are, in all probability, similar.

However, Mills pointed out some of the problems inherent in these social pathology perspectives when he said: "An individual who does not approximate these [socially approved] standards is said to be unadjusted. If he does not concern himself with living up to them, he is said to be demoralized or disorganized.[3]

The sociological literature is replete with this type of paradoxical thinking. The paradox can be specifically seen in the liter-

ature's handling of class. For example, most
sociologists do not use labels such as "immoral" or "uncivilized" in writing about the
lower class. They do, however, refer to the
lower class as being inadequately socialized,
using such terms as "unintegrated," "immature," "pathological," and "disorganized."

SUBCULTURAL

The use of the above mentioned terms
suggests values and behaviors that coalesce to
form a culture at variance within the broader
culture. However, to be meaningful as a concept this counter--or subculture must account
for specificities in behavior, attributed to
the subcultural, which are different from the
behavior that occurs outside of it. Therefore,
in order to apply subcultural theories, the
critical questions become: (1) Do the subcultural values differ significantly from the
cultural values? (2) Are urban individuals
more prone to commit crime than rural individuals because they have a greater opportunity
to be exposed to subcultures? (3) In the
behavioral process, what effect does the urban
area have vis-a-vis the rural area on the
attributes (psychological, social, or economic) deemed necessary in order to produce the
"strain," which is believed to lead to aberrant behavior? (4) Is one attribute, or a
combination of several, more important than
the others, and if not, then how do all of
these attributes function to generate these
particular behaviors? (5) How do we explain
the nondelinquent or criminal behavior of
these individuals purported to be enmeshed in
the subcultures?
Although Merton[4] stated that crime and
deviancy resulted from the inability of every-

one to achieve equal success and consequently could be structurally induced into these behaviors, he also argued that there were other behavioral alternatives. Cloward and Ohlin[5] revised Merton's anomie theory and suggested possible ways that an individual could adapt to the interfacing of goals and means. Their revision focused on the lower class youth's struggle to accumulate monetary and symbols of wealth. One can logically conclude from this that once wealth or the symbols of it are attainted, the causative factors for delinquency and crime will disappear. However, if this is true, one is still left grappling for an explanation for white collar crime.

SOCIAL CONTROL

The social control theories that have emerged in recent years implicitly suggest how middle class youths should behave. One of these was Hirschi's[6] social bond theory that argued that the individual's social bond with society is maintained through the level or degree of four bonding elements: attachment, commitment, involvement, and beliefs. Attachment according to Hirschi, could be measured by looking at the extent of attachment the youth has to significant others:[7] commitment is the investment an individual makes to conventional behavior; involvement is the behavioral side of commitment; and belief is a commitment to the social order-common values and rules. Criminal or delinquent behavior in Hirschi's social control scheme would be the resulting behavior by individuals whose allegiance to a belief system has not been properly developed or has become weakened.[8] Owing to this condition, these individuals feel free to

behave as they choose (an opposing argument to
Matza's "techniques of neutralization" explanation for delinquency).[9] In Hirschi's words,
"many persons do not have an attitude of
respect toward the rules of society; many persons feel no moral obligation to conform
regardless of personal advantage. Insofar as
the values and beliefs of these persons are
consistent with their feelings, and there
should be a tendency towards consistency,
neutralization is unnecessary; it has already
occurred."[10]

Using Hirschi's theoretical statements,
those who are inclined to commit delinquent or
criminal acts do so because the act is congru-
ent with their overall attitude (see Figure
7.1).

The most glaring weaknesses with Hirschi's argument center around the general
notion of that which constitutes an adolescent's perception of proper attitude and
respect toward the rules of society and whether commitment, attachment, and beliefs designed to measure these perceptions actually
constitute acceptance. For example, do youths
perceive these "attitudes" and "respect" as
constituting legitimate demands by the social
order? One major criticism of bonding theory
focuses on its failure to adequately account
for the occurrence of delinquent behavior that
cannot be attributed to the bonding level and
the subsequent impact that this behavior may
have on the bonding level.[11]

Nevertheless, a closer examination of the
delinquency literature is needed to determine
whether it is true that youth who are initially strongly bonded engage in less delinquent
behavior than those who are less bonded. A
ramification of this thinking is the assumption that the bond level, and therefore the
behavior, remains static. Theoretically, these
could change over time as the result of bond-

ing experiences, situational involvements, and
attitudinal changes toward the bonding condi-

Figure 7.1
Bonding Level, Attitude, and Predicted
Behavior

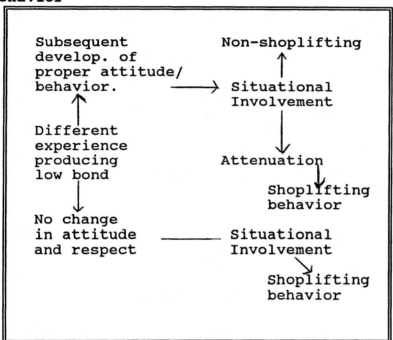

tions. Reckless[12] contended that the individual's strong self-concept and high tolerance for frustration (inner containment) and
the social norms, values, and effective supervision (external containment) helped him or
her resist temptations of internal "pushes"
(restlessness) and the external "pulls" (the
lure of deviant subcultures, minority status,
and unemployment).

In general, bonding theories provide us
with the perception that for these lower class
youths to be "socialized," they must engage in

activities that prepare them to conform to middle-class standards. Critics of Cohen[13] and Miller[14] have questioned whether lower class youth really aspire to attain middle class values.

While criminologists have made detailed studies of race,[15] poverty and other factors[16] and their correlation to delinquency, they have basically failed to coherently explain the impact of the delinquent behavior on the individual. Most accounts depict these individuals as being in pursuit of hedonism. It does seem logical to conclude that those individuals who commit and recommit delinquent and criminal acts appear to derive some satisfaction from the behavior, however, this perceptive makes the assumption that people are capable of making rational decisions in which the cost-benefit analysis is weighted in favor of pleasure prior to acting.

SOCIAL LEARNING PERSPECTIVE

For many years, Sutherland was the most influential theorist in U. S. criminology. His efforts revealed an environmental bias when examining why people learn to act in specific ways. Differential association,[17] a learning theory, contends that delinquent or criminal behavior is learned through association with those who have already learned and nurtured it. What is taught is not only the delinquent behavior but also the values, attitudes, and skills associated with it. The theory contends that when a violator's behavior is altered to the extent that it results in a delinquent or criminal act, there is normally a link primarily to people who share the same or similar sentiments.

Sutherland perceived the family and/or

gang as the source of all learning and social behavior, including delinquent behavior. In this setting, the individual learns how to define different situations and behavior as being either appropriate, law abiding, or law breaking. How individuals define a particular situation depends upon how early in life the definitions of the situation were learned, the frequency of enforcement, and the importance of the definition to those individuals.

Criminal or delinquent behavior, in the concept of the theory of differential association, can produce many possible types of behavior as a result of a weak family socialization process. More specifically, the process points out a conflict in the youth's operating milieu due to a weakness in the functioning of the family (see Figure 7.2). Exposure to this type of milieu is said to manifest itself in the form of the youth's inability or failure to acquire prosocial norms and to subsequently associate with similar delinquents who provide delinquent definitions. This process is believed to determine which youths are led to delinquent behavior.

The problems with this scheme can be demonstrated by focusing on the delinquent associations and the family support elements. For example, there are myriad youths with weak family supports who do not develop delinquent associates and/or move further into the process.

Figure 7.2
Differential Association Applied to General
Delinquent or Criminal Behavior

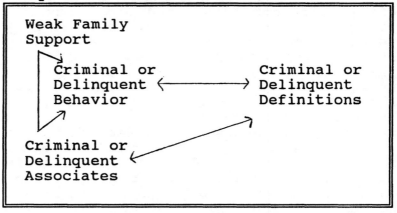

Conflict

Dahrendorf[18] and Vold[19] popularized the
conflict theory. However, they warned it
should not be stretched too far in the attempt
to explain the varying forms of criminal
behavior. Vold pointed out there are situations in which criminality is a normal response by normal people struggling in normal
situations, attempting to maintain an accus-
tomed way of life. Clinard and Quinney[20] provided an intellectual linkage between the
efforts of Lemert[21] and Dahrendorf-Vold. Despite the transition, Turk[22] sees "power" as
the root of the conflict. Wirth believed that
people who were accused of misconduct in a
culture-conflict situation behaved in a manner
which was rational and self-justified. He
stated:

> Our conduct, whatever it may consist
> of, or however, it might be judged
> by the world at large, appears moral

to us when we can get the people whom we regard as significant in our social world to accept it. One of the most convincing bits of evidence for the importance of the role played by culture conflict in the cases that have come to my attention is the frequency with which delinquents, far from exhibiting a sense of guilt, make the charge of hypocrisy. Wirth set forth the hypothesis that, "the physical and psychic tensions which express them selves in attitudes and in overt conduct may be correlated with culture conflict. This hypothesis may, to be sure, not always prove fitting.[23]

However, Merton rejected the notion that man is a bundle of impulses seeking immediate gratification and who would succeed if not controlled or imprisoned by society. Instead, he saw considerable consensus of value among individual, even in a conflict-ridden and pluralistic society. Therefore, he concluded that the attempts to bring forth a single theory to explain all instances, all people, and all types of behavior may be too ambitious.

SITUATIONAL PERSPECTIVE

The ability to predict behavior using situational stimuli is enhanced if past behavior to similar stimuli reveals a consistency with present behavior. However, behavioral congruence is only one facet of gauging situationally induced behavior, and this measure becomes less relevant if past behavior involves irrelevant information and dimensions

when applied to current situational stimuli.
Therefore, responses to previous situational
facilitants may or may not be indicators of
further behavior.

In order to address behavioral consistency, ambiguity, or inconsistency, it is
necessary to analyze an individual's attitudes
toward the current facilitants and the behavior simultaneously. Analysis of this nature
would ferret out the relevant information elements and permit the researcher to compare
phenomena that are similar. The expectation
from this procedure should provide us with
those elements that lead to behavioral consistency and a grouping of similar elements that
lead to behavioral consistency. A grouping of
similar elements should predict the behavior.

Most personality theorists and many social psychologists agree with this perspective.
However, some have presented a case against
behavioral consistency despite commonality of
elements. They argued that to expect behavioral and cognitive consistency when differing
situational stimuli are encountered would be
intrinsically unnatural and would result in
limiting the range of self-defining qualities
and behaviors necessary for effective social
interaction.

While these theorists have also pointed
out an important problem encountered in the
attempt to relate behavior to an individual's
characteristics and the situation, there still
exists a need to develop additional theoretical statements that would extend both these
positions and the empirical assessment. These
theorists were silent on past and present behavioral tendencies, given the same stimuli.
Perhaps he felt that there is no such thing as
similar stimuli over time. If stimuli are not
similar over time then, one cannot logically
group them.

Because of the differences in phenomen-
ological context or observational perspective,

individuals may interpret situational impressions and activities differently. Nevertheless,
it is assumed that individuals will respond to
stimuli in a fashion that is consistent with
past behavior. A situational stimuli paradigm
also provides a perspective that enables the
researcher to analyze the causal explanations
individuals construct to explain their behavior. These constructs perceive the behavior as
being logical and natural given the context.

Emanating from this perspective is the
suggestion that individuals do not always, if
ever have control over the way they behave.
Rather they are pushed and pulled by stimuli
designed to minimize their control. Although
the argument of free will versus determinism
is not the focus of this book, it is mentioned
to demonstrate the difficulty of operationalizing variables that inherently express values
and beliefs without considering the latitude
of freedom that is available to an individual
to exercise them. This consideration is important when variables are used to explain this
behavior.[24]

The theorists do not speak to the issue
of free will or rationality. Rather they argue
that individuals in general, in their interactions, drift in and out of delinquent and
criminal behavior, depending on the situation.[25] Despite this explanation, the fact
remains that the use of drift as a basis to
explain delinquent and criminal behavior
leaves us wondering how this interaction
works. For example, which situations are
necessary to push individuals in a drift
position from which they feel they cannot
extricate themselves? What is it about a
specific situation that leads an individual to
engage in one or another form of behavior
rather than abstaining from it?

If there exists a push-pull effect that
can be attributed to the situation, then op-

portunity theory (Spergel,[26] Stinchcombe,[27] Gould,[28] Knudsen,[29]) maybe used to explain behavior. Theoretically, if the distance between classes narrows, forms of class delinquency and crime should become less defined. Opportunity theory would appear to be a logical construct to use in an effort to determine what the situation does and does not offer from an inducement perspective.

PSYCHOGENIC PERSPECTIVE

Psychologically, there appears to be no clear syndrome that could characterize the delinquent or criminal. However, there is some agreement that certain narrow personality traits that bear directly on offenders tend to be associated with delinquent and criminal acts.

The literature suggests that if behavior can be attributed to psychological traits, the offender can then use them to rationalize behavior. Arnold, Brungart, and Tannenbaum suggest that those traits deemed to be causative factors for behavior would be more appropriate if they were conceptualized as measures. The measures could then be used to gauge both delinquent and criminal tendencies rather than be advanced as causes of the behaviors.

Lowrey agreed with this perspective:

> Despite extensive research and many ingenious efforts to delimit them, there are no such entities as "delinquent" or "criminal" personalities. To be sure, there are delinquents and criminals and naturally, each has a personality, normal or abnormal.[30]

Despite Lowrey's protestation, research continues in the attempt to determine if there are specific characteristics that predispose certain individuals to delinquency. It is imperative that these studies be thoroughly evaluated to discern what, if any, contribution they can make to enhance the explanation of delinquent and criminal behavior. Abrahamson, for example, described the psychological state of delinquent as: "many of them are neurotic, suffer from phobias, show compulsive behavior patterns, or appear to be rigid in their behavior. Some are mentally defective; some show signs of the beginning of a psychosis; others may show vague symptoms of a character disorder. All of them, however, are emotionally underdeveloped."[31]

While the validity of Abrahamson's assessment may be questionable, the salient point here is that we can deduce, among the combination of factors which are deemed to be responsible for the creation and playing out of delinquent and criminal behavior, that the psychological ones are considered by some reputable social scientists to be important. Analysis of these psychological factors leads one to conclude that they can be characterized as existing with in the individual, yet when displayed in the individual's personal social environment, they assume meaning. Furthermore, the interaction between the psychological and sociological factors provides a basis for both suggesting and predicting how an individual would or should react, given specific situational stimuli. However, there appears to be an inconsistency in this perspective when female delinquency and crime are discussed. Some of the literature suggests that delinquency or criminal behavior is performed proportionately more by boys than girls. An alternative explanation for women's involvement in most crimes and delinquency has been

explained by personal psychological maladjust-
ment rather than social circumstances. Interestingly, when women's involvement increased,
the crime itself, in some instances, took on
the trappings of femininity. For example,
theft by females became a crime requiring
psychoanalytic interpretation.[32]

Perhaps the reason why women have received clinical scrutiny for their criminal
behavior stems from traditional misconceptions
about women and men. While women are statistically under represented in crime figures, this
fact alone may augment the assumption that
female crimes require explanations different
from those that account for male crime. The
rationale being, since so few women commit
crimes, those who do must be disturbed. The
traditional view is that it is "normal" for a
certain percentage of men to engage in crime
as a natural extension of their "aggressiveness" and "competitiveness." At the same time
it has been considered abnormal, traditionally, for a woman due to her reputed "passive"
and "cooperative nature" to engage in these
antisocial impulses. Therefore a role appro-
priateness is used to provide "special" explanations. Perhaps by treating criminal women as
"sick," society can write off serious statements about increasing dissatisfaction with
position and lifestyle among women and the
consequential increase in their crime rate.
These stereotypical and subjective views of a
woman's personality and character render her
fair game for psychiatric scrutiny, despite
evidence of psychological well-being to the
contrary. Psychologically, women are seen to
be more excitable, more emotional, and more
submissive. Thus, even healthy women fit more
easily within the mental illness model than do
men. Interestingly, historical analysis of the
clinical interpretations of female delinquents
and criminals tends to parallel the general

fashions and movements in psychiatry.[33]

Throughout the last 100 years, the motivational base for their behavior appears to have shifted in line with current thoughts about the nature of mental illness. However, despite this propensity, these theories have not been derived from broad empirical studies. Instead these theories seem to parallel clinicians' experiences in the treatment and interpretation of particular cases. Whether the development of a paradigm can be erected that will enable generalization from such cases is open to speculation.

Aichhorn best summarized the general psychogenic perspective when he stated that, "There must be some thing in the child himself which the environment brings out in the form of delinquency."[34] Although it is difficult to substantiate a claim that delinquents or criminals are pathologically maladjusted, Aichhorn's second assumption regarding the function of environment and its role in the causation of delinquency deserves additional analysis. A general criticism of the psychoanalytic theories has been advanced by Gibbons, who wrote:

> Psychoanalytic theories involve contentions about the workings of instinctual sources of empirical verification. These instinctual mainsprings of lawbreaking are said to be unconscious one that the offenders are unaware of. Only a trained psychoanalyst is qualified to investigate these motivational forces, therefore other observers are unable to see them in operation. Second, psychoanalytic arguments about lawbreaking are relatively unfashionable at present.[35]

A more cursory review of the literature suggests, however, that criticism of this type may be without foundation.[36] The general criticism by criminologists tends to focus on the past attempts of psychoanalysts to single out fundamental motives in human behavior (i.e., psychic energy).[37] This criticism narrows in on the gaping lacunae in the Freudian explanation of behavior. Incidentally, this was also a problem recognized by Freud. The criticism is merited because the most obvious gap lies in Freud's inability to explain pathological behavior. His dynamic explanations intricately linked to pathological behavior also explain normal behavior. These dynamic explanations, therefore, cannot be used to logically explain pathological behavior.

These dynamic explanations are what philosophers called "necessary but not sufficient cause." For example, rapists and male seducers may be explained in terms of narcissistic needs to gain control, to transcend the Oedipal complex and to gain their father's approval. Motivationally, the objectives may be similar, but the behavior is quite different. Seduction, after all, is still a respectable social activity used to gain pleasure and gratification; whereas, subduing someone for sexual pleasure and gratification is not considered to be socially acceptable behavior.

There is another lacunae in the Freudian theory that is just as problematic as the one mentioned, because it fails to resolve the problem of why, given certain conflicts from the past, some individuals resolve the conflict by hysterical solution and others by obsessive resolution. In other words, one solution is confined to the real world (neurosis), while the other abandons reality (psychosis). Despite these two misgivings, Freud clearly articulated that behavior was motivated and purposeful in that it always

moved toward a goal. Because it was purposeful, it lacked randomness, and therefore each
action could be explained in terms of some
anticipation or desire. Behavioral actions, he
contended, could not be understood as phenomena in themselves but rather as actions on a
continuum or sequence of events from the past
which are leading to a specific future goal.
In this sense, individuals are unaware of the
determinants of their behavior because they
are determined in the "unconscious" sphere of
the mind. It is not necessary to elaborate on
the distinctions of the spheres here, except
to say that the theory suggests that we are
just as likely to respond to situational
stimuli for unconscious reasons as we are for
conscious reasons.

When we combine the concepts of unconscious determinants, the dynamic nature of
behavior and the developmental principles, the
paradigm that emerges is one of psychic determinism,[38] forces and counter forces (e.g.,
reason and cognition) that shield us against
the onslaught of passions. This shield is
crucial because, to Freud, we are all, in our
unconscious minds, pilferers, rapists, in-
cestuals, exhibitionists, voyeurs--we are all
aggressive and homicidal. Therefore, the
difference between the criminal and the average citizen is not found in the impulses, but
rather in the impulse-control mechanisms.

Establishing a causal relationship between a criminal act and mental disorder would
be equivalent to attempting to psychoanalyti-
cally connect acute heartburn to shoplifting.[39]
One is really pressed in the attempt to determine whether physical abnormalities lead to
character defects and subsequent delinquent or
criminal behavior. However, it is clear that
the character disorder concept can lead to
legal irrationalities, because it is the antisocial behavior than an individual exhibits

that defines the type and extent of mental illness.[40] Strangely, psychiatrists collectively have never successfully defined mental illness. Their professional opinions range from the assumption that all individuals suffer from mental illness to some degree, to the perception that mental illness is a myth. Nevertheless, psychogenic arguments for delinquent and criminal behavior are based on a perceived response by the individual to some kind of strain that exists within the individual. This strain is best conceptualized as the by product of some type of personality problem, immaturity, and/or mental conflict. Psychologically, it is contended that stress (strain), the by product of the conflict, is a form of psychic energy that can be both measured and demonstrated to show its positive and/or deleterious effect on behavior.

Cohen stated that, "It is instead becoming increasingly clear that it is meaning of a potential stressor that best predicts human response."[41] Simmel also pointed out that a psychogenic orientation perceived psychic energy solely as an internal attribute whose effect is too difficult to trace in a social situation. Jeffrey,[42] a former student of Sutherland, formulated a criminal behavior and learning theory. His "social alienation" theory attempted to explain crime by using a three dimensional approach that included the legal, sociological, and psychological schools of thought. However, Jeffrey's theory failed to explain how juveniles can become delinquent when they had no prior contacts with delinquent behavior patterns. The theory of social alienation is in agreement with the current trends of psychological thinking because the difference between criminal and non-criminal behavior, it is felt, can be gauged in terms of personality factors that are expressed in some form of antisocial behavior. Social alienation theory places emphasis on the feeling of rejection, emotional starvation, feelings of insecurity, psychological isolation, hostility, and so forth.

These theoretical positions cannot readily be dismissed. If we make the assumption that there is too much "psychologism" in contemporary society, then are we not guilty of relying too much on the bias inherent in our own favored research perspective? Despite the apparent shortcomings of the psychogenic paradigm, currently psychological theory is at a level that would leave one somewhat perplexed if one were to ignore its potential as a useful aid in making some assumptions about human behavior.

One result of this failure would be to provide us with a presupposed view of man through the sole use of sociological theorizing, which would tend to over stress the stability and integration of society. This would also augment a perception of the individual as being disembodied, conscience-driven, and a status-seeking phantom. If we are to reject the psychogenic hypotheses on the basis of them not being testable to our satisfaction, then perhaps an argument could be advanced that, in scientific fairness, the same criteria should be applied to differential association, subculture, strain, and cultural transmission theories.

There are many explanations for the occurrence of deviance and crime. One of these causes focus on man's nature as an explanation for his aberrant behavior. David Matza, for example, assumes that it is as much a part of man's nature to deviate as to conform. Some would agree, but most would probably share Cohen's concern for the adequacy of explaining deviance in terms of man's animal nature. Cohen points out that most people who commit deviant acts do so only occasionally. For example, most students who cheat, and even most children who steal, do so only on occasion and behave "normally" most of the time. The central concept of social disorganization, when used to account for etiology of crime and delinquency, focuses on the positions that individuals occupy in the social system. This orientation appears to provide a frame work from which to discuss both conformity and the varieties of the above behavior in terms of a simple and parsimonious conceptual schema, that is, anomie, that when individuals are experiencing strain they are mobilized individually or to deal with the stress.[43]

This mobilization can occur spontaneously with or without the aid of formal organizations. Smelzer's position is a break with traditional thought that contends that formal organizations are necessary for the development of social movements. Although this perspective may not account for delinquency it most certainly can be applied to certain criminal behaviors for example, tax revolts, riots, rebellion, etc. A less prevalent view is one that suggests that organizations may serve to impede the development of such movements.[44]

NOTES

1. Travis Hirschi, *Causes of Delinquency* (Berkeley: University of California Press, 1969).

2. Milton L. Barron, *The Juvenile in Delinquent* Society (New York: Alfred A. Knopf, Inc., 1955).

3. Wright C. Mills, "The Professional Ideology of Social Pathologists," *American Journal of Sociology* XLIX. (September 1942): 19.

4. Robert K. Merton, "Social Structure and Anomie," in *Delinquency, Crime and Social*

Process, ed. Donald R. Cressey and David A. Ward (New York: Harper and Row, 1938): 254-284.

5. Richard A. Cloward, and Lloyd E. Ohlin, *Delinquency and Opportunity: A Theory of Delinquent Gangs* (New York: Free Press, 1960).

6. Hirschi, *Causes of Delinquency.*

7. According to some theorists, social and personal control is predicated on the level of bonding one has to the social order. Delinquency, in this schema, is either the result of a failure of the bond to tie the individual to the social order, or of its attenuation, enabling the individual to engage in delinquency (See Jackson Toby "Social Disorganization and Stake in Conformity: Complementary Factors in the Predatory Behavior of Hoodlums" *Journal of Criminal Law, Criminology, and Police Science* 1957, 48: 12-17; Scott Briar and Irving Piliavin, "Delinquency, Situational Inducement, and Commitment to Conformity," *Social Problems,* 1965 (Summer) 13: 35-45; David Matza, *Delinquency and Drift* (New York: Wiley, 1964).

8. Analysis of longitudinal data shows that socialization variables, for example, lack of parental supervision, parental rejection, and parent-child involvement, are among the most powerful predictors of juvenile conduct problems, delinquency and possibly crime (See Rolf Loeber and Magda Stouthamer-Loeber, "Family Factors as Correlates and Predictors of Juvenile Conduct Problems and Delinquency" in Michael Tonry and Norval Morris eds. *Crime and Justice: An Annual Review of Research* (Chicago, Ill.: University of Chicago Press, 1986): 29-149; D. H. Olsen, et al, *Families: What Makes Them Work* (Beverly Hills, Ca.: Sage Publication, 1983); J.D. Rittenhaus and J.D. Miller, "Social Learning and Teenage Drug Use: An Analysis of Family Dyads" *Health Psychology* 3 (1984): 329-346; A. R. Tims and J. D.

Masland, "Measurement of Family Communication Patterns," *Communication Research* (1985): 12: 35-58 ; P. E. Kraus, *Yesterday's Children: A Longitudinal Study of Children from Kindergarten into Adult Years* (New York: Wiley, 1973); J. Richman, et al, *Pre-School to School: A Behavioral Study* (London: Academic Press, 1982); M. Fischer, et al, "Follow-up of a Preschool Epidemiological Sample: Cross-Age Continuities and Predictions of Later Adjustment with Internalizing and externalizing Dimensions of Behavior," *Child Development* 55 (1984): 137-150). The delinquent and criminal experiences are the result of "lax," "inadequate" or "poor" supervision (See: Travis Hirschi "Crime and Family Policy" in Ralph A. Weischeit and Robert G. Culbertson eds. *Delinquency: A Justice Perspective* (Prospect Heights, Ill., 1980): 160; Martin R. Haskell, "Toward a Reference Group Theory of Juvenile Delinquency," *Social Problems* 8 (Winter) (1960): 61-81.) offered a plausible ex-planation of how the extenuation of bonding factors could lead to socialization with peers who share similar bonding characteristics and problems. He contended that bonding extenuation occurred when: (1) the youth applies the standards taught and experienced at school by peers to conditions at home and surmises that the family and/or the home standards differ significantly or are undesirable; (2) there is a low probability of succeeding at school; (3) there is a dysjunction between the home and school in regard to goals and motivation; (4) the youth perceives him/herself as being an economic burden; (5) he/she has a perception of inferiority among family members and seeks out a group where the perception is negated; (6) gravitation is toward others sharing similar perceptions; and (7) new reference groups are formed that constitute a delinquency subculture. While the above conditions reveal much about the parent-child relationship of lower-class youths, they particularly shed light upon the extent to which the family is capable of sanctioning behavior that is not in the direction of conformity as well as indicating the importance of the family and the school in preventing nonconforming behavior.

9. P.W. Greenwood, "Differences in Criminal Behavior and Court Responses among Juveniles and Young Adults Defendants," *Crime and Justice: An Annual Review of Research*, eds. M. Tonry and N. Morris, (Chicago, Ill.: University of Chicago Press, 1968) contended that some forms of early delinquency for example, stealing, tends to be correlated with later delinquency. S. Glueck, and E.T. Glueck, *500 Criminal Careers* (New York: Knopf, 1930), cited poor supervision and lack of affection or family cohesion as strong predictors of delinquency. D. P. Farrington, *Further Analyses of a Longitudinal Survey of Crime and Delinquency* (Cambridge, England: Cambridge University Institute of Criminology, 1983), also found poor child rearing practices to be associated with delinquency and by extension crime.

10. Hirschi, *Causes of Delinquency*, 74.

11. In an extended statement on neutralization, David Matza recognized that individuals operated on a continuum between the extremes of freedom and restraint. Although some individuals act more freely than others, they exist in relative relationship between the two extremes. Drift, Matza postulate is a position mid way between freedom and constraints, a condition in which the individual flirts unevenly with one or the other, thereby drifting between criminal and nonconventional action. Although drift is a normal aspect of neutralization, which makes delinquency possible or permissible, the result is not necessarily actual delinquency (See Matza, 1964: 27-28; Robin Williams, *American Society* (New York, Knopf, 1960): 20; Graham Sykes and David

Matza, "Juvenile Delinquency and Subterranean Values," *American Sociological Review* (1961): 712-719).

12. Walter C. Reckless, Simon Dinitz, and Ellen Murray, "Self Concept as an Insulator Against Delinquency." *American Sociological Review* 26, (1956): 744-746.

13. Albert K. Cohen, *Delinquent Boys: The Culture of the Gang* (New York: Free Press, 1955).

14. Walter B. Miller "Lower Class Culture as a Generating Milieu of Gang Delinquency." *Journal of Social Issues* 14 (1958): 5-19.

15. A. Blumstein and E. Graddy, *"Prevalence and Recidivism in Index Arrests: A Feed back Model Approach,"* Law and Society 16 (1982): 265-290; and P. W. Greenwood, et al, *Youth Crimes and juvenile Justice in California: A Report to the Legislature* (Santa Monica, Ca.: Rand, 1983) demonstrated that race is clearly associated with delinquency and by extension crime. Income, social class, and the size of the family are deemed to be clearly related to delinquency (See L. C. Gould, "A Comparison of Self-Reported Indices of Delinquency for Three Racial Groups," *Social Problems*, 16 (1969): 325-335; J. P. Murray, "Status Offenders, Rules, and Reactions," *Status Offenders: A Source Book* in R.A. Weisheit and R.G. Culbertson eds. *Juvenile Delinquency: A Justice Perspective* (1983): 17-26). However, Schuster points out a problem of attempting to correlate income, social class, etc., to serious versus non-serious offenders because these terms are subject to misuse. In his study a large portion of those whose arrests were for supposed violent events, revealed upon closer inspection, that minor events occurred with little harm, for example, hair pulling incidents and neighborhood fistfights. For other youths a "serious" arrest was for behavior which could have been more appropriately labeled truant or

incorrigible (See R. L. Schuster "Violent Juveniles and Proposed Changes in Juvenile Justice: A Case of Over-kill?," *Juvenile and Family Court Journal* Nov. (1982): 27-37).

16. Cohen (1955) depicted one of the weaknesses of using a concept like legitimate social demand in his discussion of the formation of juvenile offenders among the working class. He contended that, rather than being a group of individuals engaged in the demeaning of the social order, these youths merge together in response to their shared problems that tend to center around the low status and inability to handle the demands of the social order. In this process, the demands may be perceived as never having been or no longer being relevant.

17. The theory of differential association has been sharply criticized, and Sutherland, in a 1944 paper, "The Swan Song of Differential Association" acknowledged that some of the criticisms of this theory were valid. Without criticizing Sutherland's work, it is sufficient for my purpose here to point out Birenbaum and Sagarin's criticism of his failure to give proper weight to the role of mass media. Although it is true that some forms of deviant behavior require a good deal of skill in order to perform the act and not be apprehended, this is not true of other forms. But even those acts requiring skill are often learned alone, by trial and error. Developing his theory before the television era, Sutherland lacked knowledge of the effect that the mass media would play as a criminogenic force. Television never tells anyone to do anything "wrong," but it depicts wrong, suggests it, makes known that it is taking place, shows how it is done, and offers it as an alternative to anyone watching and listening. Then it gives the arguments against that alternative. When operationalizing differential association, the weak family condition

arises when the youth fails to acquire pro-
social norms and, as a consequence, associates
with other delinquents and acquires delinquent
definitions. This is a process the youth under
goes prior to becoming involved in delinquent
behavior (Refer to Hepburn, 1963).

18. Ralf Dahrendorf, *Class and Class
Conflict in an Industrial Society* (London:
Routledge and Kegan Paul, 1959).

19. George B. Vold, *Theoretical Criminology* (New York: Oxford University Press,
1958).

20. Marshall B. Clinard and Richard
Quinney, *Criminal Behavior Systems* (New York:
Holt, Rinehart and Winston, 1973).

21. Edwin M. Lemert, *Social Pathology: A
Systematic Approach to the Theory of Socio-
pathic Behavior* (New York: McGraw-Hill, 1951).

22. Austin Turk, *Political Criminality:
The Defiance of Authority* (Beverly Hills:
Sage, 1982).

23. Louis Wirth, "*The Urban Way of Life*,"
in *On Cities and Social Life* (Chicago, Ill.:
University of Chicago Press, 1964): 28.

24. It is acknowledged t hat whatever the
determining factors for delinquent or criminal
behavior, it is felt that they are tied, in
some way (not totally explained), to the
bonding level and the social controls that an
individual experiences. If this is true, one
can logically argue that social controls (one
by-product of bonding) subjects the individual
to manipulation and a negation of free will,
and that a delinquent or criminal act may not
be elective behavior. Although it is acknowledged that there must be some degree of control over that which we choose to do and when
we choose to do it, to have some semblance of
social order, recognition of this fact predi-
cates our level of bonding which, in turn,
allows us to a large degree to be manipulated
and molded. If compliance is not by choice,
how important are the antecedent factors for

analyzing delinquent or other types of behavior? Conversely, if we believe that the social order has minimal impact on behavior, then causation can be traced to a single or a combination of variable(s). However, if we argue that individual delinquent or criminal behavior is an intentional act, then qualify that intention by acknowledging that there are conditions or events over which the individual has no control, then total exculpation of the behavior is impossible.

25. David Matza, *Becoming Deviant* (Englewood Cliffs, N.J.: Prentice-Hall, Inc. 1969): 90-197.

26. Irving Spergel, *Racketville, Slum Town and Hautberg* (Chicago: University of Chicago Press, 1964).

27. Arthur L. Stinchcombe, *Rebellion In a High School* (Chicago: Quadrangle, 1964).

28. Leroy C. Gould, *"Juvenile Entrepreneur,"* *American Journal* LXXIV, 716-18.

29. Richard Knudsen, *Crime In a Complex Society* (Homewood, Ill.: Dorsey Press, 1970): 316-25.

30. Lawson G. Lowrey, *"Delinquent and Criminal Personalities,"* in vol.# 2 of *Personality and the Behavior Disorder*, ed. J. McV. Hunt (New York: Ronald Press Company, 1944): 794.

31. David Abrahamson, *The Psychology of Crime* (New York: Columbia Press, 1960): 61.

32. In 1978, in the United Kingdom, 55.7% of all convicted females was for shoplifting. The statistical data reveals that more women are being found guilty of shoplifting, unfortunately U.S. statistics do not breakdown crime as sensitive as the United Kingdom. See Richard Knudsen, *Crime in a Complex Society* (Home wood, Ill.: Dorsey Press, 1970): 240; J. J. Eysenck *Crime and Personality* (Boston, Mass.: Houghton-Mifflin, 1964): 689; Calvin S. Hall and Lindzey Gardner, *Theories of Personality* (New York: John Wiley and Son, 1960):

457; and Gordon Trasler, *The Explanation of Criminology* (London: Routledge, 1962): 71, 74).

33. For example, see T .C. N. Gibbons, C. Palmer and J. Prince, *"Mental Health Aspects of Shoplifting,"* *British Medical Journal*, 3: (1971) 612-615; and Ann Campbell, *Girl Delinquents* (New York: St. Martin Press, 1981).

34. August Aichhorn, *Wayward Youth* (New York: The Viking Press, 1968): 15.

35. Don C. Gibbons *Delinquent Behavior*, 2 ed. (Englewood Cliffs, N. J.: Prentice-Hall, Inc., 1976), 75.

36. Psychoanalysis contains a set of vital insights about delinquent(s) and criminal development, they are: (1) moral conduct or delinquency is organically related to the structure of an individual's personality; (2) a person's moral posture is closely linked to the kind of relationship that existed between that person and his/her parents; (3) a person's moral posture is largely unconscious; and (4) adult personality is shaped, to some degree, by childhood experiences. David Abrahamson, *The Psychology of Crime* (New York: Columbia Press, 1960): 24, contended that all elements that bring about crime are specific or vague strains and stresses in the person himself, in the situation, or in both, eliciting certain reactions that may lead to criminal or delinquent acts.

Glueck S. and E. Glueck, *Unraveling Juvenile Delinquency* (Cambridge, Mass.: Harvard University, 1950): 239, found that 51.4% of the delinquents and 44.3% of the nondelinquents were mentally abnormal. However, W. Healy and A. F. Bronner, *New Light on Delinquency and Its Treatment* (New Haven, Conn.: Yale University Press, 1936): 122, when comparing a small group of delinquent children with their nondelinquent siblings, found that ninety one percent of the delinquents and thirteen percent of the nondelinquents had deep emotional disturbances. It is possible to acknowledge the existence of individual personality differences and still attribute major and primary causal significance for behavior to social context and situations. The fact that people react differently to situational stimuli does not mean that the situation is not causing the behavior (Abrahamson, 1960). External pressure may affect people differently, just as internal chemical agents do, but they affect them nonetheless. Abrahamson says that the main characteristic of the juvenile delinquent is that he acts out and is unable to postpone immediate gratification. Consequently any pressure from his environment makes him feel anxious the delinquent gains relief by acting out his impulses. (1960: 61) Here it is unclear as to whether the motivating factor for behavior is the environment or the internal impulse.

37. The term "psychic energy" owes its genesis to St. Paul whose triune of man exceed Jesus' dualistic demarcation between flesh and spirit. In St. Paul's triune, "spirit" (pneuma) was regarded as a divinely inspired life principle, "soul" (psyche) as man's life in which "spirit" manifests itself, and "body" soma) as the physical mechanism animated by "soul." Plutarch (c. AD-119) perceived the psyche as being the seat of man's emotional, sensuous, and animated state. (For additional information, see the works of Descartes, Leibniz, Aristotle, Locke, Hobbes, and Humes).

38. If each piece of behavior is causally related to the past. For example, if one does Y because of an X(X1 + X2 + X3 ad infinitum) that preceded it, and if one is going to explain Y on the basis of X, then one is forced to conclude that behavior is determined.

39. In the *Diagnostic and Statistical Manual of Mental Disorder* of the American Psychiatric Association, heartburn is listed as an example of mental disorder (006-580

Psychological gastrointestinal reaction in *DSM1*).

40. The Model Penal Code of the American Law Institute has a section dealing with criminal responsible behavior. In 1962, the Code approved attempts to serve as guides for insanity tests.

41. Cohen, *Delinquent Boys: The Culture of The Gang*, 75.

42. C. Ray Jeffrey, "An Integrated Theory of Crime and Criminal Behavior." *Journal of Criminal Law, Criminology and Police Science* 49 (1959): 533-552.

43. Mona Charen contends that the "Dream and the Nightmare: The Sixties' Legacy to the Underclass" by Myron Magnet is the book of the decade (*Chicago Tribune, Creators Syndicate*, March 22, 1993): 18. She contends that Magnet not only explodes the myths about the homeless and poverty, but also crime and joblessness. She states uncategorically that the liberals created in the inner cities a world of abject poverty, crime, degradation, and hopelessness. Despite the admittance of hopelessness, she lauds Magnet's criteria for rising out of poverty, they are: (1) finish high school; (2) work a steady job (any job); and (3) get married as an adult and stay married. These Magnet argue have been the ticket out of the slums for the Italians, for the Jews, and today for the Koreans and other immigrants, including Black immigrants.

44. Charles Tilly, "The Chaos of the Living City" in *An Urban World* (Boston: Little Brown and Company, 1974).

8

Weakness of Explanations

Sociologists and criminologists use a number of causal perspectives in the attempt to explain delinquent and criminal behavior. An example is the social control theory that focuses on the relationship between socialization and delinquency. Hirschi claimed youths form a bond to society that prevents them from becoming involved in delinquent behavior.[1] More succinctly, the theory contends that involvement in delinquency is negatively correlated to the strength of the bond the individual has to the social order. There are many problems with this conclusion, but the most glaring ones center around the issue of what constitutes adolescent's perception and acceptance of that which constitutes a bond. This is an issue of relevance if a difference in perspective exists between the youth and the social order regarding what constitutes legitimate social demands.

Cohen, for example, suggests that it is a reasonable expectation to have all youth practice and value the behavior and attitudes to which middle-class youths adhere. These middle class "measuring rods" center around traits such as ambition, individual responsibility, talent, asceticism, rationality, courtesy and

control of physical aggression. These are
decidedly different than the values perceived
to be maintained by lower-class youths. They
are values perceived to be conflictive because
they are nonutilitarian, malicious, and nega-
tivistic. Cohen argued that much of the delinquent behaviors of lower-class individuals is
motivated by interests other than rational
utilitarian gain. This utilitarian value is
the purpose of behavior attributed to middle-
class youths.[2]

Cohen discussed the issue of legitimate
social demands, not what constitute it, and
posited that the formation of juvenile offenders among the working class could be
accounted for by their merging together a
solution to their shared problems of low
status. This grouping also served to enhance
the interaction with others confronting similar problems and adjustments.

Delinquency, from Hirschi's social control perspective, results from a failure to
establish social bonds or to a subsequent
detachment of them. The following model depicts this socialization process.

Figure 8.1
Path to Delinquency

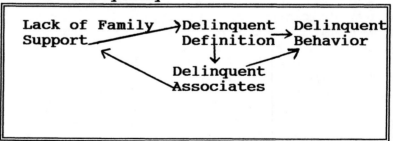

Another problem with this explanation regarding the genesis of delinquency is the emphasis
placed on primary bonding. It is clear that
due to changing social conditions that indi-

viduals confront, these may be an impediment to complete bonding. This is a socialization process entirely different from those which Cohen utilizes. Similarly, it largely ignores those youth who initially had strong bonds but some how eventually become weakened. These can also be used to account for the on set of delinquent behavior at different stages. They can also be operationalized to assess why there is an inconsistency in behavior by individuals over time. The model makes an assumption, unrealistically, that the bond level, attitudes, and behavior will be static or stable. However, the bond could change over time as a result of certain bonding experience(s).

Anomie, in certain respects, perceives the individual as being atomistic and individualistic. A person within this framework is perceived to emphasize the goals, norms, and opportunities presented by the "legitimate" social order. As a result, he/she occupies a unique spatial setting. This setting provides the incentive to internalize the goals and regulatory rules. Once they are internalized, the opportunity structures are assessed and reassessed to determine the efficacy of the goals in terms of the ability to use legitimate channels to both pursue and achieve them. In this process, some strain or tension is experienced. The manner in which the individual chooses to handle the tension is described as a behavior adaptation. Over looked by this theoretical explanation are the effects that the experiences, strains, conformity, or delinquency of other persons can have on the individual.

Cloward and Ohlin addressed these anomie "problems" by attempting to link them with a general theory of subculture.[3] The link is especially tied to the emergence and development of new subcultural forms. This approach served to link anomie with the traditional theories of Sutherland, Shaw and McKay, and Thrasher; that is, the "cultural transmission" and "differential association" perspectives of the "Chicago Schools."[4] The common element of the subcultural theory is the insistence that delinquent, as well as nondelinquent, behavior is typically the result of a collaborative social activity in which the things that other people say and do give meaning, value, and effect to one's own behavior.

The traditional sociological approach operationalized social class, ethnicity, sex, and age in the analysis of delinquency. Despite a large volume of theoretical research that used these variables, Johnstone and Tittle and Villemez point out the considerable debate regarding their usefulness due to variation in application.[5]

Cameron suggests that a more subjective technique be used to gauge the perceptions of social class because objective measures are subject to misinterpretations.[6] Studies by Cameron and Won and Yamamoto, for example, found only a moderate correlation between shoplifting and lower-class economic status.[7] These are consistent findings with others who used social class as a variable to study general delinquency.

Psychological diagnosis of offenders and non delinquent control groups points out that the difference between the two groups is not pronounced when mental pathology is considered. However, a number of characteristics identified through the Rorschach Test, that is, assertiveness, impulsiveness, and vivacity, were more common among delinquents than nondelinquents.

Hathaway and Monachesi are modest in the claims they make using the MMPI.[8] They argue that the inventory possesses some discriminatory power. Nevertheless, critics note the problems of interpretation involved in the variability of results and point out that a number of social factors correlate more highly with delinquency than do MMPI scores.

For example, a more recent study conducted retrospectively on both delinquents and nondelinquents using school records and teacher ratings, found that teachers had viewed the delinquent youth as less adjusted than nonoffenders over a seven year period. Additionally, the results of personality tests administered to the two groups indicated that the delinquents were more immature, egocentric, inconsiderate, and hostile than the non-delinquents.

However, some psychiatrists have doubts about the validity of these psychogenic assertions. For example, some argue that, on the basis of impressionistic observations from child guidance clinics, a number of types of delinquency exist in the population of official offenders, but only some of them fit the simple psychogenic model of the disturbed adolescent acting out his/her problems illegally.[9]

Jenkins dissents from the sophisticated version of psychiatry to a more simple psychogenic notion.[10] His arguments have a foundation in careful and objective research rather than clinical impressions. He claims that delinquent misconduct is not a form of neurotic behavior, for neuroticism involves a high level of inhibition, sense of duty, and introjected standards and strict super ego control, whereas delinquency is frequently the direct opposite of such a pattern.

The aggressive delinquent is seen as being poorly socialized, lacking in internalized controls, antagonistic towards his peers, and generally maladjusted. In contrast to the "maladaptive" delinquent (identified above), the more frequently encountered "adaptive" or

"pseudo-social" violator is usually the product of lower-class slums areas, who is rea-
sonably well-socialized and "normal" among
his/her peers and parents. They are seen as
being normal but having weakened inhibitions.
In addition, their loyalty and group identity
are limited to the local area and immediate
peers.

Gibbons contends that the lower-class
delinquent engages in violations against the
community with relatively little guilt or
concern.[11] These activities are construed to be
rational and goal-directed. Therefore, he
concludes that social adjustment, from this
perspective, does not justify a judgment that
the individual is maladjusted.

When applying that psychological perspective to some forms of delinquency, one is left
with the impression that these youths exhibit
behavior that is consistent with the economist's view of crime being a rational act that
results from an evaluation of the expected
utility of both delinquent and non-delinquent
opportunity. Becker indicates that the choice
selected represents the highest utility.[12]
Carroll and Cook have questioned the rational
view of delinquency formulated by the economist.[13] Their efforts suggest that potential
delinquents may make reasoned judgments in
regard to opportunity, but should not be
expected to combine information about these
opportunities and the rational expected utility rule.

Despite the divergent perspectives of
these theorists, there appears to be an under
lying consensus on the deviant vulnerability
and socialization hypotheses. They discuss and
attempt to account for the delinquent behavior
by focusing on: (1) the "strain" experienced
by youths in their major social involvement,
and (2) the peer involvement of these youths
experiencing strain and its effect on sub-

sequent behavior.[14]

However, these hypotheses, using strain, fail to account for the individualistic behavior that cannot logically be attributed to social strain as it's commonly defined. The failure lies in the inability of strain to account for the precipitating factors that lay outside the youth's major social involvement, that is, desires, spontaneous behavior, or compulsions. Nevertheless, the preponderance of sociological efforts on delinquency stress the nature of the relationship youths have with in their immediate social network and its functioning with regard to the larger social structure. Analysis of this nature also fails to address the effect(s) that the broader social structure has on specific behavior, the conditions under which it occurs, and the individual specific response to a general and/or a specific condition.

The two major criticisms of strain theories are: (1) for the theory to be correct, delinquency should be greatest when aspirations are high and expectations low; and (2) the attempt to establish a relationship between social class and delinquency is not straight forward or, as visualized, not valid. There are two compelling arguments against using strain theory to explain behavior: (1) the theory does not provide an explanation for the fact that most delinquents abandon their delinquency in late adolescence; and (2) it does not or cannot explain why delinquents may go for long intervals without committing a delinquent act.[15]

Although revisions to the strain theories state, or imply, that goal commitment should be a variable, they also suggest that adolescents are more interested in the achievement of immediate goals rather than long-range goals, that is, monetary success. More immediate goals may include peer popularity, dressing appropriately, performing well in school, and coexisting with parents. This focus on immediate-range goals would enable strain theories to explain: (1) why most juveniles abandon delinquency in late adolescence (at this time the immediate goals expressed earlier become irrelevant), (2) the sporadic nature of delinquency, and (3) those findings that are discordant with the dysjunction between aspirations and expectations. The proper test for strain theory would require an examination of the adolescent's overall achievement on a broad range of goals.

SITUATED IDENTITY

Situated identity theory provides a straight forward schemata that is useful in predicting behavior through a systematic approach. The theory is based on the assumption that the environment emits "impressions" (stimuli), and that ongoing activities in that environment are predicated by the stimuli and the individual's interaction with the stimuli. This interaction creates a situation where on going activities are selectively perceived by the individual.

In short, individuals process the stimuli, which may or may not be consistent with personal identity attributes. When behavior, which is not consistent with the identity attributes, occurs, and that behavior can logically be attributed to the situation, a situated identity is considered to have occurred. Operationally, an individual processes the perceived stimuli, negotiates his/her identity in relationship to the stimuli, and situational-specific behavior follows. This behavior may or may not be consistent with prior identity attributes and past behaviors.[16]

This perspective is consistent with Matza's pre-eminent sociological theory of deviant behavior. In his theory, human action, delinquent or other wise, is some thing that typically develops and grows in a tentative, groping, advancing, backtracking, and sounding-out process. The theoretical basis for situated identity is derived, in part, from an interactionist perspective that posits that one's attributes, and the perceptions of those attributes, determine identity. Conceptually, identity is the internal component of role, and there is a presumption that it must be related to other's identities to be understood. For example, the identity "student" (internal) does not stand in isolation of the "role" (external) student. Similarly, attributes can only have meaning when contrasted against other attributes.

In the situated identity schemata, attributes are perceived as being contingencies.[17] Presently these contingencies are unclear, although when used in the literature, they are commonly presented as race, gender, and socio-economic status. Utilization of these attributes within the situated identity schemata enables the researcher to gauge the individual's ability to anticipate and select between competing stimuli.

Another basic assumption of the theory is that selection is not predicated upon prior identity attributes. The rationale for this is the knowledge that behavioral form and context can vary almost indefinitely, and if selection options, in response to the stimuli, were limited exclusively to prior identity, differential learning would cease.[18] Empirically, the relationship between identity and various forms of delinquent behavior seems to be well established. Cohen, in a criticism of Merton's strain theory, anomie, says that to make "the assumption of discontinuity is to imply that

it treats the deviant act as though it was
an abrupt change of state. People taste and
feel their way along. They begin an act and do
not complete it. They start one thing and end
up by doing another. They extricate themselves
from progressive involvement or become further
involved to the point of commitment."[19] This
suggests that there is an association between
identity and social experience, and self-
evaluation and delinquency involvement.

However, there are a number of problems
involved in examining the complex nature of
identity and its function in a social setting.
Nevertheless, the predictive ability of situated identity theory has received support from
studies conducted in a variety of settings
ranging from novel, contrived and allegedly
"normless" laboratory deceptions, to important, every day decisions that people make.[20]
For example, situated identity theory predicts
that normative expectations about conduct will
emerge if the identity evaluations associated
with choice alternatives are differentiated in
terms of social desirability.[21]

The predictive ability of situated identity is enhanced when past behavior reveals a
consistency with present behavior. However,
behavior congruence is only one facet of
situated identity and becomes less relevant if
past behavior involves irrelevant information
and dimensions when applied to current environmental stimuli. Therefore, previous
"strain" and responses may or may not be
indicators for future behavior. To address
this ambiguity, it becomes prudent to analyze
identity attributes and "strain" simultaneously. The situated identity schemata affords an
opportunity to manipulate this interactive
process.

However, there are arguments that have
been advanced against behavior consistency.
This perspective is maintained by most person-

ality theorists and many social psychologists. They contend that behavioral and cognitive consistency across stimuli are intrinsically unnatural and limit the range of self-defining qualities and behavior necessary for elective social interaction. While this points out an important problem facing students of personality and identity and their impact on behavior, there is still a need for additional, formal theoretical statements that will extend this position and empirical assessment.

Situated identity, as an explanation for delinquent behavior, has not been used previously as a theoretical perspective, there fore a critique of the theory's efficacy is impossible at this time. This caveat aside, the theory does permit a researcher to address the causal explanations that individuals construct for their behavior by placing more attention on societal variables and less on individual constructs. Rather then perceiving sex, race, and the cognitive reaction to these attributes as individual constructs for explaining delinquent behavior, the analysis shifts to discern the effects of the situation and its impact on the individual constructs to explain behavior.

Insofar as delinquency is concerned, situated identity theory provides a theoretical framework to expand social strain theories. The balance of this chapter will attempt to link more clearly the anomie efforts of Merton, Cloward, and Ohlin; the theoretical tradition of Sutherland, Shaw and McKay; and the social control perspective of Hirschi; and to determine if they are adequate when it comes to explaining the general delinquency committed by Black youths.

Conklin stated that the evidence suggested that Blacks have higher crime rates than Whites, even when individuals of similar backgrounds are compared, but that differences between the groups are reduced in comparisons

of people of similar backgrounds.[22] This also
suggests that if Blacks and Whites of similar
backgrounds are compared, differences in the
crime rates between the groups will be reduced
or eliminated. However, Conklin then states: A
study of Murder in Philadelphia found that
when blacks and whites with similar occupations were compared blacks still committed
homicide more often than whites.[23] A study of
rape in the same city found that black committed rape about four times as often as whites
when people with similar occupations were
compared.[24] Blacks thus seem to have higher
rates of crime and delinquency than whites of
similar back ground. Although research indicates that black-white differences are reduced
when people of similar backgrounds are compared.[25]

The 1989 statistics reveal that 49.1
percent of all homicide victims were Black and
that Black males in the urban areas have about
a five percent chance of being murdered. The
rate is even worse for Black males between the
ages of fifteen and twenty-four. The rate for
this group is seven times greater than the
rest of the population. These rates have been
attributed to social class status.[26] A recent
study analyzed the correlation between employment, property crimes and Black youths, and
reported that there is a linear relationship
between race, lower employability, the occurrence of crime, and future employability.[27]
Phillips and Votey also found a correlation
between economic opportunity and differential
criminal participation.[28] Viscusi stated,
"Crime serves an economic function [for Black
youths] by providing many with a substantial
income source. A fundamental influence on
criminal behavior is the role of economic
factors, such as labor market status. [Those]
who were in school or employed were much less
likely to engage in crime."[29]

The research also shows that when conditions exist where it is more profitable to earn more money from crime than the labor market, crime will be the behavior of choice. Moore stated: "To many black kids living in a run-down housing project, the thriving drug business looks a lot more accessible and promising than school or a traditional job."[30]

This relationship is demonstrated in a later chapter. Although most studies regarding the differences between White and Black crime have concentrated on class, according to Blau and Blau the independent variable related income inequality to race.[31] In addition, when Blau and Blau controlled for class, they found that socioeconomic inequality had a positive and direct correlation to criminal violence. These conditions race, crime, delinquency and class, constitute dimensions, contexts, and situations. Nevertheless, we confront a number of problems when we attempt to make a direct correlations between these and behavior. For example, in 1992 the FBI reported that the rising number of murders, rapes, and assaults involved not only disadvantaged minority youths in urban areas, but was evident in all races, social classes, and life-styles in all parts of the country. During the decade of the 1980s, according to the FBI, the arrest rates among white juveniles accused of committing violent crimes rose forty four percent. The increase among Blacks for the same period was nineteen percent. The juvenile murder arrest rate for Blacks during this period rose 145 percent but White arrest rates for rape increased dramatically faster than the black arrest rates for the same behavior. The rates were fifty three and forty six percent for Whites and Blacks respectively. Does this violence reflect a breakdown of families, schools, and other social institutions?

Although the rates for murder are deplor-

able, they must be looked at longitudinally to
detect a trend. While in 1980, there were
21,860 murders, in 1890 a century ago, when
there were approximately 70 million people in
the United States, we had 10,652 murders. This
represented a per capita rate about twice that
of today. There were factors present in 1890
that were similar to those in 1990. For example, in 1890 the unemployed and under-em-
ployed, were left to the whims of their own
meager support systems, private charities, and
public ridicule. Many of these individuals
were immigrants to the urban areas in search
of work. Today, the same conditions exists for
individuals who are trapped in urban areas and
are unable to compete in the labor market. In
1890 these type of individuals who were un-
successful in their attempts to penetrate the
labor market, were labeled vagabonds, hoboes,
vagrants, or beggars. (Today, they are known
as the homeless, welfare queens, etc.). Others
in the 1890 environment survived through
marginal economic activities, such as rag
picking and bone gathering. This social context is demonstrated in a 1857 New York State
report that was based on a survey of slum
areas in Manhattan and Brooklyn. The following
is a description of one such group:

> "Rag-pickers' Paradise" is inhabited
> entirely by Germans, who dwell in
> small rooms in almost fabulous gre-
> gariousness. We were told of a colo-
> ny of three hundred of these people,
> who occupied a single basement,
> living on offal and scraps their
> means of livelihood, degraded as it
> is, is exceedingly precarious, espe-
> cially in severe winters, when snow
> storms, covering the ground, hide
> the rags, shreds of paper, etc., on
> the sale of which they subsist. In
> such season the children are sent

out to sweep crossings or beg, and many of the most adroit practitioners on public charity are found among these urchins, who are generally marked by a precocity and cunning, which render them, too often adept in vice at the tendere stage."[32]

The salient point is many of the older body of rules and procedures that directed the common place behavior of preindustrial village residents were no longer adequate to the exigencies of urban life. The literature on immigration is filled with examples of extended families and even of almost entire villages leaving the old country or rural areas and arriving intact to begin a new life in the city. However, this was not the primary pattern because, for the most part, the larger family units dissolved at the points of departure.

Therefore, the main family pattern was one comprised of younger members arriving as married couples or unattached individuals. The migrants tended to be young, ages fifteen to thirty-five.[33] Age and the lack of bonds presented many problems for example, for the first time many of these young people were left to their own wits and resources. They were also free from the surveillance, controls, and guidance of the older members of their families. Jane Addams described the problems of the city's youth:

Never before in civilization have such numbers of young girls been suddenly released from the protection of home and permitted to walk unattended upon city streets and to work under alien roofs. Never before have such numbers of young boys

earned money independently of the
family life, and left themselves
free to spend it as they chose in
the midst of vice deliberately dis-
guised as pressure.[34]

A large number of these people confronting trying circumstances became involved in
the marginal and some times illegal businesses
that were oriented to satisfying their desires
by abrogating the generally suppressed conventional puritan morality of the day through
behaviors like gambling, alcohol, drugs,
prostitution, and pornography.[35] During this
era, both the people in the cities and the
cities themselves were perceived to be serious
menaces to civilization. Thus, the saloon and
the resulting intemperance movement were
frequently cited, along with the growing
inequities in the class structure, as unfortunate but nevertheless dangerous by products of
urbanization and industrialization. The verac-
ity of this perception is subject, still, to
interpretation.
It is difficult now, as it was in the
1800s, to be certain to what degree the actual
rate of crime is, and was, greater in cities
than in the less urbanized areas. However, a
number of social and physical characteristics
in cities may very well generate the kinds of
conditions conducive to violations of the law.
Wolfgang provides a useful review of the more
commonly held perspective on the criminogenic
forces that are supposedly prevalent in the
cities. He stated:

Urban areas with mass populations,
greater wealth, more commercial
establishments, and more products of
our technology also provide more
frequent opportunities for theft.
Victims are impersonalized, property

is insured, consumer goods are in greater abundance, they are more vividly displayed, and they are more portable. Urban life is commonly characterized by population density, social mobility, class and ethnic heterogeneity, reduced family functions, and greater anonymity when these traits are found in high degree, and when they are combined with poverty, physical deterioration, low education, residence in industrial and commercial centers, unemployment, unskilled labor, economic dependency, marital in-stability, etc. and a cultural minority status of inferiority, it is generally assumed that deviance is more likely to emerge.[36]

Horton and Leslie are not convinced that the actual rate of crime is clearly greater in the city. They said:

Cities show higher crime rates than rural areas, but is probable that rural crime is less fully reported. The city also attracts people intending to commit crimes, as it provides more opportunities for crime and provides greater anonymity for those seeking an unconventional mode of life. But there is no evidence that country-reared persons are conspicuously less criminal than their city-reared compatriots.[37]

This contention has been lent credence by the formation of gangs in suburbs and small towns. Their emergence contradicts Thrasher's conclusions that the inevitable rise of gangs in the big cities was due to consolidated

schools that brought large number of age-
segregated young people together who are freed
from the direct control of their parents. In
between school and home, the opportunities for
congregation free from the direct surveillance
of either school officials, family, or other
formal agents of control readily abound.[38] Today, the easy access to private vehicles
provides greater geographic mobility and even
greater freedom from agents of formal control
and this contributes to the formation of
gangs, delinquency, and the crime that is now
occurring in the rural and suburban areas.

In searching for explanations to explain
the spatial patterning and distribution of
crime and delinquency, a number of theorists
have agreed that the important factor is not
location or distance from the core or central
area, but rather the social and physical
characteristics of the area in which the crime
occurs, or, equally important, in which the
offender resides. One must remember that
offenders do not always confine their illegal
activities to the areas in which they live.
From this perspective, factors such as, poverty, unemployment, poor housing, family status,
anomie, segregation, social rank, ethnic
composition, age composition, sex composition,
and degree of urbanization have been associated to one degree or another with the incidence
of delinquent and criminal behavior.[39]

The salient aspect of Schmidt's study of
Seattle was his findings that supported the
thesis that the core, skid row and contiguous
areas had the highest crime rates. He also
found that these areas were characterized by
differentiated crimes. The core areas were
characterized by high rates of shoplifting,
check fraud, residential burglaries, auto
theft, and suicides. The skid row areas, they
found, were characterized by high rates of
fighting, robbery, nonresidential burglaries

and disorderly conduct. Using this study, it becomes clear that not only are areas individuated, but the behavior is also. Given this, it become impossible to speak in terms of causation without entertaining an interactive perspective. That is to say, there are antecedent and intervening variables that coalesce to impact the dependent variable. These varying factors are conflict of institutions, spatial setting, social mobility, individuation, and anomie.

Following is an applied application of the variables that have been identified in the literature as being the factors that cause delinquent behaviors (Figure 8.2). These variables, after treatment, have been placed in an analytical model. The model disaggregates the variables into individuals elements. This procedure is critical because the variables are deemed to be multi-dimensional, and these can only be captured when reduced to their constituent parts or elements. Structurally, the individual's perception defines self-image and behavior. (These perceptions are contrived from an individual's reflective measurements.

Figure 8.2
Multidimensional Individual Stated Character-
istics (Image) and the Theorized Impact of the
Situation and the Behavior on that Image

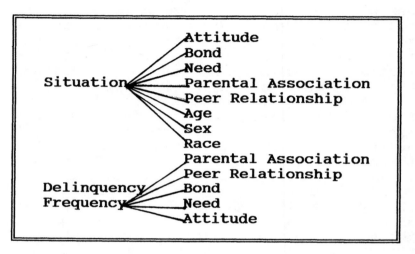

This application is accomplished by
reversing the assumed causal direction between
scale items and making the assumption that
these reflective measurements are the function
of the underlying variable, the elements, and
measurement error. When this is accomplished
one can assume that the elements form the
variable without measurable error).

These perceptions were then combined with
the situational elements to determine their
collective impact on: (1) a delinquent (shop
lifting) or criminal behavior; and (2) the
statistical importance of the situational
variable in predicting the behavior.

The use of reflective measurement is
often appropriate for measuring concepts like
socioeconomic status, attitudes, and preference. This is accomplished by using different
modes as scale items. Some inherent problems
with this type of measurement are: (1) unreli-
ability of cross sectional data; (2) each

scale item weight is model specific and is determined by the relationship that the elements of underlying variable have with other variables in the model; and (3) there must be an assumption that all relevant aspects of the underlying elements in the variables are contained within the scale item.

The individual characteristic elements make measurement and structural assumptions in that these characteristics evaluations are weighted initially with respect to the '"desired" behavior underlying that characteristics (e.g., the desired "peer association" would be fraternization with nondelinquents). The model does not make any assumptions regarding the relationships between the latent values of the variables and shoplifting or delinquency.

This model conceptually and empirically specifies the relational link(s) between the elements that represent social bonding and the empirical indicators that impacts it, for example, sex, age, and race. These indicators are regressed on delinquent behavior to determine their significance. The model does not measure the specific global attributes of bonding; instead it uses indices from a self-report to determine if they constitute the dynamics of bonding.[40] This dynamic, rather than static, perception of bonding is then combined with the situational elements to determine their relationship to the delinquent behavior.

The model is based upon the following assumptions: (1) each element, excluding situational stimuli, is a part of the individuals' perception of their bonding, and that the perception can be evaluated; (2) The elements can be combined to form distinct instruments; (3) The predicted scores associated with the instruments can serve as indices for a global scale for the elements; 4) There is enough heterogeneity among the elements to minimize impact from exogenous elements. Therefore, the variables are defined simply as being the linear combination of the individuals' predicted scores.[41]

The diverse data in my study on shop lifting were analyzed using multiple linear regression. (MLR) was used because it enabled the effects of each independent variable to be assessed and to be interpreted independently. The zero order correlation technique was also used to determine if the independent variables functioned as intervening variables on the dependent variable. Because none of the independent variables had a [r = 0], it was impossible to conclude that the independent variables explicated from the literature did not act as intervening variables.

The joint effect of the variable elements was regressed on the dependent variable, shop lifting, to gauge their independent effect "due to" or "accounted for" by the manipulation of the independent variables. In order for the independent variable, operationalized separately as an intervening variable, to be a good predictor of the dependent variable, it had to have a low R2. If the R2 score was achieved, this was interpreted to mean that the intervening variable was not accounting for the movement (+) in the dependent variables. A (-) value indicated this "good fit" for that variable in the model.

MLR enabled the use of eight independent elements which became surrogate variables to be regressed on the delinquent behavior. These eight variable were scaled to provide a prediction equation:

$$Y1=(f)(a+B1 \ X1,+b2 \ X2,+b3 \ X3,....)$$

Where: **a**= constant

X1 = value of score on the independent
variable
b1 = the weight the independent variable
has in the equation
(the lower the coefficient the less
weight).

One of the primary reasons for conducting
this research was to determine whether a
traditional variable, for example, the bonding
elements, race, etc., could predict shop
lifting behavior. If it could not, it raised
some serious question in regard to their use
in explaining the occurrence of other forms of
delinquent behaviors. It was posited that
there are a number of different aspects of
bonding, and that adolescents differed on
these facets.

In Figure 8.3 , Model 1 shows a behavioral out come consistent with the bonding level.
However, an alternative formulation (Model 3)
can be constructed to depict an attenuation of
the bonding level and the subsequent behavior.
Models 2 and 3 provide useful frameworks for
analyzing the effect of intervening factor(s),
for example, situational stimuli, on youths
experiencing stable or unstable bonding.

These configurations enhance the ability
to investigate the intervening variables when
reduced to their constituent parts, to determine their impact on the youths' stated attitudes and behavior, and to discern if there is
consistency with the stated bond level.

The three major weaknesses of Model 1 are
its inability to: (1) determine whether shop
lifting or contemplated shoplifting behavior
affects the bond level;

Figure 8.3
Bonding Level and Expected Behavior

```
┌─────────────────────────────────────────────────┐
│                    Model 1                        │
│"Normative" -------------> Nonshop-               │
│ (stable)                  lifting                 │
│ bond                                              │
│ level                                             │
│                                                   │
│                                                   │
│                    Model 2                        │
│"Abnormal" -->Intervening-->Shop                   │
│ (unstable)   factor(s)     lifting                │
│ bond level                                        │
│                                                   │
│                                                   │
│                    Model 3                        │
│"Normative" -->Intervening-->Shop                  │
│ (stable)     factor(s)     lifting                │
│ bond level                                        │
└─────────────────────────────────────────────────┘
```

(2) discern if and how "drifting" affects the stated bond level; and (3) determine what impact behavioral outcomes have on the stated bond perception.

Responding to the limitations of the analytical model presented here, it was imperative to marshall some evidence from the literature to build a logical case for one or both of the remaining models. While there is support in the literature for Model 1, it was necessary to build a case for Models 2 and 3. The best method was one proposed by Liska.[42]

The procedure makes it possible to test competing sociological variables derived from a common base. The purpose of this is to statistically reject variables or theories not supported by the data. Therefore, the statistical equation to test the analytical model became:

$$S1 = f(B, PA1, PA2, PR, N3, N4, S, ATT,$$

Age, Sex, Race).[43]

When the regression estimates (beta values) are inserted, the linear equation becomes (T values are in the brackets):

SL = f (.090536 [B] + .005343 [PA1] + - .025360 [PA2] + .023038 [PR] + [1.536] + [.096] + [-.451] + [.397] -.052647 [N3] + - .012728 [N4] + -.123775 [S] + -080707 [ATT] + [-.918] + [-.226] + [-2.117] + [-1.310] + .033862 [Age] + .116914 [Sex] + .207097 [R]. [.592] [2.060] [3.727])

R2 = .11237   F= 3.45254   Sign. F= .0002

Formulation and use of the instruments provided standardized beta weights that could be used like percentages to compare the effects of the independent instruments upon the dependent variable. The signs of the coefficients have nothing to do with the strength of the relationship of the instruments. A (-) means that one of the instruments and the dependent variable increase while the other decreases. A (+) means that the two increase together. The signs merely tell the direction of the relationship. The beta weights can be compared and used to establish a hierarchy.

The linear equation statistical values suggest that a hierarchy that uses the situation, sex, and race instruments would be superior to the use of a hierarchy comprised of bonding, peer association, parental relations, and need. The T statistic at .05 level also suggests that the situation, sex, and race variables are the most important when adolescent snitch shoplifting is analyzed. However, when a zero correlation was run using the instruments individually to determine its relationship their shoplifting, only the situation instrument was reduced to show that

no (zero) relationship existed between the
other independent instruments and shoplifting
behavior.

Multiple linear regression does exactly
what it implies. It provides a coefficient, a
statistic, R, which reveals how well we may
predict the dependent variable from the several independent variables used in the equation.
The R2 explains the variation caused in the
dependent variable by multiple independent
variables.

Delinquency problems can rarely be stated
in terms of a simple relationship between A
and B or Y and X. Normally the behavior involves some type of relationship between Y, X,
and some other variables. This has been statistically demonstrated in the research on
adolescent snitch shoplifting.

Shoplifting and other forms of delinquency have been associated with many variables
believed to be interrelated to some degree.
The beta values are often used erroneously to
make definitive interpretations. They are
improper indices because the erroneous use of
these values often leads the researcher to
treat the variables as a set despite statistical findings that they should not. To conduct
research in this fashion precludes, as discussed in chapter one, the search for the real
relation of particular variables that are
necessary for under standing delinquent and
criminal behaviors.

There is no general model that is univer-
sally agreed upon, which can encompass all the
causes of human behavior. However, we can, as
this research did, use a general theory of
social learning that has gained broad support
because it suggests that direct and vicarious
experience, accompanied with rewards and
punishment, leads to the acquisition of specific beliefs about the consequences of attitudes toward a situation. Based on the postulate that it is these beliefs that shape

behavior, the theory also suggests that how one interacts with a social situation necessitates a degree of social learning.

This research depicted one aspect of social learning, shoplifting. Social learning theory was applied to a simultaneous equation model. This model, (figure 8.4) enabled a test of relevant dimensions and their interactions, given a specific situation. It assumed that there is a reciprocal effect between behavior and attitude, that attitude was the result of delineated elements, and that these effects, attitudes, and behavior would be simultaneous, or at least proximate in time. The model enabled the use of instrumental variables (predicted scores) to determine their effect on the dependent variable (shoplifting), using multiple linear regression.

Figure 8.4

Simultaneous Model

Let:
A1 = Current attitude
B1 = Situational stimuli
A2 = Situated behavior (Behavior attributed to the situational stimuli)
B2 = Non-situated behavior (Behavior consistent with the bonding level)

SUMMARY OF FINDINGS

Insofar as snitch variety adolescent shop lifting is concerned, bonding factors, peer association, parental relationship, need, attitude and age factors were found to be less important when statistically operationalized than previously thought. However, the situational stimuli, sex and race factors were important. The attitude factor was difficult to interpret and basically unnecessary, due to its statistical insignificance.

There appears to be one seemingly apparent problem, the low R2 (the total variance between the independent variables and their effect on the dependent variable less the error term). However, criticism of the R2 value (.11237) can be dismissed by referring to the F value. Nevertheless, the low R2 value can be explained by pointing to the limited range of the item scaling (1-7), use of predicted scores rather than operationalizing the statistically significant elements for each variable, and failure to delete those that did not meet this criteria.

Although the F-statistic, 3.45254, is relatively small, the probability that the findings reported in regard to the relationship between shoplifting and the independent variables occurred by chance is less than .01. The results suggest that behavior neutralization is not a factor that can be used to explain the occurrence of this behavior by youths who are differentially bonded.

The most significant aspect of the study, using the F-value (3.45254), is Blacks and Crime the finding that the variables commonly operationalized to explain delinquent behavior in general may be more appropriate indicators of White male delinquent behavior, in these case shoplifting, than for White females, non-White males and females. This finding clashes with Klemke's.[44] However, to validate his findings, the F-values would have to be in the (1.) and (2.) ranges respectively to be construed as appropriate indicators for youths who are not White males.

NOTES

1. Hirschi, Travis, *Causes of Delinquency* (Berkeley, Calif.: University of California Press, 1969).

2. Cohen, Albert K., *Delinquent Boys: The Culture of the Gang* (New York, N.Y.: Free Press, 1955).

3. Richard A. Cloward and Lloyd E. Ohlin, *Delinquency and Opportunity: A Theory of Delinquent Gangs* (New York: Free Press, 1960).

4. Clifford Shaw and Henry D. McKay, *Juvenile Delinquency and Urban Areas* (Chicago: University of Chicago Press, 1942); Frederic M. Thrasher, *The Gang: A Study of 1,313 Gangs in Chicago* (Chicago: University of Chicago Press, 1927).

5. John W.C. Johnstone, "Social Class, Social Areas, and Delinquency." *Sociology and Social Research*, 63, (1978): 49-72; Charles R. Tittle, "Labeling and Crime: An Empirical Analysis" in *The Labeling of Deviance*, ed. Walter R. Gove, (Beverly Hills: Sage, 1975), 241-63; Charles R. Tittle and Wayne J. Villemez and Douglas A. Smith, "The Myth of Social Class and Criminality: An Empirical Assessment of the Empirical Evidence," *American Sociological Review* 43 (October 1978): 643-656.

6. Mary Owen Cameron, *The Booster and the Snitch* (New York: Free Press, 1964).

7. George Won and George Yamamoto "Social Structure and Deviant Behavior: A Study of Shoplifting," *Sociology and Social Research* 53 (1968): 44-55.

8. Starke R. Hathaway and Elio D. Monachesi, *Analyzing and Predicting Juvenile Delinquency with the MMPI Minneapolis* (University of Minnesota Press, 1953).

9. Research shows that a number of vio-

lent offenders suffer from sort of personality for example, and these would fit the psychogenic models. Sorrell's study of juvenile murderers found that many of these youths could be described in terms of being "overly hostile," "explosive," "anxious," or "volatile." See James Sorrell "Kids Who Kill," *Crime and Delinquency* 23 (1977), 312-320; Richard Rosner, et al., "Adolescents Accused of Murder and Manslaughter: A Five-Year Descriptive Study," *Bulletin of the American Academy of Psychiatry and the Law* 7 (1979), 342-351; Walter Mischel, *Introduction to Personality* 4th ed. (New York: Holt, Rinehart and Winston, 1989); Sheldon Glueck and Elanor Glueck, *Unraveling Juvenile Delinquency* (Cambridge, Mass.: Harvard University, 1950),and Hans Eysenck, *Personality and Individual Differences* (New York: Plenum, 1985).

10. Richard L. Jenkins "Adaptive and Maladaptive Delinquency," *Nervous Child* 2 (October 1955): 9-11.

11. Don C. Gibbons, "Crime and Punishment: A Study of Social Attitudes." *Social Forces* 47 (June 1969): 391-397.

12. Howard S. Becker, *Outsiders: Studies in the Sociology of Deviance* (New York: Free Press, 1973).

13. Leo Carroll and Pamela I. Jackson "Inequality Opportunity, and Crime Rates in Central Cities." *Criminology* 21, (1983): 170-194; Philip J. Cook, *Robbery in the United States: An Analysis of Recent Trends* Washington, D.C.: U.S. Department of Justice, 1983).

14. This process, anomie, is demonstrated in chapter 11.

15. Matza maintains that motivational or deterministic characteristics purported by the strain theories in regard to the offender do not ring true. He contends that they fail to account for maturational reform and for the fact that the large number of juvenile offenders desist from further misconduct near the

end of the adolescent period.

He views the delinquent, as well as the non-delinquent, as transitly existing in limbo between convention and crime, responding in turn to the demands of each, flirting now with one, now the other, but postponing commitment and evading decision. Thus, the adolescent drifts between criminal and conventional behavior. Matza views delinquency as being episodic behavior by many youths not because they are driven into it, but because their usual attachment to pro-social conduct norms is temporarily broken by various neutralization techniques. The major differences between this argument and that formulated by Hirschi is that the latter suggests that detachment from social controls is a relatively permanent state. Thus, delinquents do not drift in and out of conventional attachments.

16. For example, when joyriding is the result of operator carelessness (leaving the keys in the ignition), and this behavior is committed by an individual who has never offended in this fashion, a situated identity can be said to have occurred. The elements of this "transaction" includes (1) environmental stimuli: the unlocked car and keys in the ignition, (2) innovative behavior, and (3) behavior that may or may not be consistent with past "behavior". This interaction can be modeled by making an analysis of acts by assessing prior attributes. This requires t he use of a general association model that makes no assumptions about the level of measurement of the variables. The model captures each two-way association with a single parameter that shifts the distribution of one variable upward or downward as the other variable is moved. The model, general log-linear, is specified as:

$$O_{ij} = F_{ij}F_{i+1, j+1}/F_{i+1, j}F_{i, j+1} = 0$$

Where: i=1 to 1=1 and j=1 to j-1

In this manner the model implies differences among the elements of the "basic set of interaction" (L. A. Goodman, "Simple Models for the Analysis of Doubly Ordered Cross Classifications," *Journal of the American Statistical Association* 74 (1979), 537-552. The model is one of independence and its fit to differentiate stimuli (uf ($_i$)) and acts (uAj): LN (Fij) = u + uF($_i$) + ua(j)

Where:

Σu_i F(i)=Σu_i A(j)=o

The association between stimuli and behavior is the likely ratio statistic:

I J

L2=2Σ $\Sigma f_i j LN(f_i j/F_i j)$
　$_ij$

which is distributed approximately as chi-square with (I-1) (J-1) degrees of freedom.

Note: There are two different stimuli and only two possible behaviors in this illustration. Theoretically, there are a number of behavior options in any environmental interaction. In this illustration, 0 = no change or behavior consistent with prior identity attributes; 1 = change in behavior inconsistent with prior attributes. This methodology was utilized in the research reported in the last part of this chapter.

HYPOTHETICAL FRAMEWORK

Stimulus Behavior	Observed	LL/UA	Indep
1 Auto Unlocked	0	391	300.6
			88.1
	1	106	135.2
			112.6
2 Keys in Ignition	0	135	150.3
			137.6
	1	84	77.1
			67.6

17. Contingencies, in regard to an attribute, are conceptualized as being a method of explaining both the uniqueness and complexity of that attribute, that is, age is more than an attribute that denotes chronological state; it can also depict a position, behavior, or perspective.

18. Sutherland's Differential association principles would be rendered irrelevant (as well as the efforts of Merton).

19. Cohen, *Delinquent Boys*: 1955.

20. See C.N. Alexander and G. W. Knight, "Situated Identities and Social Psychological Experimentation", *Sociometry*, 34: (1971): 65-82; P.E. Tetlock, "Explaining teacher Explanations of Pupil Performance: A Self Presentation Interpretation," *Social Psychology Quarterly*, 3: (1980): 283-290; D.J. Bem, and D.C. Funder, "Predicting More of the People More of the Time: Assessing the Personality of Situations, "*Psychological Review*, 85: (1978): 485-501; P.J. Burke, and D.C. Reitzes,"The Link Between Identity and Role Performance," *Social Psychology Quarterly*, 44: (1981): 83-92; R. Christie and F. L. Geis, *Studies in Machiavellianism* (New York; Academic Press, 1970).

21. Alexander and Lauderdale cite a study conducted by Alexander and Knight where people were given the opportunity to check "how much" they liked or disliked their task on a scale that ranged from -5 to +5. Situated identity theory predicted the model response as well as the distribution of responses among all the alternatives of four conditions (See Alexander and Knight, 1971). Situated identity theory has also been used to go beyond the tested hypothesis that other theories generate, concerning how people conform more often to others who have high levels of task ability than they do to those with low ability levels. This hypothesis is fairly obvious. Situated identity theory goes a step further to predict how much more, and at what specific level conformity, it will be manifested. Situated identity, in other words, predicts the particular mean and model response and the variance of the distribution of responses among alternatives (See Alexander and Lauderdale, "Situated Identities and Social Influences.")

22. John E. Conklin, *Criminology* (New York: MacMillan Publishing Company, 1992).

23. Marvin E. Wolfgang, *Patterns in Criminal Homicide* (Philadelphia: University of Pennsylvania Press, 1958).

24. Menachem Amir, *Patterns in Forcible Rape* (Chicago: University of Chicago Press, 1971).

25. Edward Green, "Race Social Status, and Criminal Arrest," *American Sociological Review* 35 (June 1970): 476-490; Marvin E. Wolfgang, Robert M. Figlio, and Thorsten Sellin *Delinquency in a Birth Cohort* (Chicago: University of Chicago Press, 1972).

26. When the relationship between class and crime are explored using self-reports, there is a modest correlation between the two variables. However, Braithwaite reported that no study reported a higher rate for the middle than lower class. See John Braithwaite, *In-

equality, Crime, and Public Policy (London: Rondledge and Kegan Paul, 1981): 35-58.

27. David H. Good and Maureen A. Pirog-Good "A Simultaneous Probit Model of Crime and Employment for Black and White Teenage Males," *The Review of Black Political Economy* 16 (1987): 109-127.

28. Liad Phillips and Harold Votey "Rational Choice Models of Crimes by Youth." *The Review of Black Politic-al Economy* 16 (1987): 129-87.

29. W. Kip Viscusi " Market Incentives for Criminal Behavior," in *The Black Youth Employment Crisis*, ed. Richard B. Freeman and Harry J. Holzer (Chicago: The University of Chicago Press, 1986): 301-46.

30. Thomas Moore "The Black-on-Black Crime Plague," *U.S. News and World Report* August 22 (1988): 49-55.

31. Judith R. Blau and Peter M. Blau, "The Cost of Inequality: Metropolitan Structure and Violent Crime," *American Sociological Review* 47 (1982): 114-29.

32. Charles N. Glaab, *The American City: A Documentary History* (Homewood, Ill: Dorsey Press, 1963): 277-78.

33. Amos H. Hawley, *Urban Society* (New York: Ronald Press, 1971).

34. Jane Addams, *The Spirit of Youth and the City Streets* (New York: C.F. Glaab, 1910).

35. Daniel Bell, "Crime as An American Way of Life." *Antioch Review* 13 (Summer 1953): 131-54.

36. Marvin E. Wolfgang, "Crime in Urban America." In *The Threat of Crime in America* (Newark: University of Delaware Press, 1969): 31.

37. Paul Horton and Gerald Leslie, *The Sociology of Social Problems* 5th ed. (Englewood Cliffs, N. J,: Prentice-Hall, 1974), 126.

38. M. Thrasher, "The Gang: A Study of 1313 Gangs in Chicago," in E.W. Burgess and D.J. Bogue, eds., *Contributions to Urban*

Sociology (Chicago: University of Chicago
Press, 1964), 655-59.
    39. See Edgar Butler, *Urban Sociology*
(New York: Harper & Row, Publisher, 1976),
109-20; Sara L. Boggs, "Urban Crime patterns,"
American Sociological Review 30 (December
1965): 899-908; Calvin F. Schmidt, "Urban
Crime Areas: Part 1," *American Sociological
Review* 25 (October 1960): 655-78; Karl
Schuessler, "Components of Variations in City
Crime Rates," *Social Problems* (Spring 1962):
314-23; Clifford Shaw, *Delinquency Areas* Chicago: University of Chicago Press, 1929);
Clifford Shaw and H. D. McKay, *Juvenile Delinquency and Urban Areas*. rev. ed. (Chicago:
University of Chicago Press, 1969).
    40. A copy of the S & R can be obtained
from the author.
    41. Global refers to this study exclu-
sively.
    42. A Pearsonian Correlation Coefficient
was computed for each of the zero-order correlations to examine the effects of these intervening variables on shoplifting behavior. The
logic behind this is the relationship between
each bonding element and the dependent variable (shoplifting) should be reduced to zero
if the test is one of measuring the intervening variables. Reduction provided an indica-
tion of whether or not the bonding factors
operate on shoplifting behavior through the
situational stimuli. However, this method was
rejected in favor of partial correlation, because analyses of this type would constitute a
complete book. Partialling of the variables
was performed to determine the relative beta
weights of the sub-elements of each variable.
Those sub-elements that did not achieve a
significant T-value at .05 provided a basis
for elimination, thus enabling interpretation
of the importance of the sub-elements. It is
also enabled deciphering of the importance of
the sub-elements from the predicted scores

compiled for each subject. Also See: Liska, A. E. "Interpreting the Causal Structure of Differential Association Theory," *Social Problems* 16, (1969): 485-492.

43. The partialling and predicted scores are available on request from the author.

44. Lloyd W. Klemke, "Exploring Juvenile Shoplifting," *Sociology and Social Research* 67 (October, 1982), 59-75.

9

Race, Delinquency, and Crime

The significance of the race factor in determining criminal justice outcomes has been one
of the most widely debated issues in criminal
justice during recent years. Conservative
scholars, practitioners and a large part of
the general public contend that outcomes are
always based on individual characteristics of
the person and the case. However, this contention appears to be ahistorical. This perception is consistent with the first generation
of American sociologists, Ward, Small, and
Ross whose goals were to make intransigent
individuals and groups of different races,
nationalities, ethnic origins, creeds, reli-
gions, and economic statuses behave like white
protestants in the middle class. Using this as
the norm, when violations occurred, race was
not an issue of concern. These were individuals who basically studied the social institutions within the context of a set of explicit
assumptions. These assumptions specified what
society should be like and how people are to
behave within it.

The explicit assumptions revolved around
the concept of capitalism that were deemed to
be the adhesion which held its people together
through money ties. These ties were deemed to
epitomize the acquisitive urges of a business

civilization. Perhaps it would be more useful
to think of the culture of capitalism as being
centered around two interrelated concepts:
individualism and the free market. Individualism is both a theory of human behavior and a
doctrine espoused in justification of laissez
faire. As a theory, it tries to explain man's
conduct in terms of a pleasure-pain calculus.
In this paradigm, man is assumed to pursue his
self-interest because it is seen in economic
terms: we acquire and consume material goods
(pleasure); we avoid economic loss (pain). As
doctrine, individuals pursue self-interest
with minimal interference. This doctrine can
best be grasped first as a set of beliefs
about what should be and another set of beliefs regarding what is. These beliefs are:

> 1. The individual should strive
> to be successful in competition with
> others, under the rules of the game.
> 2. These rules involve "fair
> play":
> a. Everyone should start with
> equal opportunity;
> b. No one should take unfair
> advantage through force, fraud
> or pull.
> 3. The test of reward should be
> ability (especially ability to con-
> tribute to the productive and other
> purposes of the social order. There
> should be unequal reward for unequal
> talents and unequal contributions.

However accurate this image of capitalism
may be, it is marked by a crucial shortcoming:
it appears to be drawn exclusively from the
upper and lower echelons of our society, but
it is applicable to a very few. These shortcomings manifest themselves in our criminal
justice and other social systems. Clearly, as
previously stated, there are at least two

cultures in America. One culture is comprised of poverty and the other is fixated on, among other things, alienation and loathesomeness toward the impoverished class in general, and Blacks and other minority groups specifically. This alienation and loathesomeness have many ramifications for the individual, but the most crucial are those that give rise to conditions which are pathogenic, painful, and disordering. These conditions have manifested themselves in differentiated outcomes in the varying criminal justice systems.

This condition exists because the justice system, although it advocates it, lacks a clear notion of fairness and equity. There are many reasons that can be advanced to explain this failure, but it occurs mainly because the system fails to adhere to the concepts that comprise the basic rudiments of capitalism. The concept of equity, a concern for fairness, can be found in the Bible: "And thou shalt do what is right and good in the sight of the Lord."[1] Thus, it is not good enough to "do that which is right," to act in accord with the letter of the law. One must also act fairly-- do that which is "good in the sight of the Lord." The Hebrew concept of *yosher* is based on this biblical imperative, according to which an individual must act beyond mere rule of law (din) whenever the latter involves harshness or causes hardship. In more contemporary times, the issue remains: should a rule(s) be applied mechanically, no matter how outlandish or unfair the out come, an approach advocated by German philosopher Immanuel Kant (1724-1804), or should there be room for ensuring a fair and reasonable outcome?

The term "equity", from the Latin *aequitas* meaning equality or justice, evolved from the Roman concept of natural law. It referred to fairness or equality of treatment between Roman citizens and foreigners in matters before the Praetors or magistrates in

Justinian ome. Although the legal culture in
the United States has reflected the general
culture's commitment to the idea of equality,
though equality of a particular in the mind of
some, it is one of a limited sort. It is
limited because we have clung to the idea that
the rule of the law implies only that the
playing field be level, not that every player
on it be similarly endowed or treated. As a
result, equality of status (the idea that all
persons should be similarly situated as a consequence of the law) has been alien to most
Americans and, also, to the legal culture.

Our legal history reflects generations of
pragmatic decision making rather than a quest
for ideological purity and consistency. History reveals that personal and groups interests have always ordered the course of legal
development, therefore instrumentalism has
been the function of law. Who have been the
winners and the losers? The answer is hardly
clear cut. However, it is clear that the rule
of law, in America's history, has made possible wide spread economic and political power.

Yet our legal past and present is studded
with injustice. Neither wealth, political
power, social standing, nor civil liberties
and civil rights have ever been equally distributed. Often the legal system has abetted
racial and gender discrimination, maldistribu-
tion of wealth, exploitation, and political
powerlessness. Through a system of popular
justice, lacking any vestige of equity, Americans have frequently and savagely stepped
outside the law to administer "criminal justice."[2]

This system of popular justice occurs in
those areas that generally have large black
populations. These areas also generally experience higher levels of inequality. These
inequalities are manifested in political
participation,[3] differential income levels,[4]
and Occupational status.[5] Given this condition,

there is a suggestion that these factors are the result of perceived threats by Whites of minorities. Stated differently, the threat is generally described as the actual or perceived potential of a minority group to pose a realistic challenge to the existing White political or economic control base.

Jacob reported that in metropolitan areas, police strength and the nature of the relationship between the races are interrelated.[6] Jackson and Carroll, testing this hypothesis, used racial composition, level of Black mobilization activity, and the frequency of riots in the 1960s as factors to determine if it was possible to predict police strength by sampling 90 non-Southern cities during 1971.[7] Their findings suggest that there is a curvilinear relationship between the size of the minority population and the perceived threat felt by the dominant group. These and other related findings suggest that theories using these factors may be relevant for predicting geographical patterns of arrest and imprisonment rates. To the extent that race-related societal forces exert an influence on police strength, such social sentiments may also be expected to influence the entire justice process. It can be hypothesized that the racial power threat can influence the behavior of the police, prosecuting attorneys, judges, probation and parole officers. Considering this power-threat hypothesis, we can speculate regarding the linkage between Black population size and variations in their incarceration rates.

Blumstein conducted a study regarding the determinants of disproportionality of the prison population in the United States.[8] His study analyzed the country as a whole, and he found that during the late 1970s, the differences in arrest and incarceration rates were accounted for by using racial factors. Despite this finding, he found a twenty percent ratio difference regarding the actual Black-white rates of imprisonment which, he felt, remained unexplained by the arrest data. In attempting to account for this ratio, he suggested that: (A) Legitimate race-related variation in criminal activity or criminal processing may account for some of the difference for example, over representation of Blacks among crimes with less mitigating qualities, longer criminal records and the effects of low levels of education and occupational status on perceptions of the ability of the offender to function within the legitimate economy, (B) An analysis of race differences by crime types showed the unexplained difference, he stated, to be only 2.8 percent and 5.2 percent for homicide and aggravated assault, but nearly fifty percent for larceny/auto theft and drug violations. Thus he contended that there was a differential imprisonment rate, but that it was based on the type of offense, (C) That there were possible biasing effects due to aggregation. For example, some regions may discriminate against Blacks while another may be more lenient, and (D) Finally, he suggested that these attempts at explanation do not argue that discrimination is absent from the criminal justice system or that the amount of discrimination is negligibly small or insignificant. But he clearly found that there is a need to empirically assess the separate effects of legal and extra legal factors on differential imprisonment by race.

Not only has race been demonstrated to be a critical factor in arrest and incarceration rates, it is also a factor in capital punishment. A report prepared by death penalty foes, named the Death Penalty Information Center of Washington, and submitted to the House Judiciary Subcommittee on Civil and Constitutional Rights focused on a six county area along the banks of the Chattahoochee River in Georgia. The study was not concerned with how many people were condemned to death nor with their race but rather the race of their victim. They found that based upon the fashion in which the killer was prosecuted and the degree of assiduousness the court system accorded the bereaved survivors, it was unquestioned that the legal apparatus placed a higher premium on the lives of Whites compared to Blacks. Their data also showed that while whites represented thirty five percent of the murder victims, eighty five percent of capital cases brought by local prosecutors involved White victims. This meant that the prosecutors sought the death penalty in one of three murders involving Whites when Blacks were the victims, the ratio dropped to 1 in 17. In addition, prosecutors sought executions of nearly half of those convicted of killing White women and thirty percent of persons killing White men, but when the victims were Black, the numbers were only 9.4 percent and 2.6 percent, respectively. It is clear from this study that the race of the victim was a crucial factor in the concept and exercising of the death penalty. George Kendall said: "The tradition of the black codes and slave codes, which provided different and harsher punishment for offenders who harmed whites than blacks, remain today in places like Columbus."[9] Despite this data, the U.S. Supreme Court has held that such statistical evidence is irrelevant when applied to particular cases and can not be used when appeals are brought before the court.[10]

There are four distinct obstacles, among many, confronting Blacks who kill Whites and attempt to avoid capital punishment in the six county area (1) poverty, which suggests that they confront difficulty in hiring competent counsel; (2) all of the judges hearing capital cases are white;[11] (3) all of the prosecuting attorneys who ask for the death penalty are white; and (4) until recently virtually all juries deciding these type of cases were

White.[12]

The basis that one can use to argue against the contention that Blacks and other minority members receive differential sanctioning by the criminal justice system is very slim. Given the conditions discussed, one is perplexed regarding the response by law enforcement officials, the police in particular, to the rap lyrics contained in Ice Tea's *O.G. Original Gangster*. Ice Tea writes about catching the police chief, then Daryl Gates, in traffic without a vest and doing bodily harm to him. In this rough allegory, the main moral point is to remove the chief's head.

The rap is crude but it speaks to and for the sentiments that are prevalent in South Central Los Angeles and many other communities in this society. Are these types of lyrics really irresponsible as some critics suggest? Perhaps that which is most shameful regarding the song is its opening lines which discusses being born in America while questioning whether South Centrals' qualities are indicative of America to any one other than Blacks.

It is true that rap music makes a large part of the United States uneasy. This uneasiness is attributed to the lyrics that create a real life imagery, which does not glorify but rather depicts daily existence in Central Los Angeles and similar areas. This imagery is laced with guns, gangs, and violence. This violence is a response to decades of neglect, inurement to human suffering, and affluence constantly flaunted but unattainable to these people. It is also a response to the violence that has been meted out by the hired guardians of the affluent, the police. It is true that Ice Tea's lyrics called for the virtual assassination of the then police chief, Daryl Gates. It is also true that Daryl Gates systematically permitted and condoned the use of illegal force against these people. It is force that citizens in a truly civilized society should, but do not, find difficult to endorse. A large portion of this society endorsed the violence sanctioned by Gates and others like Rizzo. Society has not concerned itself with the violence being meted out by the law enforcement apparatus in any spatial setting where Blacks and other minorities are deemed to be problematic. This violence takes the form of officially sanctioned murders, beatings, indiscriminate use of police dogs, crippling injuries, contrived evidence, and a host of other behaviors that should be, but seemingly are not, beneath the dignity of a large portion of these "professional" public servants. When indignities of this nature and insensitivities are continuously heaped upon people, many of them, like Ice Tea, contend that their resentment and bitterness is justifiable. Given these police behaviors and the inurement by the generally more affluent, it is easy to understand why people in the "hood" agree with Tea when he perplexes as to why people with the ability to comprehend cannot understand that hard core people on the streets will rap about hard core experiences.

This social order has advanced many reasons for the varying degrees of enforcement that have been utilized against these people. The most current rationale for this force is the scourge of drugs and what it is doing to this social order. Does anyone outside of these lower-class neighborhoods really care about the amount of drugs available and being used in these areas?

History and social policies indicate that the answer is a resounding no! Why then is there a fixation on control of these substances in these areas? Let me suggest that it is because we have been fed a lot of myths about drugs and drug pushing. Let me challenge you to look in every nook and cranny in your city, town, or hamlet and find one pusher. I am confident that you will not find one drug pusher. These are the type of people that provide interesting action stories for television shows like "Top Cop," "Cops," and a host of other imitations. Despite their heroics they have yet to catch a pusher. This is because there are no pushers. It is a simple truism, you do not need pushers when demand is as it is now and has always been, plentiful. The pusher is a figment of the law enforcers and public's imagination, a figment not unlike Santa or the tooth fairy. There are no pushers, because pushing never has been nor will it ever be a profitable activity. This is because drugs are extremely expensive and those involved in the marketing aspect of the business are dealers, or business people, who sell only to customers with the money and desire to buy the commodity. This is not a play on words because there are clear distinctions between the terms pusher and dealer. Drug dealers do not waste their time attempting to push anyone who refuses to buy their product. I challenge you to walk the streets where you live or visit to test this distinction. In the process you will be able to, if you know where to go which is practically everywhere, to have the "opportunity" to see a drug dealer. After you have found this "pusher" and you say no or, better, claim that you want the drug but lack the money to purchase it, watch how fast the "pusher" moves on to someone who has both the inclination to purchase and the money to consummate the deal. Where can you find these "pushers," I mean dealers? In needle strewn alleys, waterfront condominiums, nightclubs, schools, business establishments, churches, and every other conceivable place where people go. The dealer would not exist if millions of people did not feel compelled to shape their personal reality with drugs. This is the reality, people buy drugs, so dealers sell. No one pushes them!

How could we attack drug use or wage war

against the commodity with out an identifiable enemy? Because drugs exist everywhere in our social order and traffickers, suppliers, distributors, and dealers are identifiable, with some effort, therefore they become the enemy. We shift the blame from personal behavioral choices to the enemy, mislabel them and force them underground. After we have accomplished this, we then find solace in and operate on our assumption that drugs are something that must be forced or pushed on people. How can we rationally combat a problem when we have difficulty defining it and the actors properly?

The question is asked repetitively, how do children growing up in America's inner cities cope with the constant exposure to violence, drugs, danger, and fear? These children are resilient and despite the popular perception, quite remarkable. In 1993 the Mississippi and a host of other rivers inundated the midwest with devastating floods. Only the most callous could not feel acute sorrow for these people living along the delta areas who lost everything material they could not move out of harms way. Psychologists reflecting on the catastrophe contend that the hardest thing about enduring the floods and the incessant rains was the seeming unending nature of the calamities. The people across the country, justifiably and humanely, responded to the urgent needs of these people in their time of crisis. Both the president and vice president visited the devastated areas and were told by several mayors and citizens that they were uninterested in any government loans that would be made available through FEMA. Instead they insisted that they wanted and needed grants to rebuild their cities. They contended that the losses were too great to expect the citizens of the effected areas to bear alone. Massive aid was critical and expected. These requests were made despite the fact that there was growing concern nationally that these people created their own problems by situating in flood plains and failing to purchase flood insurance to indemnify themselves against loss.

As bad as the situation was in Sioux City and Des Moines, Iowa, and other places along the Great Mississippi and Missouri Rivers, the people effected can expect an end to their problems. But what do you tell a citizen who inhabits the varying "hoods" in the urban areas, where there is no hope of peace nor renewal of community life? What do the good people of the United States owe these people? They are less responsible for the conditions that they inhabit than the people who were victims of the flood, the earth quake in San Francisco, or the hurricane in South Florida. Why do we find it so difficult to marshall compassion for these people rather than rain our enmity upon them? There are no calls for national sympathy for these people. Every program formulated, like Rebuild L.A. and similar plans oriented theoretically to save, reinvigorate, or energize the inner city, are scuttled by political representatives from the states now urgently pleading for help. Their problems, they deemed, are acute and they must be addressed equitably, meaning fully, because the help is essential in maintaining middle American values and maintenance of the public's trust.

A recent study indicated the disproportionate fixation of values and the importance of the public official's concerns. The study relates that prenatal drug exposure disrupts children's ability to form relationships.[13] The study is both insightful and interesting because it placed forth notions that on their face can not be construed as anything but frivolous research or an exercise in nonsense. Let me clarify, the research as a scholarly pursuit is far from nonsense, the question is:

what is its purpose? To whom are the findings supposed to be applied? The study stated that prenatal exposure to illegal drugs, particularly powdered cocaine and its smokeable derivative, crack, seems to be "interfering with the central core of what it is to be human."[14] Corey states that without help, the children of these addicted mother may be unable to develop into adults with basic employment skills and unable to form close relationships. Given the environment that these youths and their parents currently inhabit, does it really matter that they may not develop basic employment skills? Of course not! The economic deprivation, racial hatred, and law enforcement violence will ensure that they do not develop as "humans." In addition, they have other things that command their undivided attention for example, gangs, community disruption, early death, high morbidity rates, high mortality rates, an uncaring social order that deems that they belong where they are situated socially, and drugs. Given a legacy of these conditions, how can one ponder the results of the study, take ameliorative steps, or be perplexed with Ice Tea's lyrics? What merits displeasure by Daryl Gates? What right does any one in this society, not subjected to these conditions, have to be repulsed by any reaction by these people when they find it extremely difficult to appeal to and be comforted by the larger society or to know that their sense of community is merely disrupted for a short period of time rather than a way of life?

Surprising that when these people have had enough and respond, we do become repulsed by their behavior with considerable ease. We do not stop with repulsion, we go even further by placing blame on the victim rather than on the real culprits. Like Santa we create and believe in our fantasies. It is not just the people, it is the political leaders, people we

expect to know better after all of the studies
they have conducted or commissioned to be
undertaken. Consider the inanity of the
following incident that took place in Chicago.[15] A five year old boy became another victim
of a constant danger for many of the children
living in building #8 in the Rockwell Gardens
complex, a public housing project in Chicago.
This child fell thirteen stories to his death
through a open and unprotected window. The
parents were charged with misdemeanor child
neglect. The tenants say that at least three
children have been seriously injured in falls
from unprotected windows in another CHA,
Chicago Housing Authority, complex, Robert
Taylor Homes. Another child, two-years old,
was killed in this building by falling out of
an unprotected window. A twenty two month old
boy was critically injured when he fell from
an eighth floor window at another CPA complex,
Ickes Homes. These tragic events could have
been prevented if the CHA had found it important enough to place screens or bars on the
windows in the apartments. The CHA spokesper-
son said, "we have started to put child guards
on the windows at Rockwell Gardens, but [Jeff-
rey's building, where the five year old was
the latest to fall] particular building did
not have them yet. They are slated to be in-
stalled in the next year to 18 months." What
sense of logic led the law enforcers in Chicago to arrest, incarcerate, and subsequently
release Jeffrey's parents, pending trial, on
misdemeanor charges when the negligence or
criminal fault clearly lies with the housing
authority? These parents' grief was simply
compounded by an insensitive social structure
that is inured to the well-being of helpless
children, and they were further victimized.
Could this and other incidents be attributed
to race and its manifestations?

Armstrong Williams, host of the seemingly
omnipresent vehicle for hate mongers, talk

radio, told his mainly Black audience on station WOL in Washington, D.C.: "If African Americans look only for injustice and overlook instances of kindness and fairness in whites, they cannot help but have their worst fears confirmed. A balanced view will require giving the system the benefit of the doubt when things don't go your way. The system is some-times flawed, but it is fair."[16] Not only is Williams wrong, he could be dead wrong. This probability was driven home on July 17, 1993, when the FBI arrested six White youths, who called themselves the Fourth Reich Skinheads, and an two adults who plotted, they thought the perfect scenario, for initiating a race riot involving Blacks and Whites. Their dia-bolical plot involved killing members of Los Angeles most prominent church, First African Methodist. This was to be accomplished by either the tossing of grenades or the shooting of these people with machine guns. In addi-tion, their level of insanity was demonstrated when they began to formulate plans to kill a famous major league base ball player, Rodney King, and a number of other Black national leaders.

These seriously disturbed people, accord-ing to the FBI, are tied to two White suprema-cist groups, the Florida based Church of the Creator and the San Diego based White Aryan Resistance. WAR is the same group whose lead-er,Tom Metzger and his son, were ordered to pay $12.5 million dollar to the family of the Ethiopian man after they were convicted of being responsible for his murder, committed by deranged skin heads. These "sissy warriors" fronting for older and even sicker and gutless warriors bragged that they had carried out a number of pipe bombings prior to their latest threats in the Los Angeles area. When cap-tured, these mighty mites and intellectual midgets claimed that first they were entrapped and that their ill feelings toward minorities

and fears of reverse discrimination were
stoked by undercover FBI agents. In effect,
what they were intimating was that they did
not really mean it, rather they were suckered
in and coerced into this behavior, not by WAR
or COC, but rather by the FBI.

Williams would be well advised to remember the words of David Duke, ex-GOP candidate
for governor, White supremacist, conservative
Republican, avowed Nazi activist and
sympathizer, and "ex-Ku Klux Klan" member,
when he said,

> I appreciate the honorable people
> who have not been intimidated, who
> know that the time has come in this
> country to stand up for us, to stand
> up for our heritage and our way of
> life.[17]

It would be interesting to learn how Williams and the large number of Duke supporters
interpreted this. Ruth Rickey, a New Orleans
Republican, said after listening to his extended diatribe, of 40 to 50 hours:

> He is a racial ideologue of a type
> that I have yet to encounter in my
> entire lifetime. He is not a George
> Wallace. He is beyond that. He is
> truly a type that one would find in
> the 1930's in Germany. He sees him
> self as this Messiah, that he's
> going to save the white race.[18]

Thomas says, "Too many black 'leaders'
continue to portray all blacks as victims of
white oppression, this is a form of racism
that is rarely addressed."[19] This is a curious
application of the term, but we must give
Thomas the benefit of the doubt. However, the
evidence strongly suggests that reactions by
Blacks and minorities to perceived and real

threats can hardly be called a form of racism. Perhaps he meant to use the word racialist to describe that which he deemed to be problematic. Furthermore, Thomas would understand more clearly the correlation between White racism and the current conditions of minorities in the inner cities if he objectively explored the nexus between these factors, rather than resort to the espousing of Republican jingos and slogans to obfuscate the issues.

It is not solely the traditional disaffected who are engaging in violence. In recent months, the work place has been saturated with violence. Violence that was thought to be limited primarily to the inner city has increasingly found its way into fashionable and up scale business sites. The Centers for Disease Control reports that there were more than 750 work place homicides in 1992. The center has declared work place homicide to be an epidemic. However, homicides constitute an insignificant part of the total violence that occurs in the work place. For every murder, statistically, there are scores of injuries, beatings, stabbings, suicides, shootings, rapes, near-suicides, psychological traumas, and assorted mental health pathologies. This violence is perceived to contribute to or is part of work place drug and alcohol abuse, absenteeism, and many other factors that impede business operations and productivity.

This increase in violence is deemed to be a reflection both of a stressed-out, downsized business environment and a changing moral value structure. Previously, this aggressive behavior was mitigated by factors for example, family, neighbors, life-time employment, etc. These seemingly stable and enduring factors, as discussed in previous chapters, are not as prevalent today as they once were. Nevertheless, these individuals are receiving a modicum of help because the businesses affected were forced to comprise strategies to deal

with the violence. These strategies include
the development of threat assessment teams,
training for supervisors and managers, behavioral screening, prevention planning when
downsizing, and--post incident analysis. Still
we are confronted with the issue regarding how
to sanction the general violence that occurs
when the traditional bedrock factors of the
social order become porous.

NOTES

1. Deut. 6:18.
2. F. M. Danbaugh "Racially Disproportionate Rates of Incarceration in the United
States," *Prison Monitor* 25 (March, 1979): 219-
22; S. Christianson "Our Black Prisons,"
Crime and Delinquency 27 (July, 1981): 364-
75.
3. V. O. Key, Jr. *Southern Politics* (New
York: Alfred A. Knopf, 1949); D. M. Heer "The
Sentiment of White Supremacy: An Ecological
Study." *American Journal of Sociology* 64 (May,
1959): 592-98.
4. H. M. Blalock "Economic Discrimination
and Negro-Increase." *American Sociological
Review* 21, (Oct., 1956): 584-88; H. M. Blalock
"Percent Non-White and discrimination in the
South." *American Sociological Review* 22 (Dec.,
1957): 677-82; W. P. Frisbie and L. Neidert
"Inequality and the Relative Size of Minority
Populations: a Comparative Analysis." *American
Journal of Sociology* 82 (March, 1977): 1007-
30.
5. N. D. Glenn "The Relative Size of the
Negro Population and Negro Occupational Status," *Social Forces* 43 (Oct., 1964): 42-49; N.
D. Glenn "Occupational Benefits to Whites from
the Subordination of Negroes." *American Sociological Review* 28 (June, 1963): 443-48.
6. D. Jacobs "Inequality and Police

Strength: Conflict Theory and Coercive Control in Metropolitan Areas," *American Sociological Review* 44 (Dec., 1979): 913-25.

7. P. I. Jackson and L. Carroll "Race and the War on Crime: The Socio-political Determinants of Municipal Police Expenditures in 90 Non-Southern U.S. Cities," *American Sociological Review* 46 (June, 1981): 290-305.

8. A. Blumstein "On the Racial Disproportionality of the United States' Prison Populations," *The Journal of Criminal Law and Criminology* 73. (Fall 1982): 1259-81.

9. George Kendall is a lawyer with the NAACP Legal Defense and Educational Fund Inc. Reported in David Margolick, "Foes of Death Penalty Says Georgia Values White Lives Over Black," *New York Times New Service*, July 12, 1991.

10. This was decided in **Jerome Bowden v Georgia**, [(435 U.S. 937, 55 L.Ed. 2d 533)], In this case, race data were presented in the appeal process. Bowden was executed in 1986 for killing a white female neighbor. The House was considering using the data compiled by the death penalty foes and submitting it to the House Judiciary Subcommittee on Civil and Constitutional Rights, but the Bush administration opposed the measure as the **Fairness in Death Sentencing Act** passed in 1990 without including the measure. The substitute legislation, entitled the **Equal Justice Act**, prohibits jurors from considering race in determining a defendant's sentence, but bars the use of statistical data for invaliding the sentence.

11. Albert Thompson is the only Black to ever serve on the Chattahoochie Judicial Circuit's Superior Court. Thompson was a gubernatorial appointee who lost his bid for election after a brief tenure.

12. The United States Supreme Court decided that race was not a factor in determining whether an individual had a jury com-

prised of his/her peers. Therefore, Blacks are systemically excused from jury duty during the voir dire process.

13. S. Blakeslee "Crack Babies Show Emotional Problems" *New York Times News Service*, Feb. 7, 1992.

14. Coryl Jones, a research psychologist at the National Institute of Drug Abuse, located in Bethesda Md. made this observation which was reported in Blakeslee, "Crack Babies."

15. James Hill "Boy, 5, Dies After Fall From A CHA Window," *Chicago Tribune*, July 19, 1993. Sec. 1, 8.

16. Quoted from Cal Thomas,"Contrast in Black and White Reaction," *Los Angeles Time Syndicate*, Sept. 15, 1992.

17. P. Applebone "David Duke: A Wolf Dressed in Sheep Clothing?" *The Oregonian*, Nov. 13, 1991, 1-3. Applebone is a columnist for the *New York Times News Service*.

18. Ibid. 3.

19. Thomas, "Contrast in Black and White Reaction."

10

Hate, Crimes, Social Structure Elements

The definition of crime must encompass clearly the individual and the nature of the social behavior. When clearly defined a crime becomes understandable to social control agencies and its agents. It can also delineate methods which these individual can use to deal with the behavior. A clearly defined crime also identifies why the behavior is important to the social order. A clear definition of crime does more than reflect the attributes of the individual involved in the behavior it also provides a clear definition, which underscores the importance of its causes and the need for control.

Hate crimes are behaviors which are irrationally motivated by a victim's race, ethnicity, religion, sexual preference, gender, and nationality. This behavior is defined in at least nine different ways in seven different nations. Not only is this behavior defined differently internationally, it is explained differently nationally, regionally, intrastate, county, and in varying urban areas. For example, they have been described as hate crimes, hate motivated crimes, bias crimes, bias-motivated crimes and ethnic-violence. These various terms often feed community divisiveness, especially in racially charged times, therefore the police in several urban

departments have created the label possible
bias crimes in an effort to contain media
attention and hostile reactions from special
interest groups.

Nationally, hate crime (alternatively
referred to as right wing violence, racist
violence, etc.,) must be conceptualized as a
movement toward racism. This is so because it
is racism (not homophobia, and certainly not
misogyny) that fuels, Ku Klux Klan, skinheads,
white power, Christian Patriots, Christian
identity, Kingdom Covenant, Aryan Nation,
Black Power, and other groups e.g., the Weath-
ermen, Symbionese Liberation Army to violence
in this country.

Racism as distinguished from race, is
not a fact of life, but an ideology, and the
deeds it leads to are not reflective actions,
but deliberate acts based on pseudo-scientific
theories. Violence in interracial struggles
are always murderous, but it is not irrational, it is the natural consequence of racism.
Race prejudice, no matter how reprehensible in
itself, is a profoundly human phenomenon. It
is, as Park suggested, reflections of our
thoughts, actions and justification in our
efforts to achieve ends. We are biased by our
own purposes, and in the final analysis, knowledge is relative to them. However, common
sense suggest that prejudice can not be justified on general or rational grounds. Nevertheless, all of our sentiments, love, loyalty,
patriotism, homesickness, contempt, arrogance,
hate, are based upon and supported by prejudices. Race prejudice like class and caste
prejudice are merely one variety of a species.
However, prejudice premised on race, class and
caste in its more naive manifestations is
merely the resistance to social change.[1]

In the United States, skin heads, neo-
nazis and other white hate groups have been
implicated in the murder of more than one-
hundred young Afro-Americans, third world

immigrants, at least four homicide against gay men, nearly four-hundred assaults against black males, more than three-hundred cross-burnings, fourteen fire bombing of Afro-American churches, more than two-hundred assaults against gays and lesbians, desecrations of more than forty Jewish cemeteries, assorted acts of violence against worshipers at Jewish synagogues, including one attempted murder in Dallas, Texas, and the killing of two marshals in Idaho. These offenses were motivated by the victim's race, ethnicity, religion and those who attempted to prevent the perpetrators from carrying out their crimes.

Hate crime is a behavior is a social problem and must be analyzed in terms of why this is the best behavioral response to the conditions haters confront. The analysis can be conducted using social exchange theory. However, this theory would not completely explain the behavior which leads to hate crimes. To understand the behavior one must begin with three theoretical assumptions regarding it. First, the motivation toward becoming engaged in the behavior is grounded in an ideology of racism. Second, because the behavior is perceived to be ideologically motivated, it is rational to the perpetrator. Third, hate crimes, like all behavior are differentiated.[2] Hate crimes are characterized by the premeditated violence which is performed in terms of heroic ecstasy or hedonism. Its expressed function is to prevent that which they perceive to be social disequilibrium. In order to achieve this the offenders attempt to negate all adaptation responses to the means and goals schema except rigid conformity. Interestingly, it is an adaptation they have failed to achieve. Nevertheless, they expect and demand that every individual in the social order adhere to their values. Those who choose to abrogate their demands are

singled out for punishment. This form of
behavior is not unique to skin heads, rather
it appears to be behavior which is indicative
of all hate groups. The behavior in these
groups becomes parodical and irrationally
tautological. Perhaps this aspect of irrationality warrants that the behavior be labeled domestic terrorism. This would serve, in
addition to the hedonism characteristic, to
differentiate it from other forms of violence
which are commonly characterized as criminal
behavior.[3]

Neo-Nazi skin heads are not the first,
nor will they in all probability be the last,
to engage in hate motivated crime. One of the
most difficult tasks confronted by individuals
in our social world is to realize the pain or
injury that we visit upon each other. We
seemed to be so preoccupied with how we feel
and how we think, our own value system and
belief that it is often impossible to understand how what we do or think can harm others.
The insensitivities that we practice on a
daily basis comes back to haunt us repetitively. They are magnified in the actions of our
children and how they come to view the world
and the way they treat people whom they interact with or select to ignore. Although in many
instances our behavior seems to be covert and
it serves to condone a mean spiritedness in a
overt manner.

We do not wish to consider the humanity
of those we consider different. This simple
denial make individuals non-people and eligi-
ble for acts of violence and hatred which
would be unthinkable to do to "real people."
Police agencies across the country are finding
out how vicious and prevalent this attitude
has become. Consider Houston, Texas, which
recently discovered the extent of gay-bashing
which was occurring in their city in a fashionable section called Montrose.

Montrose is a suburban area which has

shops, art galleries, popular restaurants in addition to gay bars. It also has "wild" packs of "straight" young men who are homophobic. These "moral entrepreneurs" go to these bars, specifically after dark to harass and attack people which they assume to be homosexual. In July, 1991 a young Houston banker minding his own business, was beaten and stabbed to death. This occurred after he and his two companions left a gay bar and were chased by 10 young men armed with boards and knives. This mindless predatory behavior sparked activists to march in protest through the affluent suburb of The Woodlands, where most of the "predatory pack" members lived. Initially, the police stated that no evidence existed which could be used to classify the attack as being a hate crime. This was because the department's definition of hate crimes did not include crimes against homosexuals.

In August of the same year they were forced to change their definition when undercover police began to walk the streets of Montrose posing as gay potential victims to lure gay bashers. Within two hours, two undercover officers were attacked and sprayed with mace by gay bashers. Two days later they beat another officer with a baseball bat. All of the gay bashers were men who resided outside of Montrose but who thought that their victims were homosexuals. The arrests were televised and when a reporter asked one of the attackers about the crime he said: "What's the big deal?" "The big deal is that you hit a police officer," an officer responded. "I apologize for that," said the man in custody. "I thought he was a queer." That was it. There was no other excuse or provocation for the attack. The victims were judged by the clothes they wore, the part of town they were in and suddenly they became instant targets for assault.

Houston, like the 16,000 other police departments in this country, expressed amaze-

ment at the frequency and intensity of the
assaultive acts against people like these.
They at long agonizing last have come to
perceive it as a problem but it did not become
one, at least in Houston, until they personally experienced the rancor and hatred. Hatred
which was raw, wanton, unmitigated and casual-
ly accepted. These attitude were translated
into violence which can be described in the
same manner. Once the Houston police became
involved as victims, they understood how out
of control the hatred and violence was.

It would be a mistake to think that this
behavior only occurs in Houston just as it
would be to attribute this degree of inhumani-
ty only to gay-bashing. In this case, it was
homosexuals. In another, it is racial or
religious or political "provocation." It is a
rising tide of intolerance that seems to negate common sense, civility and encourage
violence and destruction. This negation of
common sense has its genesis at home and
quickly validated by the community that either
practice, condone or ignore the kind of slurs
that dehumanize people for their differences.
Individuals in these settings who do not
challenge the stupidity that their children
begin to overtly react to is in effect endors-
ing it by their silence. Through this process
entire groups of people become worthy of being
taunted, beaten or even killed. It is a process we have honed in our society to a fine
art during times of war. We never kill people,
it is always Krauts, Gooks, VC, Rakies, Li-
meys, Rebs, Yanks, Chinks, Spics, Niggers,
etc.-never real people.

Consider the events which occurred in
Aug. 1992 in Nampa Idaho. Angry neighbors of
Randy Weaver, charged with criminal assault
and abetting in the killing of a deputy U.S.
Marshall, felt that he was justified in breaking the law because war was being waged
against the white sons of Isaac. Weaver, a

member of the Yahweh religious movement considered the federal governments and federal official to be "Baal," the "Edomites," the "Queen of Babylon" and the "one-world beastly government." Collectively, these were, in their minds, at war against the awakening Saxons. In response to this aggression they contended that the tyrants' blood will flow. This was to be accomplished by a group of individuals unified, beginning in 1983, in their opposition to the United States government, which they call Z.O.G. (Zionist Occupation Government), or the "New World Order" for the purpose of advancing their views of 'white' or 'aryan' supremacy or separation. Z.O.G.'s rationale for existing was to provoke and sustain a violent confrontation with federal, state and/or local law enforcement officers or agents in furtherance of their prediction and belief that a 'Great Tribulation' would occur. It was clearly stated by these adherents, "whether we live or whether we die, we will not obey your lawless government."

This conflict had its genesis and reached the national stage with the deeds of Robert J. Mathews, of Metaline Falls, Washington in 1984. Mathews was co-founder and leader of the white supremacist group called the Order, an offshoot of the white supremacist Church of Jesus Christ Christians/Aryan Nations, based in Hayden Lake, Idaho. His notoriety was enhanced when he exchanged gun fire with FBI agents at a Northeast Portland motel in November 1984. It was to be his last hurrah, for he was killed a few weeks later in a shoot out and fire on Whidbey Island, Washington. Religious perception was not the cause of Mathew's death, rather it was the theft and hijacking of armored cars and assorted other criminal acts.

Weaver, a follower of this group's ideology was indicted in December 1990 for selling

sawed-off shot guns to a federal agent. After
his arrest and release on his own recognizance
the following month he retreated to his isolated mountain top cabin. After repeatedly
ignoring warrants he was destined to have a
stand off with the system. The standoff ended
with Weaver's surrender, eleven days after
holding off authorities. In the aftermath of
this action a federal agent, Weaver's wife,
Vicki and son, Samuel were dead.[4]

Tom Metzger does not fit the standard
perception one holds of the red-neck racist.
Born in Indianapolis, Metzger says that he was
not exposed to people of other races until he
joined the U.S. Army. There, he contends, he
began to develop a world view of other cultures and other races. He brags that it took
many years to develop into what he is to day.
He began his journey into racism by involving
himself first in conventional politics, working for Republican Sen. Barry Goldwater's
presidential campaign in 1964. He later joined
and left the John Birch Society because he
believed that he was not free to criticize the
Jews. He then began to campaign for George
Wallace's 1968 American Independent Party
presidential campaign. In 1975, he joined the
Knights of the Ku Klux Klan and became the
grand Dragon, or chief regional officer, of
its southern California branch. He dropped his
association with the Klan in 1982 and founded
the White American Political Association, aka
the White Aryan Resistance. His involvement in
the killing of an Ethiopian immigrant in Portland Oregon in 1968 led to a finding of conspiracy by a jury and resulted in his loss of
a tort suit.

The hatred is occurring even among groups
who are supposed to be protecting us. August
23, 1991 the FBI said that it had disciplined
eight employees for their role in the harassment of a black agent in a case that had come
to symbolize the racial bitterness within the

agency. Two field agents and six managers, including five at the FBI's headquarters comprised the "pack" at the bureau in Chicago. The victim's complaints of death threats and other intimidating acts in the Omaha and Chicago offices of the FBI were sustained in an administrative hearing held by the Justice Department and Equal Employment Opportunity Commission.

A report issued by Special Counsel James G. Kolts, a retired Superior court judge in Los Angeles found a "deeply disturbing" pattern of excessive force and brutality being exercised by the Los Angeles County Sheriff Department. The report detailed the routine abuse and violence perpetrated on the citizens, particularly minorities. Validating the Christopher Commission's finding, Kolts' staff identified 62 officers who were particularly problematic. These were individuals who repetitively used excessive force and had multiple complaints lodged against them. Despite histories of questionable conduct, nearly all of these abusers continued to patrol the streets.

In their analysis of civil lawsuits the county was forced to pay, the investigators found patterns in the originating incidents. Many of the cases involved people mistakenly identified as suspects. Blacks and Hispanics were the most common victims of this abuse. To compound matters, the department's complaint procedures made it difficult for these citizens to file a complaint against a deputy. Those who did file were subjected to harassment by sheriff department officials. In several instances, people who tried to lodge a complaint at the sheriff stations were placed under arrest of fabricated charges. The report said that, in general deputies are usually disciplined more harshly for traffic violation than they are for incidents of brutality. This, despite the fact that the county has had to pay out millions of dollars in settlements.

The Kolt Commission found that over the past decade, sheriff investigators referred 382 cases of "questionable" shootings to the district attorney, but that only one of these cases was prosecuted. The commission also cited acts of misconduct by deputies assigned to the jails, including cross-burnings and severe beatings of inmates.[5]

"They marched, they yelled racial epithets, they stormed the steps of City Hall and blockaded the Brooklyn Bridge, prompting a tense stand off with uniformed police officers. The unruly demonstrators were 10,000 off-duty police officers, protesting a proposed all-civilian review board."[6] "It was a horrible scene," said Detective Robert Rivers head of the Guardian Association, an organization which represents 3,000 black officers in the city police department. Rivers continued by stating: "If it had been a black group, people would have been arrested....The majority of the people there were white police officers. There were no arrests."[7] The head of the NYC Patrolman's Benevolent Association contends that the officers are humiliated and dehumanized when they must justify their actions before an all-civilian board. The group he defended is one in which uniformed officers did little to control their protesting off-duty cohorts, and in some cases reportedly egged them on. This is the same group who yelled racial slurs as they marched. Still they find it reprehensible that there is some concern by segments of the public when they deal with those individuals who were and are the object of their racial slurs and hatred.

This is also the same agency from which two officers beat to death a 25 year old mugging suspect who was unarmed, in Sept 1989. The police said that their actions were justified because he had violently resisted arrest. However, witnesses said that the first two arresting officers, a man and a woman, shouted racial insults at the handcuffed victim while they beat and kicked him in the head and groin. Some witnesses said the beating stopped when other police officers began arriving, but others said the violence continued as regular police and transit officers arrived. Despite being double handcuffed the officers felt that the racial slurs, somehow, would aid them in subduing the suspect. "He was lying on the ground and they kept hitting him", said Marla Jiminez, a fifth floor resident who watched from her window. "It lasted at least 20 to 25 minutes. He kept saying, "Help me, help me, but the police, forget it, they kept hitting him. I felt I should call the police, but this was the police. I wanted to help, but I didn't want to go outside. I was so scared" she said. Miguel Flores, standing approximately 25 feet away from the arresting officers, said: "They were hitting him in the groin. She was beating him in the body while he was doing a job on the head. "Flores said, that when he and other bystanders approached the officers and said, "Stop beating him, you are going to kill him. The male officer held his gun in the air and cursing, warned them to stay back."

At a news conference later that day regarding the incident, the 41st Precinct Assistant Chief John J. Holmes, commander of patrol for the Bronx said, "I don't believe there were any beatings." The radio tapes from transmissions by police cruisers reveals that the police at 5:43 AM reported that they had sighted a running man and begun a foot and car chase; at 5:52 AM they reported that they had a man in custody; at 6:04 am the paramedics pronounced the suspect dead.[8]

Oregon, which is required by law, has one of the best hate crime tracking systems in the U.S. The state' 1991-92 statistics, through September, reported the most incidents in the Northwest region with 317. Washington, whose 1992 legislative session failed to pass a

hate-crime reporting law and characterized
over the past few years by a few homophobic
members who have held the bill hostage because
they did not want passage of the language that
would included sexual orientation in the
states' definition of hate crime, reported the
second highest number of incidents, 180. Idaho
reported 35, Montana 12 and Wyoming none. The
incidents ranged from swastikas painted on
churches to racially motivated homicide. Among
the reports were: (1) chemical lawn killer
used to burn swastikas, crosses and profani-
ties into the lawn of 13 out of 15 homes in a
Nampa Idaho neighborhood, where a black family
move in 1992; (2) a group of white supremacist
skin heads celebrating Adolf Hitler's birthday
at a Portland, Oregon park attacked and beat
up two black teenagers; and (3) in Federal
Way, Washington, a car load of white high
school students harassed three black students
near a school bus stop.

These events like the above demonstrate
United States' failure to deal with the conditions which gives rise to inequities and injustices. These failures have manifested them
selves to create climates of fear, lawlessness
and alienation. The failures which gave rise
to the inequalities and injustices are exacerbated by a political system which is unwilling
or unable to deal with acute problems ranging
from the national debt-to the collapse of the
infrastructures--to the loss of well paying
jobs. The political leadership has responded
to these problems by making scapegoats of
black criminals, Japanese, welfare recipients,
immigrants and other vulnerable groups. This
political leadership appears to be incompetent, selfish and dishonest. Scapegoating, to
them, seems to be preferable to dealing with
real problems, which none of these groups
caused, like the looting of the savings and
loan institutions and the Iran-Contra corrup-
tion. This political behavior has perpetuated

a disproportionate amount of economic and social violence on people of color. However, these problems have not been confined solely to these people. In the United States there are growing number of poor whites and increasing number of middle-class whites who are slipping in to poverty. These are people, like the blacks, who are experiencing a growing sense of betrayal by the system and an increase in anger as a response. Rather than responding to the government's ineptness the newly minted poor whites begin to behave like the government-scapegoat. Consider the response to political ineptness in Dubuque. Dubuque, Iowa has approximately 57,000 white citizens, exactly 331 black citizens and a very serious racial problem. The city also has an image of the 1930's much like the one depicted in the movie, Mississippi Burning. The chairman of the city's Human Right Commission contends that the town's very whiteness breeds racism. The citizens evidently do not know that their behavior is racism, because they blame their actions on the lack of opportunities to associate with different people and cultures. The chair of the committee contends that this is a form of rationalization to conceal the real problem which is covert and knowing deep seated racism to keep Dubuque as white as it can possibly be.

Dubuque is primarily a blue-collar town in which thousands are employed in the meat packaging and construction industries at John Deere and FDL Foods. It also has an unemployment rate which fluctuates between 8-10 percent fort the past three years. In this environment, the Iowa Dept of Employment Services approved a "constructive integration plan" to attract 20 minority families a year for five years. A city council member, who approved the integration plan was voted out of office because of his stand on the issue.

Some of the white citizens perceived the

plan to be a threat to their jobs and a form of reverse discrimination. One individual, interviewed on television, expressed his concern that the influx of blacks would increase the crime rate. This individual neglected to say, during the interview, that not only was he a convicted felon but was a one-man crime wave and currently on parole. Tom McDermott, a laid off construction worker said;

> They want to bring 100 minorities in, and we just don't have the jobs for these people. If they want to move here, they should move here on their own.

However, his real sentiments were revealed when he further stated:

> It would be nice for them not to even come in. Dubuque been pretty much a white town, and it's been a nice little town. They are going to bring them in, and there's going to be all sorts of problems.

He and a few cohorts, in response to this impending threat, want to form a chapter of the National Association for the Advancement of White People. This would be a subsidiary of the organization founded by David Duke, "ex Klan man turned humanistic and egalitarian." One of the cohorts, age 18, said:

> Everyone is trying to say we're racist, we're just trying to stick up for the whites. It seems like every time you stick up for the whites, you get called a racist. It's not fair, you know? You get hammered.

Two years prior to the utterance of these profound and insightful statements at age sixteen, this youth placed a burning cross carved with the words "KKK Lives" next to a black couple's garage. He was convicted for the crime and spent 17 months in prison.[9]

In September 1989, police in International Falls, Minnesota, located in the bastion of conservatism, had to use tear gas to turn back demonstrators who burned temporary housing and overturned cars in a protest of the hiring of non-union construction labor at a Boise Cascade paper mill. Starting from a wildcat strike in July, sporadic violence continued to escalate until September 10 which, at that time, culminated in an estimated $250,000 arson. In this town of 6,500 people, 400 'law abiding' building trade activists had seemingly gone berserk. They were anti-right to work individuals and racists. They were angry because they felt that the company was hiring black and Hispanics primarily. Therefore, these individuals and their nonunion status justified their being targets and the protestors' anger. Labor protestors from North Dakota, Wisconsin and Michigan came to International Falls to join the fray. A spokesman for Boise Cascade said that the governor, Perpich, was playing politics and siding with labor by putting National Guardsmen on alert rather than sending them immediately to quell the disorder.

May 2, 1991, a riot broke out, within vision of the Nation's capitol, in Mount Pleasant. This is east of the National Zoo where a Hispanic man was shot in the chest by a female police officer. Her reaction, she contends, was justified because he attacked her with a knife after she tried to arrest him for disorderly conduct. Two nights later, following fires, looting, tear gas and an imposed 7 pm to 5 am curfew the violence subsided. The Sunday night shooting was only the catalyst, according to the Hispanic residents, or the spark which touched off a volatile situation. A situation characterized by high unemployment rates, lack of political empowerment, fears of deportations, and a lack of a sense of respect by the government agents. It is also a situation exacerbated many times when people are beaten while being arrested. These things conspired to make these people feel that others thought that they were not human beings.

This major incident occurred in the same city where Oliver North defended remarks he made at a Republican roast for former Congressman Stan Parris of Virginia. North insisted fellow roasters Charles Black and Virginia State Senator Warren E. Barry had not made racist statements, nor had he slurred gays when he quipped that he could not get a call through to the White House until he lisped, "Ekscuthe Me." Black had said President Clinton wanted to include the words "Don we now our gay apparels" in the Marine Corp hymn. Barry had referred to Clinton's "fag-in-the fox hole" policy, and joked that Parris' dispute with black District of Columbia officials over a bridge had led Parris to call it "the longest bridge in the world because it connects Virginia with Africa." Not surprising, when brought to their attentions, none of these three saw anything offensive in their remarks.[10]

Price Food Market is an anomaly in South Central Los Angeles. It is unique because it is a Korean owned enterprise where most of the 40 employees are black and Hispanic. It is also unique because it is one of the few minority owned businesses in this area which is prospering. The store grosses $100,000 a week in sales. Nine blocks from Price Foods is Jr. Liquor Market. It too was once a thriving business. However, now it sits virtually empty, its shutters tightly drawn, the shelves

half empty and boxes crammed with all of the
amenities plus liquor which are essential to
run a food dispensing business. Anger is the
reason for the variance in these two enterprises. Anger directed at the violence which
has escalated between black customers and
Korean merchants. It also includes a tremen-
dous amount of tension which reached the
boiling point and erupted over a simple delinquent behavior. These problems boiled over
first at Jr.'s when Sam Park killed a black
man alleged to had robbed him and when grocer
Soon Da Ju shot 15 year old Latasha Harlins
inside the Du family store over the accusation
that she shoplifted a $1.79 bottle of orange
juice. To add fuel to the fire, Superior Court
Judge Joyce Harlin handed down a sentence
deemed to be too lenient by stunned black
individuals. These individuals vowed to take
their protests to the street, this time in
front of Harlin's home. Both the Jr. Market
and The Du family store are in the throes of
black boycotts.

David Kim, Southern California president
of the National Korean American Grocers Association, acknowledges that some Korean grocers
are suspicious of blacks and don't hire their
employees from the community. As a result,
blacks resent the Koreans because they perceive this to be a form of exploitation. In
addition, they feel that they are being pushed
further down the economic ladder by yet another immigrant group. The situation will remain
volatile because the Los Angeles' Korean
population has grown from 9,000 over the past
twenty years to 250,000. The demographics for
this portion of the city reveals that Hispanics now account for 40 percent of the 3.5
million and remain a slight majority in South
Central; blacks comprise 14 percent; and
Asians 9 percent.[11]

The abortion battle in Congress has been
fought around the margins since the Supreme

Court gave constitutional protection to
abortion in the **Roe vs. Wade** decision in 1973.
Operation Rescue, cultish in its structures
and behavior, engenders a dangerous and zealous intolerance of religious and ideological
diversity. They trample on every notion of
democracy and freedom of conscience and religion. They are a group so convinced of the
rightness of their cause that they defy court
orders with out fear of being held in contempt. They have been guilty of harassment,
assault, criminal trespassing, arson and
murder. These behaviors have all been condoned
by them as being the work of God. In carrying
out his work and plan they deem themselves to
be good stewards.

This sense of good stewardship lead to
the killing of a doctor in Pensacola, Florida
in 1993. The doctor, David Gunn, had been sen-
tenced to death because he performed abort-
ions. He was shot several times in the back as
he got out of his car at the Women's Medical
Service clinic he opened one month earlier.
The anti-abortion protester who allegedly
killed Gunn was Michael F. Griffin. Despite
the sniper attack John Burt, the organizer of
the protest and affiliated with Rescue America
a Houston based anti-abortion group that
organizes clinic blockage, said "I think all
life is sacred, and Dr. Gunn and Michael
Griffin are both victims of abortion."[12] According to the National abortion Federation,
which represents 200 clinics, incidents of
reported vandalism more than doubled from
1992, and cases of arson rose from four in
1990 to 12 in 1992. In March, 1992, The fire
bombing of a clinic in Corpus Christi, Texas,
razed a building and caused $1 million dollars
in damage. In California, four health care
workers were hospitalized with respiratory
problems after butyric acid was sprayed into
eight clinics Riverside and San Diego coun-
ties.

Many of the anti-abortionist deplore the violence on the physical structures and the death of the doctor. Don Treshman and Randall Terry, head of the equally militant Operation Rescue contend, in response to the murder, that it is wrong to take life. Every life has a value, even if it's an abortionist. While they saw Gunn's death as being unfortunate, they contended that quite a number of babies' lives will be saved.

The tactics used by the anti-abortionist had shifted, prior to the murder, from block-ading clinics to harassment of clinic patients and workers. Florida had become the training ground for the newest techniques by preparing 22 future anti-abortion leaders, after spending twelve weeks in an Operation Rescue National "boot camp" to learn the latest tactics. Part of their training was to learn how to identify and trace license plates of women seeking abortion. They would then mail a letter to the woman, and if she returned to the clinic they would isolate and personalize her by calling out her name and imploring her not to kill her baby.

At The Ladies Center abortion clinic in Pensacola, anti-abortionists purchased the adjoining property on which to stage protests and to erect a bronze statue titled *Holy Innocents Plot*. Pickets have been stationed outside of the homes of current and former employees of the clinics. The employees are followed to and from work. They have received bomb and death threats. They have jammed the lines at the clinics. Their goal is to humili-ate, embarrass, shame and expose them accord-ing to Randall Terry.

Among many descriptions this is terror-ism. They encourage violence, intimidation, death threats and constant harassment. These are not First Amendment issues but violations of the law. This is fanaticism punctuated by the stalking and the placing of Gunn's face,

address and telephone number on a wanted
poster. This violence and terrorism was deliberate, personal and political. Terry contended
that while Gunn's death was unfortunate one
has to recognize that this doctor was a mass
murderer. "Praise God," said a protester after
hearing that Gunn was murdered, "one of the
(baby) killers is dead!"

How did we get to this conflict over one
person's freedom of speech and another's
freedom of choice? There has always been a
disrespect for our fellowman. However, the
genesis of the recent conflicts, and the
profundity of hate crimes can be traced to the
Reagan-Bush administrations which made it
tolerable for radical anti-abortion groups
like Operation Rescue and Rescue America were
coddled. During this era they were pandered to
as though they were honorable protesters
engaged in a civil right struggle which was
premised on deep moral questions.

Resolution 3379 was adopted by the United
Nations General Assembly in 1975 on the basis
that the national liberation movement of the
Jewish people was "a form of racism and racial
discrimination." This pernicious lie acted
upon November 10 makes this one of the darkest
days in the history of the United Nations. The
result of this enactment licensed anti-Semi-
tism and granted it a new international re-
spectability. It provided the justification in
Britain to bar Jewish students from several
campuses. It also served as the "authority"
which enable Stokely Carmichael to tell an
audience at the University of Maryland: "The
only good Zionist is a dead Zionist."

These all represent hate crimes or behavior predicated on hate. There are a combination of factors responsible for their occurrences. It is too simplistic to blame the
increasing racial tensions on a faltering
economy, the growth of white supremacist
activities, and moral idealogues. These two

groups do, in fact, have a responsibility for extending this form of behavior but they can not be credited for creating the climate for its existence.

The climate was created by a right reactionary centralized government. A government which contains all of the elements of a fascist regime premised on an alliance between the wealthy whites, white land owners, and angry white middle and lower-classes. This alliance had its genesis in the Reagan administration. It occurred because these people began to question the legitimacy of the government, the welfare state, and its past attempts to solve the problems of society. These enhanced the Republican party because they drew converts as people loss both status and sources of generating wealth. The Republican party was perceived to hold hope for the failing economic conditions they confronted and it seemingly held promises for enhancing security. This security would be at the erosion of individual freedoms. These individuals, some converted democrats, joined in this republicanism which simultaneously romanticized elements of the past and surely an unfettered future. It was a convoluted republicanism which promised a return to greatness, a condition which never ever existed, through the use of rugged individualism. This promise of a glorious future required both individual sacrifice, temporarily, and harshness. Harshness which gave rise to a silent majority, Falwell, and a form of class warfare. To control the recalcitrant new laws had to be formulated and enacted to control the crime. The welfare statutes had to be altered to fight the poor. None of it was realized as history reveals. The new order led to more crime, hatred and violence in the streets.

When forced to confront a legacy of the new republicanism even President Bush invoked Rodney King words and intoned: "Please, we can

get along here, I mean we're all stuck here
for a while. Let's try to work it out. Let's
try to beat it. Let's try to work it out."
This was the same individual who vilified
Willie Horton during his quest for the presidency. The official response by the administration was to blame the Los Angeles riots and
all of the other social ills on the liberal
social programs of President Johnson and
Carter. However, when the presidential spokes-
man, Marlin Fitzwater was asked to provide
examples, he responded limply by saying,"I
don't have a list with me."[13]

The searing clarity of racism as a cause
was not vivid to Fitzwater, the administrations and a large portion of the public. The
riots could not, they reasoned, be a response
to the elements of hatred and fascism growing
unabated in this country. Nor could they
correlate the genesis of the riot, in part to
this new Fascism manifested in the "sanctioned" attack by a "blue gang" on individuals
like Rodney King. Sanctioned because it
occurred at the behest of a sympathetic white
public. Given the fascist condition, the
attack and the other behaviors, are consistent
with the existing social exchange mechanism.

NOTES

1. Robert Ezra Park, *Race and Culture*.
(New York: Free Press, 1950): 231-5.
2. Mark S. Hamm, *American Skinheads: The
Criminology and Control of Hate Crime*.
(Praeger: Westport, Conn., 1983).
3. Ibid.
4. Richard Cockle, "Vicki Weaver's Letter." *The Oregonian*. Aug. 26, 1992, B-12.
5. Hector Tobar and Kenneth Reich, "Report Finds Pattern of Brutality in Los Angeles
Sheriff's Deputies." *LA Times-Washington Post*

Service. May, 8, 1992. A-13.

   6. Virginia Byrne, "NYC Police Protest All-Civilian Review Board. *The Associate Press*," Sept. 9, 1992, B-4.

   7. Ibid.

   8. See: Howard W. French, "Witnesses Say Police Beat Suspect To Death." *New York Times News Service*, Sept. 16, 1989, B-12.

   9. Greg Smith, "Racist Incidents Plague Dubuque." *The Associated Press*, April 22, 1992, A-19.

   10. Sarah Overstreet, *Newspaper Enterprise Association,* November 22, 1991, B-14.

   11. James Anderson, "Racial Tensions Reach Crescendo in South LA." *The Associated Press*, May 11, 1992 A-12.

   12. *New York Times News Service*, August 7, 1992, A-5.

   13. Clarence Page, "Media-Hyped Extremes Drown Out Moderate Voices." *Chicago Tribune*, May 14, 1992, B-16.

11

Employee Theft

In neo-classical theory, there is an assumption that the equilibrium wage paid reflects the worker's productivity.[1] In reality, there are other implicit-wage frameworks that reveals that (1) an increase in the productivity of on-the-job leisure distorts the equilibrium wage by lowering productivity. This behavior results in the raising of the employee's wage; and (2) any increase in employee compensation attributed to theft is a net increase in the employees' implicit wage frame work. There is a suggestion that employees are aware of this behavior. Given these additional premises, there is the contention that, in reality, workers will sort themselves among employers for a number of reasons, and two of these depend on their taste for leisure on the job and the employer's ability to provide it and theft opportunities. These do not negate the traditional notion that to become an employee, there has to be an acceptance of the prevailing marginal wage, which is based on other supply and demand elements.

However, the trade-off between prevailing marginal wages, supply and demand, shirking and employee theft is not that clear cut when potential employees confront less than ideal market conditions. These market conditions occur when there is excess labor when compared to available jobs. During this time maximize profits by being competitive to other similar firms in the market. This competitive objective must be juxtaposed against the employee's expectation of what constitutes legitimate equilibrium wage, wage growth, and other individualistic pertinent factors; when there is incongruence between perceptions, conflict arises regarding the implicit and explicit contract. To analyze this conflict between the explicit and implicit notions, I will modified a labor "shirking" model. The modification operationalizes these and other factors in a reciprocal causal structure. An analysis of this type is consistent with existing theories and provides more accurate specification of the causal processes involved in the etiology of a criminal behavior, more specifically, employee theft. The combined models, "shirking" model and reciprocal causal structure model, make it possible to structure a nonrecursive model to analyze the relationship between employee theft and differential market conditions.

Although some theorist question the financial motivation for the behavior, there are those who believe that employee theft can be a result of under-payment or perceived wage inequity. These perceptions concerning the etiology of the behavior can be subsumed under one of four theoretical perspectives. They are social control, strain, social learning, or integrative models, which combine elements of two or more of these theories into a more general body of explanatory principles. These four approaches stress different causal factors as being responsible for criminal involvement. The modified model used here to explain employee theft asserts that various social factors are the etiology for this behavior and that these causes are embedded in a reciprocal causal structure.

Although the majority of criminological researchers understand that while the reciprocal relationship X → Y is not appropriate, and X ⇄ Y is appropriate to explain all forms of behavior, relatively little research has been conducted to investigate the reciprocal causal influences of on employee theft or on any other criminal behavior. The literature suggests that there are three causal relationships that should not a priori be assumed to be unidirectional and one of these is a person's behavior and beliefs, for example, beliefs about perceived conventional morality and employee theft.

MODEL ASSUMPTION

A. Theft can increase the employees' marginal utility.

B. Employee theft is a function of the differential in perception between the employee's position in the pay structure and their perception of real worth.

C. Employee theft is an instrumental increase in the wage rate that has not been bargained or legislated.

D. Employee theft serves a eufunction (benefit) in the market because it addresses issues of differential productivity by operationalizing wage differentials that are unexplained by conventional notions of human capital, demographics, and other variables.

E. Employee theft is perceived to be a form of spoilage, a normal aspect of business.

F. The issue of employee theft is unilaterally determined and is the sole important decision the employee can make in regard to compensation.

ECONOMIC ASSUMPTIONS

Wages are deemed to be an economic variable and as such it can be examined in terms of utility maximization. A model based on utility maximization would enable one to predict, with certain fine tuning, when involvement in licit activities will be chosen over illicit activities. Individuals will, and do, choose illicit activities despite the knowledge that there are uncertainties and higher costs entailed that are associated with apprehension. Utility theory posits that as the returns one receives from illicit activities increases, licit activities become less attractive. Thus, to hypothesize that the wage rate in an homogenous market and employee theft are reciprocally related and when treated explicitly, the hypothesis is consistent with a number of etiological theories regarding criminal behavior.

An employee is an employee because he has signed an explicit agreement covering conditions and wages. The explicit arrangement assumes a profit or utility maximization. This arrangement will remain constant only if the parties to the agreement are interested in keeping it. The agreement will cease or be modified by one of the parties if it is no longer deemed to be in their short term interest. We can also hypothesize that agreements of this type will only be sustained if a surplus is generated for the two parties. Initially, this surplus occurs when one or both of the principals to the agreement are either receiving higher wages than all other alternatives present, and the other principal is not earning less. A surplus is needed because both parties to the agreement are potential cheaters. Notice that in this model, it is not solely the negotiated wage that determines the surplus to the employee, but in addition it is also the excess that the

employee can obtain in wages over the negotiated amount.

The Shirking model suggests that this
increase in wage surplus, can be obtained by
"shirking" on the job. This simply is the
increasing of leisure time relative to the
stipulated working time. Theoretically, if the
stipulated working time is eight hours at
$4.50 per hour and the shirking time is four
hours, not only is this behavior a form of
employee theft but an increase in wage that
exceeds the equilibrium. In this example, the
wage is no longer $4.50 per hour, but rather
$9.00. Therefore, the equilibrium wage is not
factored by the wage that was equal to the
wage received by the last marginal worker, but
rather it now must be perceived to be an
efficiency wage. These same conditions and
results apply to employee theft.

When either of these conditions occur,
the employer is confronted with options (1)
increase monitoring of the workers; (2) increase the severity of sanctions that are
imposed on those who are detected engaging in
illicit efficiency wage generating; (3) control the loss to employee theft by increasing
the wage. Neo-classical theory suggests that
each approach will be applied to impact the
behavior to the point where the marginal
reduction in theft costs equals the marginal
cost of the approach.

SPECIFICATION OF THE MODEL

I will denote the equilibrium wage at T_i
by E^{Ti}:

where:

E_{ti} = equilibrium wage
T_1 = Time one

As stated, the employee will honor this implicit arrangement as long as there is a perceived benefit. When the employee no longer perceives the arrangement as being beneficial, there will be an adjustment in the equilibrium wage. This is denoted by:

$$E^{Tz} = f(Ap_i \pm E^{Ti})$$

where:

E^{Tz} = illicit wage that is different from the negotiated explicit level.

Ap_i = apprehension probability

The model becomes reciprocal because it suggests a relationship between wages (W) and employee-theft (E). At the point of contract inception wage and employee theft are construed to exogenous variables with a zero-order correlation. However, they become endogenous factors when the issue of surplus arises. Therefore, the specified reciprocal model is:

$$u_{wt2} = f(E^{Ti} + b_1 \pm A^{pi} \pm S_z + a_1 + E)$$

where:

u = utility
S_z = Surplus - a surrogate variable for the restructured unilateral wage structures:

a_1 = coefficient for equilibrium
b_1 = coefficient for employee theft

The model specification becomes:

A $E_{Tz} = f(E^{Ti} + b_1 + A_{pi} + S_z)$

where:

A_1 E_{Tz} = differential employee theft
B_1 E_{Tz} = $f(E^{Ti}+b_1+S_z+A_i)$
C_1 E_{Tz} = $f(A_{pi}+E^{Ti})$

Employee theft can be accounted for in terms of instantaneous and lagged effects. This behavior has an instantaneous effect because it can impact the ability of an individual to continue to draw the wage at T_1. It has a lagged effect because apprehension could, among other negative reactions, impact the probability of future employment in the homogeneous market. The model does not, but could, control for factors, such as, race, social status, and gender. However, this model, as specified, is better suited to assess subjects from blue-collar backgrounds.

Employee theft is contingent on employment. In the (A) equation, the relationship between these two variables are linear. Despite this linear relationship, there are parameters (b_1) or coefficients that are determined by the employer regarding how much theft is too much. This (b_1) is factored into the wage equation during the negotiated explicit contract. It is also a factor when there is a question regarding the equilibrium wage. This coefficient also becomes more critical in employment areas that are less sensitive or responsive to market conditions. These employment areas are enterprises that employ stock clerks, delivery boys, fast food workers. There are objective reasons, which focus around economic considerations, as to why an individual normally would not consider this type of job but subsequently fills one. One of these reasons is that these types of jobs offer fairly regular employment despite the low wage. Another seemingly important advantage, but no less important, is that they frequently offer an opportunity for stealing while on the job.

Equation (A) makes the assumption that employers frequently expect or anticipate employee theft and adjust the wage accordingly. By adjusting the wage, it is hypothesized that the employer has established (b_1). For example, the equilibrium wage may be negotiated as $4.50 per hour. However, the employer anticipating employee theft and attempting to accommodate it while maintaining a surplus arrives at this contrived figure rather than pay the fair wage which, hypothetically may be $5.50 an hour.[2] This condition is discussed in Liebow's book. He reported that: "Tonk's employer frequently anticipates employee stealing and adjusts the wage accordingly the employer explained why he was paying Tonk $35 for a 55-60 workweek. These men will steal, he said. Although he keeps close watch on Tonk, he estimates that Tonk steals from $35 to $40 a week. The employer said he did not mind this because Tonk is worth that much to the business."[3]

When this condition occurs (A_{pz}) is relevant only when the employer feels that he is paying the absolute equilibrium wage and there is no consideration being made for (b_1). The employer, given this condition, increases surveillance measures to enhance the probability of apprehending the thief because the employer cannot through the wage structure withstand this type of loss. Therefore, (S_z) becomes a negative factor in E^{T2} because the probability of committing theft successfully to increase the equilibrium wage diminishes because there has been a factoring out of (b_1) and an increase in (Ap). Linearly, given this configuration, theft cannot logically be attributed to the factors in equation (c).

However, given the condition that Liebow describes, and the one I hypothesize as being indicative of homogeneous markets employing blue-collar workers at minimum wage, the coefficients (a_1) must be combined with (b_1) in order for the underpaid employee to receive a surplus (s_i). This wage arrangement, according to Liebow and the model, has a built-in provision for stealing in the wage structure which is satisfactory to both parties. When this theft occurs, it is clear that the employee has maximized wage utility (U_{WT2}), but why would this arrangement be satisfactory to the employer? This occurs in two ways: first, the employer's (s_z) was maximized due to the ability to obtain the employee below equilibrium rate; finally, as long as the employee can avoid paying the efficiency wage, surplus continues to accrue, and finally the expenditures used to detect theft are minimized because there is a tacit under standing that some will be tolerated to the marginal level (b_1). When ($a_1 - b_1 + E^{T1}$) are combined the employer enjoys more surplus than he would if he had operationalized (E^T).

There is another theft condition in regard to reciprocity that must be considered. That is the situation in which the employee theft is based on the employer's perception of what the employee can get away with despite his best efforts to prevent it. To address this condition, model (B) was operationalized because it addresses differential employee theft. This is a condition when the behavior occurs despite (E^{T1}) and (Ap_2). When this condition is present, the theft that attributes to the surplus varies because of the stringency of (Ap_2). Theoretically, the wage at (T_2) will never be less than the wage at (T_1), but the possibility of (S) becomes extremely variable. The net results may be, if not caught and fired, a manipulation of the equilibrium rate. This represents a trade-off for the employer, but his choices are limited because they range only between paying an efficiency wage or the marginal cost of increasing the (Ap).

Given this range, the employer knowingly provides the conditions that provide the employee with the motivation to steal the unpaid value of his labor.

APPLICATION OF THE MODEL

This model is applied to a union bakery in Portland, Oregon, which supplied a major grocery chain with its wholesale products to be retailed. This bakery, like others, contained a provision in the negotiated union contract that permitted employees to take as much bread, but only bread, as they wanted at the end of their shift. This perk was in fact a wage increase because a loaf of bread had a retail value of $1.02 and, at that time, a production cost of .03. Since the employee's wages and the bakery's expenses were subsumed as the $.03, the accrued benefit to the employee was a wage increase of $1.02 (X) as many loaves that they could take. The initial objective was for the employee to take no more than he or his immediate family could consume. At that time, the contract minimum was $9.02. Assuming that this type of employee only took (4) four loaves, this would amount to $9.59 or an increase of $.57 per hour. Therefore, one loaf of bread would create a surplus of $1.02 to the employee and if not taken, a $.99 surplus to the employer. This contract provision was beneficial to both the employer and employee. However, this practice was stopped after the contract expired because the employer discovered that over the life of the labor contract the employees were exceeding the personal or family consumption rule of 1-4 loaves daily. Instead, some were engaging in outright theft of 15-75 loaves, which were used to establish bread routes among their friends and acquaintances.

During the duration of the contract, this excess removal of bread was both observed and tolerated by the employer until the next negotiating period. Because it was tolerated, one has to assume that it was also satisfactory to the employer. Why did this behavior appear to be satisfactory between the employee and employer? We need to analyze this in terms of (S_i). Prior to settlement of the contract, there was a concession made on the wage issue. Management included the bread "freebie" because in actuality it represented a wage increase of $1.02 to the employee and a cost to the employer of $.03. Therefore, if an employee only took four loaves a day as intended, the employee's hourly wage was increased from $9.02 per hour to $9.53 per hour. This would be true because the employee would not, assuming that he ate bread, have to purchase it at the market price. Therefore, the employee's surplus for the week would be $20.40 (assuming he took four loaves everyday) or $1,060.80 for the year. These figures adjusted the marginal or equilibrium wage to a level that represented the efficiency wage.

However, these employees realized shortly after ratification of the contract that they could not possibly consume 4 loaves a day, nor could the two males who took seventy-five loaves daily. These individuals responded to this largesse by establishing bread routes. Their enterprises were in direct competition with the bakery and they quickly became problematic. It was estimated that the average daily bread theft was fifteen loaves. The employees sold the bread on their daily routes for $.85 a loaf or $.17 cheaper than the bakery's retail outlets. This theft netted the employee who sold 15 loaves $12.75 per day or an hourly wage increase of $1.59; those two who retailed 75 loaves earned an additional $63.75 per day or $7.94 per hour for their

theft. These net earnings were an increase in
the (S). The (S_i) varied due to the number of
loaves the employee chose to take. A guessti-
mate by the bakery concluded that this theft
exceeded $800,000 in retail sales for that
contract year. However, the actual production
loss was only $24,000. This $24,000 loss was
actually an increase in (S) for the employer
because it was less than paying the efficiency
wages to the employees. Nevertheless, this
provision was negotiated out of the next union
contract.

This form of employee theft can be
explained by using Model C. Although theft
parameters were not initially established,
they were later operationalized by management
without increasing (Ap). These same conditions
have occurred in slaughter houses, butcher
shops and other homogeneous blue-collar settings.

What occurred after this perk was negotiated out? Model C best explains this condition. There was no (b_i), but an increase in
(Ap) occurred and E^{Tz} varied, which is to say
that the differential employer theft did not
occur with the tacit approval of the employer.
When this condition occurred, the estimated
losses in retail sales declined to $40,000 or
$1,200 in production loss. This increase in
the employer's (S) was accomplished by relocating the employees' parking lot further from
the loading dock and placing the foreman at
that specific entrance during shift changes.
While it did not eliminate employee theft
completely, it seriously impacted it. The
employer's (S) resulted in a wage reduction to
the equilibrium level for the employee, and it
seriously impacted them because the surplus
was being used to enjoy externalities that the
equilibrium wage could not support. In addition, except in that seemingly rare case when
they were successful in stealing it, employees

had to purchase their own bread.

Why did this condition persist at this bakery and at other homogeneous blue collar enterprises? The answer is relatively simple and straightforward. Unless the loss involves cash, the actual loss is only a fraction of the retail, usual reported, loss. These losses, which are in essence bad employer decisions with regard to hiring employees and an unwillingness to secure the job environment against theft can be passed on to the public as losses attributable to shoplifting. When attributed to shoplifting rather than employee theft, the cost can justifiably be recovered by adjusting the retail cost of their merchandise. The amount they can recover is limited only by the amount of merchandise that they can retail. In addition, they have conditioned the public consumer to believe that the largest part of a plant or business shrinkage is attributable to shoplifting.

Employee theft can not readily be passed on to the consumer. Instead the loss is most often adjusted by an insurance company under their bonding capacity, assuming that the employee was bonded. When this occurs, an actual loss, not imagined retailed one, must be declared and this loss is subjected to the employees' disavowal. The actual loss a bonding company will pay constitutes, in most cases, replacement or production loss, rather than retail cost. Therefore, it is not in the employer's interest to pursue employee thefts through their insurance company because the compensation would be considerably less. In addition, a claim always runs the risk of generating higher premiums for the employer, which is an increase in the marginal cost of conducting business. This is one of the reasons that bonding companies do not routinely bond-blue collar enterprises.

CONCLUSION

The model and explanation indicate support for the reciprocal effects predicted by the theoretical specifications. The theoretical model can be adjusted to account for the reciprocal relationship between employee theft and the major demographic subgroups for example, juveniles, races, and the sexes. It can also be modified to count for the time decay factor. That is to say, when the model is applied, one would expect a differential in the time at which an employee negates the explicit contract on wages and begins to engage in theft. An adjustment to the model would look like:

$$E^{T2} = f \; (R \pm \; , \; S_x \pm \; , \; E_T \; , \; E^{TI} \pm \; , \; b_1 \pm \; , \; Ap_i \pm \; S_i \; , \; \pm \; a_1)$$

Where:

R_i = race
S_i = sex
E_t = employment type

One can hypothesize that the effect parameters (b_1 and a_1) may vary by social background, but that they will not by employment type (E_s). Consistent with this model are traditional theories that suggest a significant relationship between social factors and crime. The control thesis used suggests that these perspectives are too limiting when utilized from a unidirectional approach. However, it would be more correct to demonstrate that criminal involvement and a variety of other process variables mutually influence one another over time. This shirking model disaggregate these variables and to discuss the correlation between them and their reciprocal causal components.

NOTES

1. In neoclassical economics the equilibrium wage is equal to the revenue received by the product produced by the last (i.e., marginal) worker. Employers who attempt to pay below the equilibrium wage will be unable to attract and retain qualified workers. Sorenson and Kalleberg suggest that the quality of work from the worker tends toward equilibrium in the sense that the quantity supplied by the worker is corrected to the quantity demanded by the employer. In this situation, all workers of a given quality are paid the equilibrium wage. This equilibrium wage will shift only if there are disturbances in the market, such as, the demand or supply curve shifts.

This presupposes that employees paid more than their value can be interchanged with others who are willing to work at the rate for wages which represent equal marginal productivity. Therefore, workers of a given skill level can be treated as a commodity whose price (i.e., wage) is determined by the market forces of supply and demand. This study utilized both the neo-classic paradigm and the interactionalist approach to discuss a form of deviant behavior, employee theft. Rational explanations offered for the behavior must include the actor's definition of the phenomenon, aspects of the work place mechanisms and the incentives and inducements which leads to the behavior.

The research model to be used for testing is specified as being:

$$E^{T2} = f \ (R \ \pm, \ S_x \ \pm, \ E_T, \ E^{T1} \ \pm \ b_i \ \pm, \ A_{pi} \ \pm \ S_i, \ \pm \ a_i)$$

2. This figure may represent the A_{Pi} and b_1 costs based on the employer's experience.

    3. Elliott Liebow, *Tally's Corner* (Boston, Mass.: Little Brown and Co., 1967): 37.

12

Economic Decline and Males

Plant shutdowns, mass furloughs, and restructuring of the labor force have become a serious problem in the United States since the
mid-1970's.[1] Between 1975 and 1981, approximately 13,000 plants employing 2.2 million
workers applied for Trade Adjustment assistance. These figures do not include termina-
tions due to restructuring of firms or industries. Harrison and Bluestone state that, for
the period 1969-1976, 31 million workers were
terminated and 4.4 million jobs were relocated
annually.

However, more recent U.S. Dept. of Labor
data suggest that these figures are conservative. A 1984 study conducted by the Department
of Labor contends that 11.5 million workers,
age 20 and over, had lost jobs because of
plant closures or layoffs. These changes
reflect the economic downturn experienced by
some communities, a condition which not only
affects the workers but their families as
well.[2] Although many communities in the United
States have developed strategies for coping
with unemployment, the problems of most workers remain because many of these communities
lack alternatives for similar employment.

Between 1978 and 1987, one of the hardest

hit states in the country was Oregon. The construction industry in the state lost more than 14,000 jobs. Others that experienced high job declines were the railroad which experienced a decline from 7,500 jobs in 1978 to 3,900 in 1987 or forty eight percent decrease, related manufacturing, down from 17,100 to 12,100 or a thirty percent decrease, and employment in the lumber and forest product industries, down to 67,400 from 81,400 or an eighteen percent decline.

In 1978, the state's per capita income was $8,296, approximately $160 above the national average. By 1986, per capita income was $13,217 or at ninety one percent of the national average. A regional comparison of per capita income shows that Oregon's 1978 figure was $519 less than Washington's and $1,115 less than California's. By 1986, the per capita income for Oregon, when compared to these two states, was $1,681 and $3,576 less respectively.

One can assess how job loss further affected the state by looking at its impact on the individual. For example, the Oregon worker, who twelve years ago earned $10.50 an hour at a union shop, earns about $7 an hour today in a non-union shop. If the 1976 wages were adjusted for inflation as reflected by the Consumer Price Index, earnings in 1986 would have been $20 an hour.

More importantly for this analysis is the conclusion that suggests that the personal consequences of job loss varied with the capacity of the individual to cope with this new condition. Coping, an adaptation process, must be juxtaposed with a general pattern of behavior that individuals have exhibited in response to economic decline. These behaviors include negative concept and dissatisfaction with self;[3] psychological disorders, for example, depression,[4] aggression, and an increase in suicide rates;[5] and reaction formation.

This study hypothesizes that the impact on individual workers and their social world is exacerbated by the prolonged duration of the inability to find employment at a comparable rate, and that this factor ushers in pathologies or social strains. To assess the hypothesis, Black working class male heads of house holds were analyzed to identify behavior changes and their correlation to economic decline or a plant closure.

UNIT OF ANALYSIS

Black working class households,[6] which are more likely to be nuclear in structure and dependent on dual incomes, were selected because their emotional, psychological, social, and biological stability and lifestyle were hypothesized to be the ones that would be threatened if job loss or reduction occurred.[7] Historically, it has been these families who have been the most vulnerable when there is a job interruption due to employee reduction or plant closure.[8] The behavior of concern has been attributed to ingrained pathologies in the black family as a unit. However, it is suggested here that the behavioral changes that occur are due to the inability of the male to find comparable employment.[9] Although there have been attempts to limit behavioral changes due to unanticipated hardships by providing compensation in the form of state provided unemployment insurance, job retraining programs, and public assistance, these males are still at risk. Therefore, this paper assesses the risk, and contends that, despite efforts taken by the state or plant, the Black male head of household families will rapidly disintegrate, both functionally and structurally[10] due to a feeling of anomie and the differential access to the job market.

That is to say, the deterioration of the

familial structure is predicated on the conditions of unemployment and a sense of economic
deprivation. When these conditions occur,
there is an increase in dissatisfaction,
reduced social interaction, and incremental
destruction of the once integrated closely
knit patterns of life both inside and out of
the plant.[11] This condition is referred to as
the general state of anomie.

While the issue of differential impact of
plant closures is important, the research base
for assessing it as being a function giving
rise to the etiology of specific individual
criminal behavior, a pathology, (see figure
12.1) is relatively limited.[12]

Figure 12.1
Interactive Process of Support, Situational
Change and Behavior

```
+-----------------------------------------------------+
|                                                     |
|                     Model                           |
|                                                     |
|      Development/                                    |
|      maintenance                                    |
|      of support               Non-                  |
|      system      Equilibrium  Assaultive            |
|                               behavior              |
|                                                     |
|      Individual                                     |
|      personal                 Situational           |
|      world        Anomie      change                |
|                                                     |
|      Nondevelopment                                 |
|      Assaultive                                     |
|      behavior                                       |
|                                                     |
|           Disequilibrium          maintenance       |
|                                       of            |
|                                   support           |
|                                   system            |
|                                                     |
+-----------------------------------------------------+
```

A number of predisposing factors or processes of varying degrees of testability and theoretical value have been suggested in the explanation of assaultive and criminal behavior. In order to discuss an associative relationship between economic decline and assaultive behavior, there has to be an identifiable conditional or interactive process. This means that the probability of the criterion or dependent variable, assaultive behavior, should be higher when the individual is exposed to the stipulated situation, economic change, and other precipitating factor(s) than to those not similarly exposed. The analysis is then conducted using simple or complex interactive effects of the situation and the dependent variable.

However, this model assumes a precipitating factor, alcohol use, which differentially impacts the perception of economic decline and behavior. In a practical sense, assaultive behavior can vary independently due to the above stated factors. Nevertheless, this analytical model conceptualizes assaultive behavior as being the differentiated association between economic decline, level of frustration, aggression, and alcohol use.[13]

The measurement of alcohol use is the quantifying of drinking patterns prior to, during, and after plant closure. This is operationalized by using the stated changes in the individual's personal world hypothesis. The hypothesis makes the assumption that when working class males confront economic decline, a sense of anomie and drifting occurs. It is further suggested that when an individual confronts this anomic state, which is exemplified by heightened frustration, this results in a greater use of alcohol in the attempt to cope.

The relationship between the variables, increased alcohol consumption, plant closures, and assaultive behavior can then be analyzed to determine if changes in the pattern of alcohol use is, in fact, a precipitating factor for assaultive behavior. When this is done, the direct measurement of changes in alcohol use in the schemata cannot, then, be logically considered to be spurious.

The model specification then becomes:

$$As = f(Pc_i, (+)Rc_i, (+)C_i, (+)A_i, (+)E_i)$$

Where:

As	=	Assaultive behavior
Pc	=	Plant closure
Rc	=	Reduction in critical support
C	=	Individual coping ability
A	=	Change in alcohol consumption pattern
E	=	Time unemployed

Therefore, the model and equation specify a stipulated behavior, the interactive and the conditional variables. Anomie is a surrogate variable that represents the stipulated changes in the individual's world. This conditional variable will be used to assess the linear relationship between alcohol consumption pattern and assaultive behavior. This relationship is specified as

As_i	=	$f(A_i)$ where:
As_i	=	Assaultive behavior
A_i	=	anomie state

Assaultive behavior in this study has been limited in definition to the carrying out of violent physical contact toward a family member. Operationalized as a dependent variable, assaultive behavior is specifically perceived to be the result of displaced aggression. This displacement is hypothesized to result from changes in the workers routine work world. The model attempts to assess this behavior in terms of anomie by analyzing the changes in Rc, C, and A. It is further hypothesized that changes in these areas determines both the magnitude and expression of aggression, and that these changes result in assaultive behavior. To accomplish this, it needs to be determined whether the aggression was a response to Rc, C, and A; or whether this was routine prior behavior. It is also critically important to determine if the behavior occurred or did not occur due to an increase in (C) while (Rc) decreased, or can the behavior be attributed to a reduction in both Rc, and C. It is further hypothesized that (Rc) and (C), without intervening factors, normally helps to control or influence this and other behaviors toward those who are both spatially close and significant.

ALCOHOL THE INTERACTIVE VARIABLE

The literature suggests, and it is hypothesized, that the explanation for the increased use of alcohol by Black-working class males who are confronting or experiencing plant closure can be attributed to a feeling or sense of powerlessness. Some of the literature has connected this increased use to both underemployed and unemployed Black males. Therefore, the research data suggests that differential alcohol use can be viewed as a mechanism utilized by those individuals to escape from and/or cope with the emotional strains and stresses that occur as a result of the loss of meaningful employment.

Operationally, any change in the routine consumption pattern can be correlated to crises confronting these individuals. The alcohol use impact of differential consumption patterns in terms of potential structural and functional changes within and on the family structure has not previously been assessed.

However, changes that can have impacts range
from dissolution, withdrawal, and isolation,
to increased physical aggression.

When examining the contextual aspect of
alcohol consumption, the framework context is
used to refer to a range of social environmental variables that include ethnic and cultural
identity and peer and family factors associated with alcohol consuming behavior. Stark and
Flitcraft contend that the male control over
women, not female pathology, environmental
"stress," or family history leads to battering. They also report that the differences in
battering by class, race, and employment
status are small.[14] Currently, alcohol use is
perceived not to be the cause of violence, but
rather it permits its occurrence by lowering
restraints against its expression. When applied to assaultive behavior, it must be
considered concomitantly with other factors
like personality disorders, sexual inequality,
stress, and the feeling of compulsive masculinity. While these factors are all relevant
specifications of variables like sexual inequality and the feeling of compulsive masculinity, they would not be straightforward and
become problematic when attempts are made to
operationalize them. Therefore, this variable
becomes more or less linear when coherently
specified.

ANOMIE

Congruence theories tend to suggest that
the social system is in a state of harmony
that ushers in a sense of homeostasis for the
individual where there exists realistic means
for achieving the prescribed internalized
success goals. Homeostasis is distorted when
stress and strain occur thus creating a feeling of alienation to which the individual must
respond. One response would be for the indi-

vidual to engage in noncongruent behavior. (It is non-congruent because it is not part of past anomic response). This behavior can take many forms, one of them being criminal assaultive behavior. It has been theorized that when individuals confront disequilibrium, they typically express concerns regarding their homeostatic state, one which ideally would be similar to that which they previously experienced.

Consistent with control or bonding theories, when a person is occupying a state of disequilibrium, he/she may feel free to commit deviant, criminal, or delinquent acts due to the severance of routine ties to the conventual order. While, conceptually, assaultive behavior can occur due to the presence of anomie, an operationalization can reveal that stress and strains, caused by a precipitating factor like plant closure, can seriously impact the supporting bonds that enhance the individual's ability to cope which in turn can either mitigate or exacerbate this condition.

In this anomic state, the individual must make a decision regarding behavior despite the supporting bonds. The behavior can be determined by the individual's coping ability and can be oriented to conventional expectations or directed toward an adjustment of those expectations. The adjustment behavior may be at dissonance from past behavior. In these instances, the individual confronts a conflict between moral obligations to behave as the social order mandates or to respond to the dysfunction by resorting to any behavior, even illegitimate, to attain goals and to theorize the dysfunction. Illegitimate adaptation modes are chosen when the individual perceives that the options to utilize legitimate means to achieve the socially desired state are closed. When this occurs, Merton contends, the individual confronts realistic behavioral options: innovation, ritualism, retreatism, and/or rebellion. The conflict can only be brought to closure by eliminating the precipitating factors of stress and frustration. Theoretically, this would eliminate aggression, and this would be achieved through re-employment that would usher in a sense of normalcy and a reduction or the extinguishing of the frustration and stress.

SUPPORT

Until recently, the typical offender-victim pattern of spousal assault was one in which the male was the aggressor and the female the victim. However, Steinmetz and Fields and Kirschner suggest that this depiction is incorrect. They base this on a reverse pattern where the wife as the perpetrator occurs with more frequency and severity. It is believed to be under reported due to the fear of humiliation. Langly and Levy estimate that 12 million men are physically abused in this fashion at some point in their marriage.

ABILITY TO COPE

Curiously, the Black males in this study confronted an anomic condition individually, but societally their new status, unemployment, is the expected state. Because of this broader expectation, hostility, alienation, and disillusionment are the normative expectations rather than determination to regain the prior level of legitimacy. It is postulated, and historically self-correct, that when Black males confront this alienation and disillusionment, they engage in self-destructive behavior, for example, hostility, aggression, crime, and alcohol and drug abuse. Therefore, these individuals confront a triple bind, that which the broader society is conditioned to expect as normative in regard to status and behavior, that which has become normative to the individual and the dissonance he now confronts, and that which his family expects.

The status of Black males in the United States is not monolithic due to the differential socioeconomic factors and commitment to family responsibilities. Therefore, it would not be fruitful to operationalize variables or concepts like masculine identity or the research on batterers to explain the differential occurrence of assaultive behavior by Black males.[15]

RE-EMPLOYMENT

Because this study was conducted during a time of structural unemployment, factors that are indicative of this state for example, age, sex, race or minority status, educational attainment, work experience, and sectoral (specific industries) conditions, must be operationalized to discuss the time span that covers unemployment. Because the nature of the job was not correlated to educational attainment or to females, these two variables out of the equation were factored. In addition to the included variables, the difference between re-employment chances, seasonal variations that result in layoffs, reduced job demands, and the total amount of regional or national unemployment must be factored in to properly identify and discuss structural unemployment.[16]

THE SAMPLE

Three hundred (N=300) working-class white and Black male workers in Portland, Oregon, were culled from a broader population of 430 men who confronted the possibility, and subsequently experienced, permanent furlough from a steel processing foundry in 1983 and 1984.

These individuals had been employed by the firm, with sporadic short term layoffs, for periods ranging from 1 to 25 years. This firm enjoyed a fine reputation for safety concerns, fair wages, an integrated work force, and a good management-employment relationship. Confronting a loss of market share, a restructuring of the labor force was mandated.

One hundred and thirty of these workers were eliminated from the sample population (N= 300) because they failed to meet the research design criteria that were: 1) employed at the firm for at least five years; 2) had a nuclear family; 3) spouse was employed; and 4) was between the ages of 25 and 55. In addition, sixteen White males who met the criteria were eliminated to provide an equal numbers subpopulation.

The individuals in the White subpopulation were used to: 1) establish performance levels on the criterion variables and to assess differences between the two populations; and 2) to hypothesize regarding the differential perceptions of the causation of anomia that resulted in assaultive behavior. These individuals (N=300) were assessed initially in 1983 and again in 1984. This time frame enabled sampling one year prior to furlough and one year after.[17]

METHODOLOGY

To assess the relationship between the hypothesized and assaultive behavior, the respondents' answers to a self-report questionnaire were analyzed. The self-report was comprised of thirty "Have you ever" types of items that could be scaled in a Likert-type fashion, except for the nominal scaling of the concerned that was reported.

CONSTRUCTION OF THE INSTRUMENTS

The economic variable, for example, was comprised of five elements (items): (1) perception of change to be experienced in relative economic position as a result of closure (t1); (2) perception of change experienced in relative economic position as a result of closure (t2); (3) perception of change in realms of disposable income (t1); (4) reported change in disposable income attributed to plant closure (t2); and (5) reported change in relative economic position attributed to plant closure (t2). These dimensions were measured in Likert fashion with scores ranging from 1 - 9. When these elements were regressed on economic position (high, medium, and low), the regression betas and (t) values indicated that, collectively, they were good predictors of the dependent variable. Therefore, they were all retained to form this instrument.

The critical support variable was comprised of eight elements (questions) that were asked at (t_1 and t_2): (1) my family is the cause of most of my frustration; (2) I get along fairly well with the other people in my home; (3) I have pushed, punched, or slapped my wife or children because I lost control due to my drinking; (4) I have never pushed, punched, or slapped my wife or children; (5) my wife is too bossy about how I spend my time; (6) my wife does not concern herself with how I spend my time; (7) my family has been real supportive lately; (9) I punched, pushed or slapped my wife because of excessive nagging; (10) my layoff has put strains on the marriage that were not there before; and (11) my layoff will not put strains on my marriage if I'm unemployed for three to six months. Statistically significant elements, measured similarly, were grouped to comprise this instrumental variable.

The coping ability variable is comprised

of 27 elements that provide insight into role options, mental state, and personal mechanisms for coping. The variable was operationalized and discussed in a framework of "masculine identity" which most likely would be invoked in a given situation.[18] Although, these identity elements involve self-worth and are tied to the societal structure, norms, and values, when dysfunction occurs in or between the individual's personal and social world, the potential for anomie and assaultive behavior are established.

Therefore:

$$As_{t1} = f(E_f, (+) \ Au_f, (+) \ Cs_f, (+) \ Ca_f, (+) \ Wm, \ Bm)$$

$$As_{T2} = f(E_f, (+) \ Au_f, (+) \ Cs_f, (+) \ Ca_f, (+) \ Wm, \ Bm)$$

Where:

t	=	time
1	=	initial survey
2	=	follow up survey
E	=	employment condition
Au	=	alcohol use
Cs	=	critical support
As	=	assaultive behavior
Ca	=	coping ability
Wm	=	white males
Bm	=	black males

Structurally, the individual's perception of defined aggression and frustration levels are contrived from reflective measurement. This technique represents the classical approach to measuring an underlying concept. This is done by reversing the assumed causal direction between scale items and the measurement error $S= f(F)$ and $F= f(A)$. The reflective responses make the assumption that they form the variable without measurable error. The reflective measurement is appropriate for measuring concepts like socioeconomic status, attitude, and preference.[19]

FINDINGS

The results indicate that Black workers confronting plant closure, in general, experience a more profound change in their social and personal world than do their White cohorts. The most indicative measure of this change is the difference in the reported unmanageable frustration levels experienced by Black males when compared to White males. The statistical finding reveal a significant differences between the populations when undergoing or experiencing a one year change in economic conditions due to plant closure. This change contrasts significantly to the reporting of unmanageable frustration by both groups prior to closure. At (t_1) reported manageable frustration was statistically insignificant.

An analysis of the statistical data revealed a reported increase in family directed aggression of fifty six percent for Blacks and fifteen percent for Whites from (T_1) to (T_2). The data also reveal that this aggressive behavior resulted in a thirty eight increase of assaultive behavior in Black families compared to a decrease of 8.4 percent for White ones. At this point, we can conclude that frustration resulting from plant closure directed aggression toward the family or $A_i = f(E_i + Ca_i)$.

However, when the dependent variables, **E (+) Au (+) Cs (+)** (changes in the economic condition, alcohol use, critical support and coping ability), were regressed on assaultive behavior, the results reveal that, for individuals between the ages of 26-45, they are fairly good predictors of black family directed assaultive behavior. The data also showed

the change over time that can be attributed to
coping and critical support.

DISCUSSION

The findings suggest that plant closure
resulted in profound changes in these Black
workers' individual, personal world and were
manifested in their ability to cope at (T2),
they perceived a commensurate decline in
critical support from their spouse. This conclusion is drawn from those individuals who
reported an increase in unmanaged frustration.
It was further validated when the data was
manipulated to directly measured the correlation between frustration and economic conditions.

In the attempt to cope, those individuals
in the sample who drank increased their consumption. Those respondents who used alcohol
had a history of frequenting those taverns and
private clubs near the plant in small groups
at least once a week, generally immediately
after their shift on Friday. This drinking was
perceived to be instrumental because it both
developed and strengthened relationships, provided an informal forum for discussing job-
related tasks and associations; it was also
just for fun, and it provided a time and a
place for the adjusting of attitudes to get
into the right frame of mind prior to becoming
involved in direct family interaction.

In the absence of this important socialization time, other processes were tentatively
tried and implemented, one of which was the
continual cohort meetings (minus those who no
longer were affected because they had found
other jobs) to discuss the job condition(s),
concomitant uncertainties, and their general
frustrations.[20] This process was characterized
by its shortness in duration (each session
grew shorter in actual time spent talking and

drinking, as well as the frequency of their occurrence), loss of affinity (as the unemployed men became re-employed, they lost their sense of belonging to the group), loss of group heterogeneity (the group was rapidly becoming homogenized primarily by unemployed Black individuals), and a rise and change in the drinking which was a partial response to the changing group's dynamics and composition with a passage of time. In general, after six months those individuals changed the loci of this drinking from this setting to their home or to the homes of close cohorts.

It was suggested and confirmed, when the remaining group members were asked, that this increase and change in drinking by the Blacks males was associated with a commensurate increase in the feelings of helplessness, the sense of a loss of affinity to significant others, a perception of a reduction in critical support from their spouse, and an escalation in the feelings of frustration. The data from this study suggest that the longer an individual was subjected to this condition, the greater the probability of family-directed aggressive behavior occurring. This finding was surprising, but an analysis of the subpopulations enables me to hypothesize that given these conditions family directed aggressive behavior appears to be culturally neutral. This is because the findings suggest that it is also applicable to White working-class males who are forced to endure the same conditions, processes, and duration. This is a significant finding that will be discussed later.

An analysis of $(Au = f(A_i, +Ec_i, +F_i, +Ag_i)$, reveals that individuals between the ages of 26-45 are most at risk. There are many factors that may account for the increased alcohol consumption by Black males in this age range, in addition to those already discussed. One reason may be that these men are firmly en-

trenched in their financial commitments, and
therefore any alterations or disruptions would
be catastrophic and trigger nonroutine responses. While financial commitments during
this age range are a cultural phenomena, they
are exacerbated by the inability of the Black
individual to find comparable re-employment.
To suggest why there is a contrast in this
behavior by those individuals in the 20-25 age
group, probably these individuals have more
flexibility when it comes to being rehired,
and they can do it at less than their pre-
furlough wages because they do not confront
similar fiscal strictures. In addition, starting new life styles is easier because they are
not generally as entrenched or committed to
one as those in the 26-45 group. This can be
interpreted to mean that they confront less
stress in regard to any life style alteration.
The population data reveal that the 30-45 age
group also had more potentially explosive
elements, given the probability of having both
a spouse and children at home.

A large percentage of the group reported
that they were causal drinkers at **(T1)**, but
employment furlough appeared to have exacerbated the problem at **(T2)**. This behavior was
uniform for both subpopulations. How ever, the
Black males appeared to have been differentially impacted due to their prolonged period
of unemployment, as compared to their White
cohorts, therefore, $A_{ui} = f(P_c E_i)$.

Interestingly, Black males in the 46-55
age group had fewer children at home and reported less of an increase in drinking after
plant closure. This could be attributed to the
probability that they had more flexibility in
being capable of making a situational economic
adjustment. Perhaps this can be attributed to
them being less extended financially, the presence of a nest egg to handle adverse economic
situations, and a past history of having to
cope with economic downturns. Despite this,

these individuals also reported a slight reduction in critical support behavior (T1) and
(T2). Interestingly, but not surprisingly,
these males had the lowest success rate in
finding comparable re-employment within the
study period, but they were the most likely to
have spouses who were employed.

Although the findings suggest that for
Black males ages 26-45, any prolonged change
in the economic condition would be an important factor in the occurrence of family-directed assaultive behavior, there still exists
the need to relate alcohol usage to the behavior. Perhaps it is not the consumption, but an
alteration in the pattern where the alcohol is
consumed, that becomes a criminogenic factor.
This change in consumption site to the home
can be correlated to the decline in critical
support, because the behavior maybe disrup-
tive, or be perceived to be so, to the home.
With this disruption, the spouse may feel a
necessity to focus on this anomic state to the
inurement of focusing primarily on the male's
feelings of frustration, stress, etc. In addition, this change in locus suggests a further
minimization of the individual's ability to
cope.[21]

The data suggest that the differences in
performances on these variables can be attributed to the differential ability to be re-
employed shortly after experiencing economic
disruption.[22] This is borne out by the fact
that sixty-six percent of the White males were
able to find re-employment within the first
six months, and ninety-four percent did so by
the end of the first year. These figures compare to 20.3 percent and 59.2 percent respectively for Black males. This ability to become
quickly re-employed seemed to minimize the
probability of becoming involved in family-
directed assaultive behavior if it had not
previously occurred. For example, 3.9 percent
of the Black males who were re-employed within

the first sixth months reported family-directed assaultive behavior, compared to 24.3 percent for those who were unemployed longer than
six months. This compares to .34 percent and
.17 percent respectively for White males.

Despite the fact that this population of
males were homogeneous, it appears that the
significant heterogeneous factor, race, effected the time factor regarding the ability
to find comparable re-employment. This factor
then is correlated to frustration and aggression that is manifested in an increase of
assaultive behavior. There fore, the time
factor must be considered when one assesses
the efficacy of the operational model.

Although the change in alcohol consumption patterns and locus were significant factors when frustration, aggression, and family-
directed assaultive behavior were analyzed for
Black males ranging in age from 26-45, the F-
statistic was greater when the alcohol use
variable was regressed on assaultive behavior
than any of the other variables. This suggests, since all of the variables were significant except aggression level, that alcohol,
despite the change in consumption pattern or
locus, had both an additive and an instrumental effect that tended to exacerbate an already bad condition for the 26-45 age group.

Interestingly, alcohol use was not a
significant factor in the occurrence of assaultive behavior for Black males, age 26-30.
This may be attributed to their ability to
more readily become re-employed than those in
the 26-45 age group. Not surprisingly, all of
the factors in the model become insignificant
after age 45. The economic factor, a correlate
of assaultive behavior, is interesting because
it depicts the hopelessness confronted by
Black males that is manifested in the change
of relative economic position. This study reveals that 42.2 percent of the black males
experienced this decline in relative economic

position compared to 4.9 percent of the White males after being unemployed for a period exceeding one year. Black males, age 46 and over, suffered the most in this area. Only 38 percent of the males reported an ability to become re-employed at a wage level that maintained their pre-shutdown economic position. This compares to 72.2 percent for the White males.

Causal explanations, not descriptions, of Black or White male assaultive behavior are few to be found. How ever, it can simply be stated that Black males, like all abusers, abuse family members because they can and they deem that the situation warrants it. In addition, there are rewards for being abusive, for example, getting someone to stop doing something, inflicting pain as a revenge, controlling behavior, and to have power. All of these rewards are evident in any social setting. How ever, there are differences in the cost-benefit utility equation regarding assaultive behavior. For example, when one assaults one's spouse or children, the cost is relatively low when compared to assaulting a person not part of the family configuration.

However, to attribute black male assaultive behavior to peculiar indigenous factors confronted by these individuals is to engage in an exchange form of theoretical thinking that enables the abuser to account for the etiology of the behavior in terms of the behavior. For example, offenders may use explanations like: I feel terrible about it, but she made me so mad; I could not help myself because I drank too much; I am angry because I can not find work because of the racists, etc. One problem with using exchange theory to provide an etiology for the behavior concerns the tautology of explanation: I assaulted her because she made me mad; I was mad, so I assaulted her.

This method of accounting for the behav-

ior is nonsensical. Gelles stated, "It is
generally agreed now that, at most, ten percent of wife abuse and child abuse cases are
attributable to mental illness and character
or, in other words, to "kind of people."[23]
These are individuals who are characterized by
their inability to control aggression. The
other ninety percent of the abusers defy
clinical classification as suffering from
individual aberrations. They are not different, psychologically, from other people.

Past explanations for assaultive and
other forms of criminality by and against the
black family and its differential members have
serious flaws because they are premised on
either the exchange theory or one of two perspectives cultural deviant or cultural variant. In the cultural deviant perspective, researchers contend that members of Black families do differ from those in White families.
These differences are perceived as being
deviant, therefore the Black family, as an
entity, by logical extension is pathological.
The basis for the pathology results from the
deviation from the middle-class values and
norms that are used to describe that which is
normative. The deviations are perceived to be
dysfunctions. Another logical extension means
that all Black families are dysfunctional
because they are not White and do not share
the same norms, life style, and values. This,
of course, is the popular explanation for the
deterioration of the fabric that comprises the
Black society. The cultural variant perspective acknowledges that the Black culture is
different, but not necessarily aberrant or
pathological. Variations in the family are
recognized and explained in terms of structure
and functioning. Cultural variant analysis
acknowledges that Black family patterns, like
any other, are adaptive to environmental demands.[24]

If assaultive behavior is assessed in

terms of cultural equivalent theory, one makes the assumption that there are no cultural differences in White and Black families. The differentials that appear in functioning should be attributed to social class distinctions. That is to say, if racism was not used as a criterion variable to assess both the structure and function, and the economic factors were held constant, Black and White families would be structured and function similarly around homogeneous or differentiated social class norms. In other words, a difference could not be discerned between White and Black families as we analyze those families capable of transcending the class strata.

Consistent with social disorganization and lower-class based theories, the Black family has been perceived as the fundamental element for the condition and perpetuation of a subculture that includes violence. These theoretical perceptions have been used to account for all criminality including family-directed assaultive behavior. However, these are flawed in an important manner, because they imply that criminality exists within the family structure, which serves to prescribe violent conduct and that is passed on from one generation to the next. There is a contention that this perspective has validity that can be traced to the "machismo syndrome." This contention suggests that there is a relationship between assertions of masculinity and mother-dominated homes.[25] The mother-dominated home factor would be more compelling etiologically if this was a phenomenon that occurred solely among Blacks. However, census data reveal that approximately 40 percent of all families in the United States are headed by a single parent, the majority of these are females. In addition, Billingsley, Hill, and McAdoo argue against the notion of the universality of a Black matriarchy in the United States. Another problem arises when the Black family is used as the focal point for the subculture of violence. It should be remembered that due to variations in the socioeconomic characteristics of a subculture, all members do not share the same values, beliefs, and behaviors. Because every member in a subculture is not equally subjected to these values, beliefs, and behaviors, the theoretical paradigms based on subculture become suspect.

The life-styles of Black families are heterogeneous in terms of geographical location, structure, values, and social status. Therefore, one would expect differential responses to the environmental stimuli these family structures have to confront. The Black workers in Portland, Oregon, by all accounts, were functioning well within their social order with a knowledge of the vagarities they confronted in the labor market prior to and during their dislocation. An analysis of the variables at (T1) that assessed these vagarities cannot logically be directly correlated to their increase in family-directed assaultive behavior. However, reassessment at T2 suggests that these vagarities played a significant role in the protracted unemployment, and an increase in alcohol consumption, frustration, aggression, and pathologies in the family structure and in the unemployed worker. These led to the onset of assaultive behavior after the first six months. However, this conclusion becomes speculative and is not consistent when we analyze the differentiated performances by age groups.

The presence of alcohol is a criminogenic factor usually present in family violence. It should be noted that the drinker need not be an alcoholic or a problem drinker to engage in assaultive behavior toward the family. The majority of the workers in this study did not fall into either one of these categories. They all described themselves as being light or moderate drinkers. It is hypothesized that because the Black and White subjects had an artificial "extended family net work" comprised of coworkers this served to mitigate against family directed assault.[26] When drinking was confined primarily to this network, consumption was not problematic. When this network, comprised of significant others, was in transition or closed, the mechanism for frustration release was no longer an option. Therefore, the frustration had to be vented in the friends network or in the family home.

Given the homogeneity of characteristics that all these men shared, it would be incorrect to account for the increase in assaultive behavior by Black males in terms of cultural baggage, that is, character flaws or pathologies within the family structure. Rather, it would be more appropriate to account for the changes in their behavioral pattern in terms of it being one form of adaptation among many broad cultural adaptation choices. More specifically, the behavior can be explained as follows: when there are dysfunctions in the environment and there exists a lack of legitimate methods to circumvent or handle them, then family-directed abusive behavior can be initiated or escalate. This explanation is consistent with the rationale used to account for the increase in White violence or assaultive behavior against Blacks during periods of economic downturns.

CONCLUSION

Merton was correct when he postulated that when a dysfunction occurs, a state of anomia sets in. In this normless state, individuals grope to maintain vestiges of the pre-anomic state. One of the findings that is ambivalent is the instrumental drinking. It appears to have a positive component in that

it functioned to maintain social ties. However-
er, it also increased frustration the more
chronic the unemployment experience.

The change in instrumental behavior and
loci became problematic to the family and may
attributed to the changes in the level of
critical support and the general ability to
cope with a fundamental change in the individual's personal world. These changes, to paraphrase Cohen and Felson, bring potential
offenders and victims together in a nonroutine
manner and contribute to the occurrences of
family-directed assaultive behavior.

It is difficult to generalize these findings to existing studies because they are
generally analyses of the macro, aggregate,
effects of race on economic well-being after
closure, success of transferring employees,
retraining, and community impact. It also
differs from studies that analyze criminal
behavior from an assumption that the social
institutions pluralistically provide the
stimuli, for example, racism or sexism, and
that individual responses are predictable.

NOTES

1. This study reports the findings of
research conducted on the relationship between
changes in the economic structure and increased opportunities for occurrence of assaultive behavior by Black working- class
males. Theoretically, when a severe disruption
in a spatial and temporal structure of routine
activities occurs, it is hypothesized that the
quantity of non routine behavior will increase. This study was presented in a modified
form at a symposium at the Urban and Public
Affairs Conference in Albuquerque, New Mexico,
March, 1988. Revised editions were presented
in a colloquiums at Indiana State University

and Purdue University October, 1992.

2. J. P. Sordius, P. Jarle, and L. A. Ferman, "Plant Closings and Economic Dislocation," *The W. E. Upjohn Institute for Employment Research*, (Kalamazoo, 1981).

3. M. Aiken, L. A. Ferman, and H. L. Sheppard, *Economic Failure, Alienation* (University of Michigan Press, 1968).

4. See S. V. Kasl, S. Cobb, and S. W. Brooks, "Changes in Serum Uric Acid and Cholesterol Levels in Men Undergoing Job Loss," *Journal of the American Medical Assoc.* CCVI (Nov. 1968): 1500-1507; and S. V. Kasl and S. Cobb, "Blood Pressure Changes in Men Undergoing Job Loss," *Psychosomatic Medicine* XXXII (Jan.-Feb. 1970): 19 - 38.

5. A. F. Henry and J. F. Short, *Suicide and Homicide: Some Economic, Sociological and Psychological Aspects of Aggression* (Glencoe, Ill.: The Free Press, 1954); see also D. S. Thomas, *Social Aspects of the Business Cycle* (London: Routledge, 1925).

6. The author realizes that the nuclear family is too limited in characterizing the Black-working class family because it fails to acknowledge families headed by single working class males and females. For more see E. Smith, "The Black Family," *Humboldt Journal of Social Relations* 14, (1987), 281-305.

7. See C. V. Willie, *A New Look at Black Families* 2 ed. (Bayside, N.Y.: General Hall, 1981). Willie points out that the well-being of these families is dependent on these dual incomes.

8. J. M. Lewis and J. G. Looney, *The Long Struggle: Well Functioning Working Class Black Families* (New York: Brunner/Mazel, 1982). Lewis and Looney suggest that there may be a critical level below which it is difficult to maintain the family structure; and W. J. Gorde "Family Disorganization" in R. K. Merton and R. A. Nisbet, eds., *Contemporary Social Problems* (New York: Harcourt, Brace and World,

Inc., 1961), 479-480; R. L. Taylor, "Black
Youth in Crisis," *Humboldt Journal of Social
Relations* 14 (1987): 108.

9. For discussions on protracted unemployment after shutdown, see J. L. Stern,
"Consequences of Plant Closure," *The Journal
of Human Resources* 7 (1972): 4- 25; R. C.
Wilcock and W. H. Fronke, *Permanent Lay-offs
and Long Term Unemployment* (New York: Free
Press, 1963).

10. See S. S. Mick, "Social and Personal
Costs of Plant Shutdowns," *Industrial Relations* 14, (May, 1965): 203-208. For a more
definitive discussion of economic impact, see
Smith, "The Black Family." 292.

11. For discussions of economic deprivation associated with destruction of integrated, closely knit patterns of life inside and
outside the plant, see A. Slote, *Termination:
The Closing at Baker Plant* (Indianapolis:
Bobbs-Merrill, 1969); L. A. Ferman and M. T.
Aiken, "The Adjustment of Older Workers to Job
Displacement" in A. B. Shostak and W. Gombert,
eds., *Blue Collar World: Studies of the American Worker* (Englewood Cliffs, NJ: Prentice-
Hall, 1964).

12. There are arguments concerning whether a plant closure can be considered as con-
tributing to economic decline because, theoretically, other entities move in to fill the
void. For more see Stern, "Consequences of
Plant Closure," 5, "the expansion of govern-
ment-sponsored manpower programs and the
maintenance of relatively full employment in
the latter part of the last decade any have
created the impression that there is the
opportunity for a rapid and relatively complete recovery from the earning loss suffered
in plant closings."

13. For more on this relationship, see L.
Lenke, *Violent Crime and Alcohol: A Study of
the Developments in Assaultive Crime* (Stock-
holm: Dept. of Criminology, Univ. of Stock-

holm, 1975).

14. E. Stark, and T. Flitcraft, "A Violence Among Intimates: An epidemic logical review." in *Handbook of Family Violence*, ed. V. N. Nasselt, (New York: Plenum Press, 1987).

15. See G. R. Liem and J. H. Liem, "Support and Stress: Some General Issues and Their Applications to the Problems of Unemployment," in *Mental Health and The Economy*, L. A. Fermjan and J. P. Gorduis eds., (Kalamazoo, Mich.: Upjohn Institute for Employment Research, 1979), 347-378.

16. See L. E. Gary and L. Brown eds., *Crime and Its Impact on the Black Community* (Howard University: Washington D.C., 1975), 80-81; Common wisdom identifies these criminogenic factors as being retaliation against White exploitation.

17. This longitudinal study is basically a pre- and post-analysis of how black males' behavior was impacted by plant closure. White males with similar characteristics are analyzed to determent the efficacy of the variables, model, and to draw comparative tentative conclusions.

18. C. N. Alexander, Jr., and J. E., "Problems of Dispositional Inference in Person Perception Research," *Sociometry* 32 (1969), 381-395; G. W. Allport, "Attitudes," in C. Murchison ed., *Handbook of Social Psychology* (Worcester, Mass: Clark University Press, 1935); K. J. Gergen, *The Concept of Self* (New York: Holt, Rinehart and Winston, 1971).

19. The other setting is residential drinking. The residence is most often their own where solitary drinking occurs. These men generally reject public (other than taverns or bars) or street drinking because it would be inconsistent with their most recent behavior. There is also a reluctance for these men to have their significant public aware of their idleness and a lack of affinity with those predisposed to this. See "Consequences of

Alcohol: A Comparison of Social and Solitary Drinking," *Journal of Abnormal Psychology* 83 (1974), 418-425.

20. See David J. Pittman, "Drugs, Addiction, And Crime" in Daniel Glaser, ed., *Handbook of Criminology* (Chicago: Rand McNally, 1974), 209-232; Joan Petersilia, Peter W. Greenwood, and Marvin Lavin, *Criminal Careers of Habitual Felons* (Santa Monica, CA: Rand, 1977); James J. Collins, Jr., *Alcohol Use and Criminal Behavior: An Executive Summary* (Washington, D.C.: U.S. Dept. of Justice, National Institute of Justice, 1981); (ed.) and *Drinking and Crime: Perspectives on the Relationships Between Alcohol Consumption and Criminal Behavior* (New York: Guilford Press, 1981).

21. Harriet P. McAdoo, "Levels of Stress and Support in Black Families," in H. McCubbin, A. E. Cauble, and J. Patterson eds., *Family Stress, Coping and Social Support* (Springfield, Ill.: Charles C. Thomas, 1982).

22. There are suggestions, which to date have been empirically unsubstantiated, that White workers are given preferential treatment in job training, relocation, and benefits. This is based on two premises: (1) Personnel officers perceive White workers to be easier to place in similar positions because the new industry can pick and choose which if any of the furloughed personnel they can use, and they select those that they feel fit in most readily, that fit is based on color and the perception that the most valued furloughed individual possessing the most skills are also White; and (2) Organizations operating in a cutback economy are conscious of public relations and initially make a concerted effort to place all effected employees, but they expends their greatest energy on relocating those who represent the greatest possibility of success to the organization. Those individuals coincidentally are White.

23. Richard J. Gelles, "Family Violence:

What We Know and Can Do," in *Clinical and Research Perspectives on Family Violence* eds. Eli H. Newberg and Richard Bourne (Littleton, Mass.: PSG Publishing Co.,Inc., 1985).

24. Andrew Billingsley, "Family Functioning in the Low Income Black Community" *Social Casework* 50 (1969), 568-72.

25. Walter Miller, W. B. Miller, Hildred Geertz, and H. Cutler, "Aggression in a Boy's Street-Corner Gang," *Psychiatry* 24 (1961), 283-98: M. Wolfgang and F. Ferracuti, *The Subculture of Violence: Toward an Integrated Theory of Criminology* (London: Tavistock, 1976).

26. Joseph T. Howell, *Hard Living on Clay Street,* (Garden City, N.Y.: Doubleday: 1973).

13

Adolescence Decision Process to Enter the Drug Trade

The relationship between law and economics has long been an issue of acute concern to criminologists. Part of this interest is based on the assumption that laws and differential enforcement have given rise to alternative legal arrangements in a economic system and who can participate. To analyze this arrangement one must base their assumptions on theoretical postulates which contends that, 1) differential enforcement of the laws, legal rules, and regulations have an impact on the allocation procedures and 2) that enforcements can be used to analyze economic decisions. It is posited that differential enforcement of the laws, rules, and employer's priorities determine the options that are available to individuals. When these options are unavailable, the individual must make behavioral adaptations or decisions which are contrary to the legitimate employment sector. Adolescents confronting this condition have other problems that are so intense and multifaceted that it is almost impossible to enter the conventional job market. Given these conditions, a large number of minority of adolescents make critical decisions in regard to entering the illicit work world. Work is not available in the

traditional or legal market structure because
this structure is generally receptive only to
adolescents who are or have been functioning
in a prescribed manner. Adolescents who have
dropped out of school, engaged in delinquency,
failed to obtain basic skills, and who are
minorities generally find the traditional
employment market inaccessible. Even though
the legitimate employment market is closed,
these youths require, and demand some form of
"work" to obtain both tangible rewards and
psychic satisfaction.

"Non-traditional" youth finding them
selves temporarily or permanently frozen out
of the labor market are forced to make alternative arrangements. The decision(s) they make
regarding market entry and the type of activity, not unlike adolescents entering the traditional sector, is premised on the desire to
engage in the best possible labor, receive the
best level of renumeration, and the type of
service to be supplied by the individual. This
decision process can be stated in the form of
an equation which can be used to determine the
explicit and implicit advantages of entering a
specific market.

These advantages are expressed as the
prospective or expected $e(U)$, (expected utility), a youth can anticipate from entering a
specific employment sector. Expected utility,
$e(U)$, generally depends on, 1) the size of the
market, 2) probability of penetrating the
market, 3) ability to function in the market,
and 4) the renumeration level from a specific
activity. However, one must factor in a another element, the probability of detection. In
addition, the $e(U)$ for adolescent contemplat-
ing entry into either the traditional or non-
traditional markets depends on the relative
skills of actors successfully participating in
that activity.

The fundamental axiom for employment
activity becomes, if the probability of (U) is

constant, then e*(U)* will vary inversely with
the level of activity given any enterprise.
This basic axiom also pertain to drug trafficking. Therefore, the probability of youths,
unable to penetrate the traditional employment
market and, becoming involved in the non-
traditional employment market is a function of
the elements of *(U)*, or

$$e\,(U) = f\ (M_i, + R_s, + O_a, + A_i, - D_1\ ),$$

Where:

M_i = Market size
R_s = Relative skill(s)
O_a = Other actors' relative skills
A_i = Activity level
D_i = Probability of detection

When we apply the equation to adolescents
who decide to become crack dealers (an illicit
market activity), the calculation of each
potential entrant's marginal utility (U_m) is
assessed in terms of the above factors, and
whether they are (+ or -), to the market.
Markets attractiveness is defined in terms of
the (+) and (-) factors.

Criminological theory suggest that if the
benefits exceed the cost the cost, man being
rational, will choose that activity that is
beneficial. When this is applied to crack
dealing we can identify the cost of market
entrance and conclude that the benefits exceed
the cost. The benefit factor is comprised of
varying elements to determine value. Two of
these elements are positive, the complexity of
market and its size.[1] The larger the market,
the greater the number of participants con-
testing for a portion of the activities. Thee
size of the market determines the variance in
cost for individuals desiring entry into the
market. This variance is competition and it
results in lowering both the cost and absolute

e(U), of each dealer.

This competition, on one hand, is an advantage to the new entrant because it serves to depress entry expense. However, competition in the long run depresses potential profits. The competition exists despite knowledge that the cost of entering the market, in terms of the skills and potential activity level will al-ways be above the minimum level while acquisition of supplies will be at the minimum because the bid price for the commodity (crack), results in the supply always being greater than the demand.

The elasticity of the supply and demand function increases *e(U)* because, as *(m)*, marginal utility, decreases the number of potential entrants declines.[2] When competition becomes too plentiful, a balancing of supply relative to demand occurs thereby stabilizing the retail price. This competition also, on the other hand, effects the number of new entrants because it creates an inelastic market for the specific commodity.

In addition, to the competition in the area, entrant's decisions are contingent on the "crack" quality, reputation of suppliers and dealers, the cost of "crack" to the consumer, and market accessibility. These factors help to determine the dealer's ability to operate quasi-independently from the suppliers.

Supply and demand are directly correlated to *(D)*, probability of detection. Optimal *(D)* is dependent on market location, size of the market relative to other markets, similar activities, for example, sale of heroin, cocaine, etc., and the distance between supply sources, market, and the level of law enforcement activities. *(D)* imposes additional or marginal costs because these will increase as the distance between market and supply increases. This cost is attributed to either the increased risk of detection and/ or the subsequent loss of supply. This cost can be translated into a dollar value that lowers the $e(U)$.

If all crack supplies, (the necessary ingredients used to manufacture the product), can be secured within a finite distance, which does increase D and is close to the market, price will be stabilized of price and there would be in a rise in competition to obtain the supplies.[3] This condition makes it possible for new entrants to enter the field as suppliers of raw materials. This broadens the entrance options regarding activities. Stated differently, the larger the local quantity of crack commodity, the greater the stabilization cost and activity options. Conversely, if the area from which the market input is situated at a location distant from the demand, input will increase the cost of the finished product, but not proportionately, since resources of a given quality are not spatially evenly distributed.

Suppliers and dealers attempt to gain an edge in the market by seeking to and providing "crack" quality over an area of increasing size. In addition, dealers attempt to align themselves with the best suppliers to minimize acquisition costs, stabilize transportation costs, minimize the necessity of searching for sources of input and, to minimize detection.[4]

The exposure to detection and arrest determine probability new entrant's probability of success in the drug field. This probability is a function of the number of actors operating on their differentiated level in the market. Therefore, the elasticity of the $e(U)$ function will increase as the (D) function decreases. Entrants can effect opportunity cost through the choice they make regarding the entry level they elect to operate on and, the differential segment of the drug market chosen for involvement. Opportunity can be controlled by entering on a level commensurate

with skill level which is correlated to the
(D) function.[5] Opportunity cost will rise due
to an increase in the (D) function increases.
Therefore, the patterns of behavior for new
dealers, whether specializing in crack or the
more segmented drug market, can be predicted
in terms of the (D) function which is translated into a cost factor.[6]

Low skilled entrants increase this cost
factor when they seek to maximize the (U)
factor by being a drug generalist. In the
attempt to achieve this they also maximize
(D).[7] This occurs when attempts are made to
expand the market beyond the realms of family
and, close friends, which must be accomplished
to increase market share. When this is attempted the probability of detection is also
increased.

Middle skilled individuals are different
because they attempt to reduce absolute (D)
and other cost factors through product spe-
cialization. This selectivity results, theoretically, in a corresponding reduction in the
(D) factor and an increase in e(U). Higher
skilled individuals specialize further by
handling very few drugs personally.[8] Thereby,
almost eliminating (D) and maximizing e(U).

The relationship between the type of
commodity and income can be demonstrated by
associating the expected value, e(U), and the
reward for entering the market with the dollar
cost encountered. The difference between cash
income and average income represents the
dollar acquisition cost.

Table 13.1
Expected Earnings for Adolescent
Drug Dealers[9]

Drugs	Cash	Average Income	P Income
Any Illicit Drug	$43.73	$38.36	.20
Heroin	76.90	86.37	.10
Cocaine	34.90	44.30	.25
Marijuana	29.38	29.30	.02
Crack	26.15	27.11	.08

The return is the equivalent of the cash income. However, the probability of detection must be factored in. The return must consider legal fees, time out of enterprise due to incarceration, etc. from the activity. The net cost for crack dealers would be, for example, $27.11 X .08 = 24.94. This represents the net profit without considering the total cost for legal fees and loss of income during periods of incarceration. These expected earning schemes can be further analyzed by assessing the constant cost of participating (*cpa*), in the drug trade. While this procedure is not exact, it does acknowledge the marginal costs (additional ones), which are comprised of fixed and other costs that are incurred and imposed upon entering the market. *E(U)*, then becomes a curve which represent the expected values of the earnings and its equivalent to the marginal values of the particular market(s).

If we designate skill levels as ranging

from high to low, and knew the (cpa), we could
plot the dealer's highest potential level of
marginal utility. The intersection of these
two factors identify the highest level of
marginal utility which is translated into
earnings one could expect to receive from
dealing in a specific drug. Low skilled individuals attempting to make their entry into
the "crack" drug market and function on the
medium skill level increase the constant cost,
as previously stipulated, and lower their e(U)
toward zero because, the higher the level of
participation, the higher the (cpa) due to the
level of skills required. CPA, in the drug
trade, is the calculated difference between
the ratio of earning and probability of detection.[10]

    As the drug of choice for users (cocaine,
heroin, etc.), become scarce, user are tempted
to use substitutes products, for example,
crack. To prevent this, dealers are forced to
either dilute their product or increase the
retail price to maintain their profit margin.[11]
When this occurs, many users use a substitute
because crack is an inexpensive product and a
suitable substitute, often retailing for as
little as five dollars a "rock." This expands
the trade to permit entry of new entrants because the market has created demands for their
product. This also increases the opportunity
for e(U), or economic success for new entrants. The more products consumed the broader
the market, and entrance opportunities.[12]
However, the profits will become depressed due
to the collapsing of the margin which make
profits possible.

    The success of an adolescent entering the
"crack" trade is contingent on entrepreneurial
skills which are also the functioning traits
of any entrepreneur in both legal or illegal
enterprises and the ability to avoid detection.[13] Those who succeed have a good eye for
profit, the ability to make deals, and have

also learned how to handle the tension accompanying this line of work. Tension management is primarily accomplished through a rationalization process which provides the pusher with a sense of invulnerability regarding detection and arrests. While all potential entrants have some sense of the risks involved, they are incapable of thoroughly understanding the scope of their vulnerability to detection.[14] This misconception can be attributed to the close ties they have to their initial market which tend to provide them with a misguided sense of safely.[15]

The search for and success in making a profit enables the adolescent to obtain money, the symbols of success and power.[16] These symbols can be measured in terms of fine clothes, ultrafine cars, and respect. The intangible and intangible objects serve as inducements to the trade and help explain why individuals stay committed to this form of employment.[17] Concomitant with these symbols are the perceived levels of competence and connections. These two factors address the dealer's place within the drug hierarchy. Adler discusses this ranking which is used to differentiate further between dealers. This stratification is less crucial on the lower level of pushing because it is necessary to do those things which essential to carve out a market niche. However, the sooner one can specialize, the sooner one is able to garner both the symbols of success and the desired respect in the stratified drug market.[18]

Successful new entrants to the "crack" drug market quickly learn that conspicuous consumption leads to detection and arrest. As one moves up the hierarchy this becomes easier to accomplish because one has the necessary capital to invest in activities that do not draw law enforcement scrutiny. Therefore, success is also dependent on the ability to hide both the illegal activity and the income

generated by it. Middle and higher level
dealers know that the police are aware of
their activities, but not necessarily the
extent. Therefore, they take many precaution-
ary measures to avoid detection and apprehension.[19] The novice feels that the activities
are undetected or will remain undetected,
therefore they fail to take the necessary
steps to prevent the police from connecting
them with the illegal activity.[20]

The successful entrant has a fear of detection, therefore they retail to a limited
number of customers who are usually intimates
and associates who can be relied on.[21] Once
their network is established additional buyers
are reluctantly added. To a large extent this
precaution determines the distribution network
and the e(U). This is not consistent with the
drug dealing and living style depicted by
Abler.[22]

Becoming a "crack" dealer is not a gradu-
al process, nor does it require an adherence
or commitment to the drug world's norms, values, or life style.[23] Unlike the low level
entrants described by some, crack dealers
typically are not recruited from the rank of
regular users, nor are they themselves heavy
users. Instead, the typical crack dealer has
little or no previous involvement in drug use
or trafficking. However, they do enjoy a social relationship with local dealers, usually
gang members, who select outsider for inclusion into the trade.[24]

Once the new entrant experiences a degree
of success they become economically committed.
The economic benefits supersede interactional
dynamics, associated involvements, sect image, role identification, role relationship,
and integration into the group or group's
identification.[25] In addition to economic
commitment, the individual experience an egoistic commitment which provided additional
contentment. The factors comprising e(U) are

multi-dimensional and vary between individuals in terms of importance. Nevertheless, they are consciously factored to help the adolescent determine whether to enter the trade, the stage of entry, type of commodity, and the level of renumeration which can be expected from the employment activity.

NOTES

1. See Erich Goode, *Drugs in American Society* (New York, N. Y.: Knopf, 1972); Edward Preble and John J. Casey, "Taking Care of Business: The Heroin User's Life on The Street," *International Journal of Addiction* 4 (1969):1-24.

2. Ibid.

3. These precursor chemicals are generally lead acetate, phenylacetic acid, and methylamine. These are cooked to make a stimulant known as methamphetamine, also known as "speed" or "crack."

4. See Patricia A. Abler, *Wheeling and Dealing, An Ethnography of An Upper-Level Drug Dealing and Smuggling Community* (New York, N.Y.: Columbia University Press, 1985): 35-36.

5. See Mark H. Moore, *Buy and Bust* Lexington, Mass.: Lexington Press, 1977); Lawrence J. Redlinger "Marketing and Distributing Heroin," *Journal of Psychedelic Drugs* 7 1983 331-353.

6. The opportunity cost is also increased or decreased by the threats to profits. These threats are normally factors such as: waiting time, entertaining customers and, suppliers, drug consumption, transportation, accommodation, meals, etc. Abler (1985), relates the comments of one drug dealer who depicts these threats to profits, "Once I've got a load in that I need to sell, I set myself up at the fanciest hotel in Swanky Hills, then I call

all my customers and tell them that I'm in
business. Naturally, I pay for their plane
fare, cab fare, and put them up in their own
room." Ibid: 41-42.

7. These factors also include legal
costs, capital losses from fronts which were
never repaid, "burns" (receiving inferior
quality merchandise), and rip-offs.

8. See Richard H. Blume, et al, *The Dream
Seller* (New York, N.Y.: Jossey Bass, 1972):
47.

9. See B. D. Johnson, M. A. Kaplan, and
J. Schmeidler, "Days With Drug Distribution:
Which Drugs? How many Transactions? With What
Returns?" (ed.) by Ralph Weisheit, *Drugs,
Crime and Criminal Justice System* (New York,
N. Y.: Anderson, 1990): 200.

10. Crack was not identified as a separate drug in the above utilized figure. Using
Johnson, Kaplan, and Schmeidler's procedure
(pp 198-199), I sampled N = 105 adolescents in
Frontier One, an alternative school in Portland, Oregon, to ascertain the mean cash
income and return.

11. To calculate (p) of detection, I
calculated the admitted number of crack deals
against charged "deals" through data available
through the Donald E. Long Juvenile Home,
affiliated with Multnomah County Court, in
Portland, Oregon.

12. The newcomer needs to more closely
consider the source of the merchandise, their
proximity to it, current availability of the
varying types of drugs, and the supply and
demand of the local, national, and international markets.

13. This is not driven by any notion of
an acceptable profit margin. Rather, these
individuals expect an eventual profit and this
varies with their level of participation. the
profits are determined by the location of the
transactions and drugs availability at a given
time.

14. Don Waldorf, *Doing Coke: An Ethnography of Cocaine Users and Sellers* (Washington, D. C.: Drug Abuse Council, 1977).

15. Bryan Brennan, "Official: Drug flow From Columbia Won't End Soon," *Associated Press* (1989), August, 27.

16. See Carl B. Klockars, *The Professional Fence* (New York, N. Y.: Free Press, 1974).

17. For an opposing perspective see Oakley Ray, *Drugs, Society, and Human Behavior* (St. Louis, Mo.: C. V. Mosley, 1983).

18. Erich Goode, *Drugs In American Society* (New York, N. Y.: Alfred A. Knopf, 1984).

19. James A. Inciardi, *Careers in Crime* (Chicago, Ill.: Rand McNally, 1975).

20. See James T. Carey, *The College Drug Scene* (Englewood Cliff, N. J.: Prentice hall, 1968); Mark H. Moore, John Lieb, and Sheldon Olson, "Prestige, Paranoia, and Profit: On Becoming a Dealer of Illicit Drugs in a University Community" *Journal of Drug Issues* 6 (1976): 356-369; Ray Marsh "The cycle of Abstinence and Relapse Among Heroin Addicts," *Social Problems* 9 (1961): 132-140; Ibid: Blume; Ibid: Carey; Erich Goode, *The Marijuana Smoker* (New York, N. Y.: Basic Books, 1970); Bruce D. Johnson, *Marijuana Users and Drug Sub-Culture* (New York, N. Y.: Wiley, 1973).

21. Howard Becker, "Notes on the Concept of Commitment," *American Journal of Sociology* 66 (1960): 32-42.

22. Mary Sheldon, "Investment and Involvement as Mechanisms Producing Commitment to the Organization," *Administrative Science Quarterly* 15 (1970): 473-481.

23. H. C. Kelman, "Compliance, Identification, and Internalization: three Processes of Attitude Change," *Journal of conflict Resolution* (1958): 51-60.

24. Mary J. Huntington, "The Development of a professional Self-Image," in Robert Merton, George Reader, and Patricia Kendal, (eds.) *The Student Physician* (Cambridge,

Mass.: Harvard University Press, 1951): 179-188.

25. Abler describes egoistic commitment as being the degree of personal satisfaction, enjoyment, and fulfillment which an individual derives from being involved in a give enterprise.

14

Sanctions and Compliance Norms

Law and order suggests that there is a relationship between cause and effect. That is,
law is intended to maintain the order, and
order is intended to maintain the law. It is
becoming more clear that some of our laws are
creating disorder, but there is disagreement
over the process. Crovitz, for example, believes that a legal system that fails to protect order signals flaws in the law. On the
other hand, I suggest that the formulation of
some laws serve to create a flawed social
order. It should be stated that Crovitz's and
my perspective have, erroneously, been characterized as being liberal and conservative.
Crovitz cited the 1972 case of *Papachristou
vs. City of Jacksonville*[1] to make his points
because it was overturned when it reached the
Supreme Court. The case involved several local
toughs who were arrested under a city ordi-
nance prohibiting vagrants, defined as "rogues
and vagabonds common drunkards, common night
thieves persons wandering or strolling around
place to place without any lawful purpose or
object." After being arrested in accord with
the law, one of the defendants it was discovered had possession of several packets of
heroin and others had long criminal records.[2]
The U.S. Supreme Court reversed the decision
rendered of the lower court upholding the laws

of the city of Jacksonville on the premise
that it was both too vague and unconstitutional. Justice William O. Douglas wrote the opinion and cited a former governor of Puerto Rico
to the effect that loafing "was a virtue in
his commonwealth and that it should be encouraged. Persons "wandering or strolling" from
place to place have been extolled by Walt
Whitman and Vachel Lindsay," Douglas wrote.
"We know that sleepless people walk at night,
perhaps hopeful that sleep-inducing relaxation
will result."[3]

The reversal incensed Crovitz who contends that there was no evidence of the police
arresting rambling poets or somnambulists. The
justices, he suggested, waved away evidence
that from Elizabethan times such laws had been
crucial to maintaining order. However, there
are serious flaws in Crovitz's reasoning. It
is true that criminal law depends on the quality of such acts or omissions as are prohibited under appropriate penal provisions by the
state. However, the criminal quality of an act
cannot be discerned by intuition; nor can it
be discovered by reference to any standard but
one or both of the following: is the act prohibited by penal consequences? Is the prohibited act part of the extensive field covered
by morality? However, if the moral code does
not disapprove of all acts that are prohibited
by the state, but rather single acts to be
sanctioned this only presents an argument in
defense of the legal action. In these instances, the moral code validates legal action and
legal action validates the moral code. The
domain of jurisprudence can be assessed only
by examining acts at a particular time that
are declared by the state to be crimes. Finally, state and federal regulations must be
viewed to determine if it is ultra vires as
conflicting with the constitution.[4] This means,
if legislation provides for some process to be
used against juveniles, psychopaths, crimi-

nals, etc., or other persons for who compulsory powers of control and treatment are thought to be justified, the validity of the legislation may be attacked by those who are effected. Therefore, the concept of crime and the determination of whether it is in fact criminal behavior, can not run counter to constitutional provisions.

There is a tendency to forget that there are two basic moral issues involved in the commission of a crime: 1) the morality of the law breaking per se; and 2) the intrinsic morality of the criminal act itself. These moral issues can be applied to the general dissension in the 1960s regarding desegregation sit-ins. An argument was advanced that the behavior was criminal because these protesters flagrantly broke the law. The unjustness of the law was deemed to be of no consequence. This was a conservative reaction, and social exchange elements dictating conditions that gave rise to law and the accepted procedure and apparatus one is to use in the attempts to change the law. Protesters confronted a dilemma, should they continue to behave in a fashion that would maintain social order by obeying what they perceived to be unjust laws that served to perpetuate an unjust social order and deny their sense of intrinsic morality? It is clear that ethical imperatives functioned to encourage or justify the breaking of the laws. To the protesters and the vagrants, it mattered little, ethically, that they were violating laws that had existed since Elizabethan time.

The formulation of these types of moral decisions are not difficult when individuals perceive the social order to be profoundly immoral and engaging in exploitative activities, for example, migrant working conditions, miserable wages, covert and overt racism. These are activities supported in the main by laws. As a result, individuals conclude that

criminal behavior and its consequences are no
more exploitative, immoral nor vicious than
many legal activities. The question of morality is cogently articulated in the following:

> Don't be telling me what is
> right. You talk that right jive, but
> where was you when my old man and
> the neighbors was teaching me how to
> steal and shoot dope? Where was you
> when me and my brothers and sisters
> was crazy and blind from hunger?
> Where was you when my mama was gam-
> bling away the welfare check? Where
> was you when the World was calling
> me a dirty nigger and a greasy Mexi-
> can and a poor white peckawood?
> Where was you when Wrong was my
> salvation? I'll tell you where you
> was. You was clear across town-
> Y'know, over there living in them
> big, fine houses-talking that trash
> about right and wrong. But check
> this out: There ain't no such thing
> as right or wrong in my world. Can
> you dig? Right or wrong is what a
> chump chooses to tell himself. And I
> choose to tell myself that stealing
> is right. I had a choice: to be a
> poor-assed raggedy-ass motha-fukker
> all my life or to go out into the
> streets and steal me some money so I
> could buy me a decent pair of shoes
> to wear, or shoot me some dope so I
> could forget about the rat-and roach
> infested dump I live in.
>   Yeah, I got a chip on my shoul-
> der. But it didn't get there by
> itself. And it's gonna stay up there
> until you eliminate the funky condi-
> tions that breed cats like me.[5]

Would Crovitz, or any other rational

person, deem a system that give rise to these
conditions and perceptions worth saving
through more stringent use of law? Can anyone
truly support a legal system that twenty five
years ago used to set killers of black victims
in the segregated South free? Can anyone condone a system that permitted the law to be
used to protect slayers of civil right workers
because they attempted to correct social
wrongs? Is the maintenance of law in the pursuit of order the only worthy goal?[5] History
reveals that it was the abrogation of law and
the erection of meaningful law that provided
in a broad sense remnants of justice.

Despite problems in arresting and con-
victing civil right murderers, there was a
continuous appeal for law and order. The
appeal was curious because the murders occurred during the presidencies of Eisenhower
and Nixon. Curious, because law and order, for
the social order was a major objective. Instead, they became code words for keeping the
lid on Blacks and other dissidents in Nixon's
successful presidential election campaign.
Perhaps it is ironic that a member of the
United State Senate, Strom Thurmond, R-S.C.,
lacked the courage to advocate or speak out
against the barbarities that occurred in his
state, as well as across the South, but now
staunchly advocates a federal death penalty to
cover those fourteen states that lack one
under their own laws? In the interest of social order, he and 65 other senators voted to
meet the public's demand for "real justice"
for depraved killers roaming the streets of
America.

Senator Orrin Hatch, R-Utah, who repeatedly categorized the Dred Scott case as a
frivolous appeal and a waste of the Court's
time, and Thurmond advanced a Bush proposal
that would restrict the habeas corpus appeals
for death row inmates and others in prison.[6]
Their reasoning was based on the contention

that hundreds of convicted murderers are escaping execution by endlessly filing repetitious and frivolous petitions. This perplexed Thurmond who stated: "Yet only 147 vicious murderers have been executed since 1972."[7]   Senator Joseph R. Biden, D-Del., backing an alternative reform plan by Senator Bob Graham, D-Florida, protested that the Bush proposal was too harsh. Biden asked: "Do we want blood so badly that we will have it at the expense of Justice?"[8] Obviously they did because the Bush faction won 58-40.

As a result there appears to be an urgency in these type of statutes. The enactment of these laws was directed primarily at minorities to counteract the fear that they engender. There have been other laws passed for the same reasons. Consider, for example, in response to the "de-whiting" of the United States, voters in Florida, Arizona, and California passed state constitutional amendments in the late 1980s declaring English the official language. Although later declared unconstitutional, these acts were clearly conceived and enacted in climates of fear and hate.

Similarly, in the 1980s the United States Supreme Court allowed law enforcers to use race, gender or national origin as factors in establishing reasons to search people or vehicles, to establish reasonable suspicion, and to be targeted for drug searches because they matched a profile. The NAACP, after reporting the findings of a six city study, indicated that they found the most prevalent cause of police misconduct and poor police community relations to be racism. Police racism often lead to the use of excessive force against members of minority groups in their use of sweeps, stops, and searches. The NAACP also found that excessive force, including beatings, shootings and the use of police dogs are a standard part of the arrest procedures for members of minority groups. Physical abuse, for example, being jerked from or shoved against a car is not unusual behavior in minority communities regardless of the individual's socioeconomic status. In addition, verbal abuse by police officers is considered "standard operating procedure" in these communities. Most police violence committed against minority citizens is committed by White officers, and the minority officers accept a "code of silence" to either keep their job or prevent retaliation. Disciplinary action against officers is minimal, and citizens are discouraged from filing complaints against them.

These are not conditions depicted in *Boyz N The Hood*, this is every day reality in major, and not so major, cities in the United States. Jaded law enforcement is not restricted to the police. In *Falling Down*, a film depicting life in Los Angeles, Michael Douglas played a mental character who snaps during a freeway jam, leaves his car, and goes on a violent trek through a city he perceives to be graffiti splattered and ethnically hostile. This was not an unusual film because *Falling Down* is like the late nite news in any city in the country. Because the film showed a city confounded by drive-by shootings, religious zealots, and people holding "will work for food" signs. It is a city which exhibits absurd wealth and wretched poverty with very little middle ground. The movie critics and general media misinterpreted the movie because they have made a hero of the bigoted and middle class grumbler depicted by the star. The message conveyed by the media is when fed up buy a gun and start blasting. It is true that this was a prevalent feeling prior to the film, but it became more prevalent after the media's interpretation. While reaction was mixed, one audience reacted by applauding when the crazy malcontent beat up a Korean merchant for charging too much. After dispens-

ing his brand of justice, he then trashed the
store. When this psychotic person shot a Mexi-
can-American gang member because he was ter-
rorizing a fast food restaurant after clerks
refused to serve him breakfast a minute or so
after the cut-off time, the audience could
hardly contain itself. In a demonstration that
real life imitates art, on March 13, 1993, a
White man swinging a belt and shouting anti-
Asian epithets vandalized a liquor store in
suburban Anaheim. The man left the shop, as in
the film, without stealing a thing but supposedly with psychic satisfaction.[9]

This form of aberrant behavior can happen
in environments like and different from Los
Angeles. The recent upsurge in this type of
behavior has been attributed to the recession,
which the government has never officially recognized. Its existence has had an impact on
the social exchange conditions. To further illustrate, in the spacious area bordering the
Mohave Desert, 70 miles north of Los Angeles,
is Antelope Valley. It is home to Edwards Air
Force Base and a huge aerospace plant. In this
2,000 square mile expanse is one of the highest rate of child abuse in the state. It has
become more appropriate to call it Death
Valley, rather than Antelope Valley, because
of the number of brutal murders which parents
have committed on their children. Reasons
advanced for the proliferation of this behavior in this once staid example of Americana
are the same used to account for the discord
and crime 70 miles south, hard times, drugs
and those conditions that emanates from them.

Another explanation for the behavior is
cultural deficiency. This a theoretical explanation that contends that lower and under
class source of inequality can be attributed
to one or more cultural traits. This approach
emphasizes attitudes and values rather than
prevailing biological factors or the dysfunctional elements in the social structure as

being the cause of inequalities and the responses to them. In Banfield's *Unheavenly
City*[10], inequality is perceived to be the
result of "lower class structure." This structure contains traits that are present rather
than future oriented. This emphasis is made
worse because these individuals lack work
discipline.

According to Banfield, people who share
this culture do poorly in school, which leads
to poverty and powerlessness, in turn these
two interact with each other to perpetuate
educational inequalities. In essence, the
cultural deficiency theory is a tautology.
That is to say, educational inequality lead to
poverty and powerlessness, and poverty and
powerlessness leads to educational inequality.
However, one can not deny that this is a
vicious cycle. While this theory suggests the
solution, it simultaneously reveals the hopelessness these people confront in the attempt
to sever the connecting links. Although minorities are not the sole group in the "lower and
under class cultures" they are, by all statistical measurements, over represented. This has
been attributed to historic conditions, such
as past racial discrimination. Excepting racism, the culturally deficient traits are deemed to be handicaps in language, values, and
attitudes. These attitudes both comprise and
demonstrate the values and combined it suggests a sense of fatalism. This "fatalism" is
manifested in a sense of dependency for example, welfare and other subsidies. Theoretically, this fixation precludes success orientation. These cultural values are manifested
in the youth's initial external institution,
the school, and they are perceived to lead
directly to other social problems. Due to the
values regarding school and the lack of success, these individuals are ensured of attaining a low economic and social level. This environment places them at a disadvantage in

terms of dealing with the broader culture. In this environment, individuals develop personality problems for example, feelings of inferiority and insecurity. Although these attitudes may not be problematic when these individuals are restricted to interacting within their under class culture and environment, they quickly are magnified and become impediments when it becomes essential to interface with the broader culture.[11]

Social structure theories also contend that the source of inequality is located in the total social structure of society. A structure is a regular pattern of human interaction that is either formal or informal. A formal structure refers to institutions, and an informal structure can denote an abstraction such as class. Class and caste are used to stratify people so that privileges, duties, obligations, and opportunities are unequally distributed. The formal and informal structures generate self-reinforcing inequalities for example, powerlessness, poor education, low income, and poor jobs. These in turn give rise, theoretically, to family instability, crime, drug usage, delinquency, and mental illness. As a result, people who fit these categories or behave in these manners are labeled as being dysfunctional.

This book contends that these people are not dysfunctional but rather the social culture is. Consider these statistics as we buttress our perspective: in 1959, twenty eight percent of poor families were headed by women. In 1992, that figure had grown to fifty two percent. In 1990, the number of people in poverty rose for the first time since 1983. Per person income fell by $428, 2.9 percent, to $14,387. The poverty rate rose from 12.8 percent to 13.5 percent, leaving 36 million people below the poverty line. This represented a growth of 2.1 million people when compared to 1989. The poverty level for a family of four was $13,924 in 1991. The total national population living in poverty is 14.2 percent. Blacks had the highest rate, 32.7 percent, Hispanics 28.7 percent, Pacific Islanders 13.8 percent, and Whites 10.7 percent.

The 1980s saw an increase in the number of Americans who live in poverty even while holding a job. Of the 21 million persons over the age of 14 who lived below the poverty line in 1988, 8.4 million worked at least part-time and 2 million worked year around full time. The 1988 statistic represents a twenty seven percent increase in the number of those who were the working poor in 1978 a 1.46 million person increase. It also means that the number of full-time working poor increased by forty six percent. This occurred while the federal minimum wage was being frozen at $3.35 an hour for eight years. Although it was subsequently raised, to $3.80, it did nothing to remove people from poverty. For example, using the latest minimum wage figure means that a person who worked at the minimum wage full time earned no more than $7,600 a year. This figure represents two-thirds of that which is necessary to support a family of four with the basic amenities. These negative figures grew despite the Republican administration's contention that there was economic expansion occurring in this country.

As grave as these figures are, their meanings somehow are obscured by the public. Part of this can be attributed to the fact that poverty is perceived to be primarily an urban problem because most people live in or near big cities. However, poverty is as much a fact of life in the rural areas as it is in the urban areas. It is obscured because it is more dispersed and therefore less visible. Statistics reveal that poverty is just as severe a problem in the rural areas as it is in the urban ones. The majority of the non-metropolitan poverty is concentrated in the

South where fifty five percent of the nation's poor live. In addition, the percentage of female headed households is approximately thirty percent in both the suburban and rural areas among the poor.

The Children's Defense Fund (CFD) and the U.S. Census Bureau more clearly focus the problems. The data shows that for 1989:

> 1. In thirty one percent of the United States' 100 largest cities, half or more of the Black children were poor.
> 2. In nineteen percent of the 100 cities, half or more of the Native American children were poor.
> 3. In 10 of these 100 cities, half or more of the Asian American-children were poor.
> 4. All 10 of the states with the highest child poverty rates are heavily rural.
> 5. The data also reveals that more children living in poverty are White (5.9) million than are black (3.7) million.
> 6. In 1993 A white child had a 15.5 percent chance (one in 6.45) of being poor.
> 7. An Asian child has a 19.1 percent chance (one in 5.24) of being poor.
> 8. A Hispanic child has a 36.1 percent chance (one in 2.77) of being poor.
> 9. A Native American child has a 42.0 percent chance (one in 2.3) of being poor.
> 10. A Black child has a 44.0 per cent chance (one in 2.27) of being poor. These figures demonstrate that child poverty is a nationwide problem and not one confined to a few states nor to an isolated group of

people commonly referred to as the lower-and under class in the urban areas. This is a real American problem that is manifested in children throughout our social order who are cold, sick, hungry, undereducated, deprived, and hopeless. This is a very serious problem because these children, in totality, represent a significant portion of America's future. The problems are significant because they are not only affecting brown, black, and yellow children, but white children as well. It appears to matter little to the general public that these children are the products of both two parent and single parent families.

These children and their parents, located in the rural, urban, or suburban areas, are primarily vilified and denigrated. Ronald Reagan, under who much of this growth of poverty occurred, pandering to popular political sentiment was insistent, during his administration, on characterizing poverty as being primarily a Black problem. He was successful in his ploy by utilizing loose and uniformed rhetoric calling women, "welfare queens."[12] Regrettably, he fell into the use of old stereotypes that characterized the poor as being lazy and uninspired. The media also added to the misperception by paying disproportionate attention to urban poverty. This skewed interest helped to divert attention from the conditions that continue to exist in the rural and suburban areas. The president, his administration, and the media were seemingly oblivious to the fact that in 1992, 2.1 million additional Americans fell below the poverty line. The 2.1 million figure was comprised of 1.4 million Whites, 405,000 Blacks, and 333,000 Hispanics. Why was the problem not

addressed? There is the suggestion that the
issue of poverty has been glossed over by the
majority of Americans because Whites in general tend to think of poverty as being a Black
condition which is derived from pathologies,
indigenous to these people, which are a natural outgrowth of historical and cultural factors which are not worthy of concern. When ap-
praised of the extent of White poverty and the
conditions emanating from it there are two reactions: (1) disbelief; and (2) it is too
atypical to be concerned with.

The conservatives and neo-conservatives
would articulate the "culture of poverty"
thesis that has been advanced by Banfield in
his book the *Unheavenly City: The Nature and
Future of Our urban Crisis* to explain the conditions in Los Angeles, but would be considerably reluctant to apply it to the Mojave
area.[13] They, like Banfield, would argue that
the impoverished condition of the urban dwell-
ers is different from those in the Mojave area
because the individuals in the ghettos are
there as a result of their thinking and behavior. Like Banfield, they would strongly suggest that the urban dweller's plight is attributed to their lack of the middle-class
ethos of hard work, education, good personal
hygiene, strong family life, capacity to save
for emergencies, etc. The ghettos exist because they were populated by impulsive, foul-
mouthed, aggressive, uneducated, oversexed,
and crime-prone males and females who shared
many of these characteristics and teach them
to their offspring. Banfield would also explain the collective behavior after the ac-
quittal of the police on brutality charges as
not being a response to a felt injustice, but
rather he would contend that the young men in
these areas who riot did so for fun and profit. Given these attributes of the urban dwell-
ers, in short there was nothing the government
could do for these people, and that most

efforts made in the attempt to rectify the conditions would only make them worse.

The neo-conservative perspective differs in two respects. They have not been content to diagnosis the problems without offering tentative solutions, and while critical of some of the government programs to help these individuals, they do not disagree in the principles but rather the methods utilized to implement them. Further the neo-conservatives see the under-class problem as being essentially a social-welfare problem. Stated differently, rather than making unconditional transfer payments to largely female headed-household in the form of AFDC checks, the government should force these individuals in to contracts that stipulate the steps of how to and when to get off the welfare rolls.

The liberals refute the above contentions and contend that the impoverished state is a byproduct of a complex process of economic and social changes. Wilson in the *Truly Disadvantaged: The Inner City, The Underclass, and Public Policy*[14] argues that over the past two decades a new and socially destructive class structure has emerged in the ghetto, and this can be attributed primarily to deindustrialization. The problem with Wilson's analysis is its failure to go far enough to explain the conditions that exist that are similar to those conditions supposedly indigenous to the urban ghetto areas. The same factors he cites, which constitute changing socioeconomic conditions, are also the factors that have led to the attitudinal and behavioral pathologies or culture of poverty that exists currently out side of the core urban areas.

To underscore this point, the Department of Health and Human Services says that the AFDC roll grew by 42,000 families between February and March 1993, an unusually large month-to-month increase. Since the urban ghettos are not growing spatially, this means that poverty is growing, if there is growth, in other sectors of our social order.[15]

George Wills says:

> In 1960, 5 percent of American births were illegitimate [such 'judgmental' language has not fallen from favor]. In 1988, twenty six percent were, including sixty three percent of Black babies. This behavioral change is the main reason almost one-third of all children are paupers at some point before they are 18.[16]

He continues by writing:

> In 1965, Pat Moynihan wrote: 'From the wild Irish slums of the 19th century Eastern seaboard, to the riot-torn suburbs of Los Angeles, there is one unmistakable lesson in American history: A community that allows a large number of young men to grow up in broken families, never acquiring any stable relationship to male authority, never acquiring any rational expectations about the future-that community asks for and gets chaos.' Moynihan was incorrect when he wrote this and Wills is just as incorrect when he attempts to apply it to today's social setting. A large body of psychological data suggest that for males, the mother is the most crucial role model and for females it is the father. Despite a broad collection of this type of data, writers like Will continue to tell damning lies about the ramifications of these relationships.

Will, in the same article contends that: "The inequalities that stem from the work place are now trivial in comparison to those stemming from family structure. What matters for success is not whether your father was rich or poor but whether you had a father at all." Moynihan wrote: "All this is new, children being the largest portion of paupers at some point. This circumstance did not exist during the New Deal, a half-century ago, nor during the era of the Great Society." Some Democratic staffer corrected this error to read: "This circumstance was not as recognized during the New Deal, a half-century ago, nor during the era of the Great Society."[17]

Will and Moynihan took umbrage with this correction, latter calling it flinching. According to Wills flinching has become the new liberal orthodoxy and a way of clinging to this comforting assumption: Macro-economic conditions, which government can influence, can be relied on to improve the conditions of poor people. Will contends: "That is decreasingly true for millions whose life chances are spoiled by family structure."

Will and Moynihan, among others, need to realize that governmental polices like supply side economics created a number of poor people, and this had nothing to do with family structure. These individuals need to be reminded of Harrington's book, *The Other America*, that graphically detailed how "good" things were prior to and during the New Deal era[18]. It was a realization of the magnitude of poverty, seemingly everywhere except in the hallowed hall of the U.S. Senate, which led to the "war on poverty." Perhaps these individuals have for gotten how shocked and dismayed John F. Kennedy, and supposedly a large part of this social order, was when he visited the hinterlands, Appalachia and the Ozarks, of this country and found conditions that were similar to those existing in Third World countries. Only the most cruel and ignorant can contend or even suggest that these conditions were created by these people and their value system. This perception is a derivative of conservative think tanks whose sole purposes are to effect policy and control public thought regarding all social issues. In reality, this abject poverty, which dictated family structures and behaviors, was created by decades of government policies that were inured to these individual's plight.

There are very few, if any, of these people who believe that the government is truly concerned with their plight or that they are getting fat off welfare payments. They realize that in Louisiana in 1992, the program entitled Aid to Families with Dependent Children provided grant payment of $190 a month, in Mississippi $120, in Texas $184, and in Alabama $124. This is the safety net that is increasingly utilized by those workers, which a large number of workers had fell through. They have had to utilize this grant system because the state of Louisiana pays only twenty five percent of the unemployed workers in the state. This is a state in which unemployment cascaded upward to rank among the nation's highest when oil prices collapsed. These people had no influence on OPEC or the spot market. Only the most callous and naive can state that, the inequalities that stem from the work place are now trivial in comparison to those stemming from family structure.

Deindustrialization is a correlate of poverty,"because it creates breeding grounds" for predatory street crimes, joblessness, broken homes, single parent families, and the underlying causes of crime in other social settings than the urban ghettos. As in the ghettos, when these conditions occur the neighborhood without exception becomes problematic. Collateral problems, for example, illiteracy, poor schools, drop outs, promiscuity, and other factors make these areas like slums in every respect except for the advanced decay of the physical structures and over-crowding. These areas, too, quickly become infested with rundown parks and poorly lit streets, high vacancy rates, and idle youths and young unemployed adults. In this type of environment, both crime and delinquency pro-liferates.

It should be clear that this behavior in the Mojave desert, like that which occurs in the urban areas, is not the ramifications of character flaws, but rather the manifestation of flaws of an unjust society. This perspec-tive is anathema to the conservatives and neo-conservatives because it is tantamount to blaming the victimizers. The victimizers are identified as being those individuals who holding power and who have managed to have their goals and values inculcated in the domi-nant American institutions. This inculcation is not only played out in the law and the courts, but also in electoral politics. It is these individuals who urge the down trodden socially and economically to rely on the machinery for peaceful debate and orderly change.

Much of modern law is concerned with facilities that are available for those who want to secure certain benefits. When a sig-nificant number of individuals are factored out of these benefits, despite color or eth-nicity, there is an emergency of "the new ghetto man."[19] This individual emerges with a new set of values and self-perceptions. How ever, these individuals are not confined to the urban ghettos. They can be found across the spatial setting, and they attach greater importance to the visible and physical expres-sion of dissatisfaction than to the external restraints that have traditionally inhibited this behavior. These individuals can be given names like skin heads, neo-Nazis, lower-class ethnic groups, and the marginalized. That which these individuals have in common are a change in values, even though they may be differentiated, and self-perception. The salient point is that their behavior is both reactive and proactive to the diminishing sense of self and new values. To oversimplify these individuals assume a sequence of social change-tension-aggressive release of frustration.

This sequence differs markedly from the collective behavior of Blacks in the lower strata that can be depicted as tension-increased tension-frustration- aggressive release of frustration. When the latter conceptualization is applied to the Los Angeles riot and those that occurred in Miami and other urban and rural areas in the past five years, we can then account for the participation of Hispanics, and Whites despite the media's earnest attempts to depict it as a Black riot, in Los Angeles. It is also useful in explaining the Hispanic riots in Miami and the White college student riots at various vacationing spots that occurred primarily during their spring vacations. These events were not random occurrences. They were the result of certain socioeconomic conditions that increased the chances that the immediate precipitating event would be the prologue to subsequent behavior. Stated differently, when there is an escalation in the feelings of deprivation and a sense that there is institutional malfunctioning, the slightest thing can be the precipitating factor for the occurrence of crime and its justification.[20]

The options available to the individual for solving problems are, like the problems themselves, closely bound up with the social order. The individual's social position defines to a significant extent the alternative choice regarding actions that are realistically viable. The options available to a twenty year old unemployed Black is significantly different from those available to a twenty year old unemployed White. This individualism that defines problems in individualistic terms also defines the options in individualistic terms. When the individual seeks ways to cope with the problems that confronts him/her, the socialization experience dictates the individualistic dorms of action. The majority of crime represents this type of individualistic solution to problems. These illegal options can be distinguished from the legal options that are available to the more affluent in realms of the issue of violence.

Social sanctions for the individualistic behavior are rarely strictly individualized. Rather they have a collective quality that is derived from three fundamental sources. First, it derives from the interdependence of group members. In groups that are positively connected, like-people who share the same class status, a reward received by one individual benefits the other group members similarly situated. A reward may be no more than confounding the legal authorities for example, the trafficking of drugs. This behavior occurs because of material interdependence within the group or because of altruistic orientation of group members.

Second, individual sanctions generate externalities via equal treatment norms or expectations. For example, if a drug dealer is apprehended for dealing, then all subsequent individuals similarly apprehended with the same background should expect to receive the same sanction. However, this is rarely the case when one offender is White and one is a minority. Finally, collective sanctions are supposedly derived from an explicit system of collective rewards and sanctions in which group members are held accountable for one another's conduct. The mixed character of most social sanctions has important implications

for understanding the relationship between
macro-social control processes and micro-
social norms. However, when there is great
disparity in the macro-social system, there is
ambivalence with respect to a collective sanctioning system. On the one hand, the group may
have incentives to urge one another to seek
out the accepted sources of external rewards
and to comply with the external dictates regarding behavior. On the other hand, peer
group members may also have an incentive to
help violators avoid detection and to assist
them in their struggle against the macro-
social system.

Given these differentiated dimensions and
contexts, how does a social order arrive at a
position in which it can exert sanctions and
expect individuals across the contexts to
comply with the norms? Efforts to understand
behavioral responses to sanctions have been
discussed extensively in the literature of
criminology and deviance. The literature emphasize that studies of responses to sanctions
must take into account the group's context
within which the sanctioning occurs.

For example, contrary to the deterrence
doctrine, deprived individuals may compensate
for their status by increasing the level of
opposition to the consensus norms. In this
situation, responses of this nature not only
bring rewards to the individual, but to the
group members as well. The collective violence
in Los Angeles in 1992, is an example of op-
positional responses to normative expectations.

In final analysis, sanctions can only
come about when individuals are endowed with
an internal control capacity. This capacity
can neither be developed nor nurtured when
rage is present due to inequities confronted
daily, in a system which provides preferential
treatment and pits one unfortunate   group
against another.

NOTES

1. Gordon L. Crovitz, "Law and Disorder: Disintegration of America's Criminal Justice System Began From Top Down," *National Review*, 6, May (1991). Crovitz is a member of the New York bar and assistant editorial page editor of the *Wall Street Journal* where he writes a weekly article entitled "Rule of law."

2. See G. Hughes, *"Concept of Crime: an American View,"* *Criminal Law Review* (1959): 239, 331.

3. Ibid., Crovitz.

4. Quoted in Eve Pell ed., *Maximum Security* 4 (New York: Dutton, 1972): 2.

5. Ibid., Pell.

6. Currently there are approximately 2,500 inmates on death row in the United States. The mean time on death row has been eight years. Thurmond was angered by the fact that only 147 had been executed since 1972.

7. The most notable cases are the 1963 ambush shooting of Medgar Evers the Mississippi NAACP leader; the 1965 shooting of Oneal Moore, a Black deputy sheriff who broke the color line in a sheriff's department in Louisiana, and the 1966 fire bombing of Vernon Dahmer, who urged black citizens to vote in Hattiesburg. In the Medgar Evers case, Byron De La Beckwith is finally scheduled to go on trial, (he was convicted of premeditated murder in 1994). In the Dahmer case, the Mississippi court system had its first ever victory against the Klan when a Hattiesburg prosecutor won conviction of four men. But the mastermind of the crime was twice freed after hung juries. In the Dahmer case, the defendant, Sam Bower, a Klan leader, was set free after a 11-1 verdict to convict. However, Bower later served a prison term for federal convictions in the 1964 deaths of civil rights workers James Chaney, Andrew Goodman, and Michael Schwerner. Their case was fictional-

ized in the movie *Mississippi Burning*. The case involving Oneal Moore, the deputy, remains unsolved. Bill Moore, a White from Keener Alabama died for helping Blacks register to vote. He was fatally shot in September 1961 at a cotton gin in Liberty, Mississippi by a state legislator who was eventually cleared by a coroner's jury. Finally, the case of Henry Dee and Charles Eddie Moore who died in 1964 in Meadville, Mississippi after Klansmen accused them of plotting to start a Black uprising. The accusation proved to be unfounded. Although a Klansman signed a confession detailing their abduction and beating deaths, a justice of the peace dropped all charges – without explanation and without presenting the evidence to a grand jury. Ironically, the bodies of Dee and Charles Moore were found during the search for Chaney, Goodman, and Schwerner. These individuals were killed because they dared to disrupt the legal order of Jim Crowism.

8. This sentiment was uttered by Sen. Alfonse D'Amato, R-N.Y. Using this sentiment, the Senate bill passed 65-33. Quoted from Paul Houston, "Execution List Grows to 50 in Senate Bill," *The Oregonian*, 27 June (1991).

9. Across this country theater owners bowed to police or civil pressure not to show *Boyz N The Hood* or to show it at matinee times because they feared the possible ramifications.

10. Edward Banfield, *The Unheavenly City* (Boston: Little, Brown, 1968).

11. William J. Wilson, *Truly Disadvantaged: The Inner City, The Underclass, and Public Policy* (Chicago: The University of Chicago of Chicago, Press, 1987).

12. Participation in AFDC has set records in all but two of the months since July 1989, when there were 3.76 million families on the roll. Currently the figure has topped 5 million. Of this total, 374,000 families were

headed by a married couple with an unemployed worker. The total number of children in these families is approximately 9.75 million. In addition to the AFDC checks, the federal government subsidizes food in the form of food stamps in excess of 24 billion dollars. This is slightly more than the aggregate for AFDC payments, which are 22.3 billion. This is compared to 17.24 billion spent in 1989 and 13.8 billion spent in 1983.

13. Ibid., Banfield.

14. Ibid., Wilson.

15. George Will, "Poor Values Pave Path To Poverty," *Washington Post Writers Group* 3, March (1992), A-16.

16. Ibid., Will.

17. Ibid., Will.

18. Most violent crimes, especially robbery, burglary, and murder, are committed by the poor. Middle-class and upper-class property crimes are construed to be essentially nonviolent. However, Reiman [(Jeffrey, *The Rich Get Richer and The Poor Get Prison* (Chicago, Ill.: John Wiley, 1984).] and others depict a different picture regarding the violence perpetrated on the lower and middle class by the upper class. An example is the more than 100 savings and loan defendants who stole from people of all classes escaped long prison terms in exchange for making penalty payments. To date they have repaid less than a half-penny per dollar of the $133.8 million they owe, according to an Associated Press review of federal court records.

19. Nathan Caplan, "The New Ghetto Man: A Review of Recent Empirical Studies," *The Journal of Social Issues* 26 (Winter, 1970): 59-74.

20. On April 20, 1993, the United States Supreme Court appeared on the verge of adopting a response to bias crimes by increasing the sentences for criminals who choose their victims on the basis of race, religion, or

other personal traits. The bill died for lack
of Congressional support.

Index

About the Author

JAMES A. CHAMBERS is Assistant Professor of Criminology at Indiana State University. He has published *Slavery, Philosophy, and Socioeconomic Disorder* (1993).

ISBN 0-275-94937-0

9 780275 949372

90000>

HARDCOVER BAR CODE

EAN